Trading Thalesians

Trading Thalesians

What the Ancient World Can Teach Us About Trading Today

Saeed Amen

Co-founder and Managing Director of the Thalesians, London, UK

First published 2014 by
PALGRAVE MACMILLAN

Palgrave Macmillan in the UK is an imprint of Macmillan Publishers Limited,
registered in England, company number 785998, of Houndmills, Basingstoke,
Hampshire RG21 6XS.

Palgrave Macmillan in the US is a division of St Martin's Press LLC,
175 Fifth Avenue, New York, NY 10010.

Palgrave Macmillan is the global academic imprint of the above companies
and has companies and representatives throughout the world.

Palgrave® and Macmillan® are registered trademarks in the United States,
the United Kingdom, Europe and other countries.

ISBN 978–1–137–39952–6

This book is printed on paper suitable for recycling and made from fully
managed and sustained forest sources. Logging, pulping and manufacturing
processes are expected to conform to the environmental regulations of the
country of origin.

A catalogue record for this book is available from the British Library.

A catalog record for this book is available from the Library of Congress.

For Baba and Gido, although light has turned to shadow, you will forever illuminate my path, with the cascading streams of your love.

"If it wasn't for me, I'd do brilliantly." Chamfort – every trader should learn this excuse

Baba

The wind it blows at times with air which chills,
Above the clouds, the sky with rain it fills,
The souls become sodden with waters hold,
The warm of old are the memories of gold,
Behold those thoughts of him which lie within,
Never will they be lost, etern'ty's in,
In time although the pain always will stay,
It will begin to fade further away,
Replaced by thoughts of warmer times with him,
That place where laughs and joys of many whim,
Neither the loss of him, nor this deep pain,
So should eclipse mem'ries of him in reign,
He was your king, your all, ever so more,
But most of all he wants you in the fore,
As each day it passes through simply recall,
That the memories of him will shine in all.

Contents

Figures

Foreword

When Lehman Brothers collapsed in 2008 it felt as if we were living in a different world, a world we had yet to grasp. To get a handle on this world we had to get in touch with new ways of thinking. Remembering that everything new has its roots in the well-forgotten old, we chose to build on a firm foundation: Antiquity.

When we think of Ancient Greek philosophy, we hear the names of Socrates, Plato, and Aristotle. Bertrand Russell tells us that Western philosophy begins with Thales. The words of the sage from Miletus resonate in the teachings of the founding fathers of Western academies.

And we picture in our mind the mysterious figure of Thales, the rational mystic, looking at his reflection in the waters of the Aegean. Water, according to Thales, is the first principle – and the ultimate source of his knowledge.

While remaining devoted to the element of Water, Thales proved that he was a truly balanced personality. He demonstrated that he was thoroughly grounded by using geometry to calculate the height of pyramids and the distance to enemy ships from the shore. And he showed his doubting friends that philosophers can easily get rich, should they so desire, by applying philosophy to finance.

And this takes us from the shores of the Aegean Sea of the sixth century BC to the twenty-first-century trading floor, where Saeed and I started our careers together. Our friendship goes back even further, to the lecture theatres of Imperial College. The traditional Clore lecture theatre, with its blackboards, would have pleased Thales, as would Room 311 with its cryptic numeric name and state-of-the-art technology in the Department of Computing.

Equipped with Clore's conservative rationality and 311's innovative technology, Saeed and I entered the world of the City and Canary Wharf. These tools were eminently useful in surviving the Global Financial Crisis. But it was our friendship that really saved the day.

Saeed's research reports at Lehman Brothers were always different. Clever and punchy headlines dispelled the routine. Fresh insights banished dogma. He has the rare skill of seeing the essence of things through the sea of complexity; like Thales, who succeeded in finding wisdom contemplating the sea.

I therefore advise you, the reader, to pay attention to this book. Saeed's application of Thalesian thinking to modernity is deeply personal. In its pages you will find both Thales and Saeed. For those who are seeking understanding of modern financial markets I can recommend no better guide. Only one thing can beat reading Saeed's thoughts on paper: having a chat with him over a coffee, something I have always enjoyed over the years. This book is the next best thing.

Paul Bilokon
CEO and Founder, the Thalesians
London, March 2014

Prologue

Sleep had failed to rest me. I had lain for hours in my bed, my eyes firmly closed, my mind open. Thoughts whirred uncontrollably through my mind, seizing their chance to hold back the tide of slumber. Rather than attempting to win the battle against my thoughts, I admitted defeat, deciding it would be more fruitful to leave my bed. My eyes opened, greeted by a new mid-September morning, the light of which had managed to slip through the gap between my curtains. Too lazy to find my slippers, I opted to walk barefoot around my flat.

Slowly, I made my way to the computer. I turned on the screen. As it whirred into life, I began to watch the newsfeed from Reuters. To pass the time, I inter-mittently paid attention to the price action in USD/JPY. Whilst European stock markets were still asleep, the foreign exchange market was awake, as it is every hour of every weekday. Indeed, it is only during the weekend that the foreign exchange market closes. If you look at the constant up and down moves of market prices it can become hypnotic, an ever-flowing array of numbers that appears highly random to most observers. However, to traders watching the tick, tick, tick of the market, from second to second, slowly over years, their brains somehow manage to filter the noise in order to discern patterns in the madness.

Then, emblazoned in red capital letters, I saw a headline that caught my attention. The headline declared that Lehman Brothers had filed for bankruptcy, the company that had given me my first job just over three years earlier. The headline was the final confirmation of Lehman's downfall, a com-pany which had existed for over 150 years, surviving the American Civil War, two world wars and 9/11, but seemingly unable to overcome that ever-present human trait: greed. I remembered in the summer of 2007, just over a year before the bankruptcy, we had all eagerly made our way to a 'town hall' at Lehman. A town hall was the convoluted term for a large employee meeting. During the meeting a senior executive had reassured us that Lehman was fine. He told us that we had enough money to last over a year without needing to access the markets for funding. He turned out to be right: we did survive for a year, but unfortunately not much longer than that. Yet that was, perhaps to use the most clichéd of statements, the beginning of the end.

1
Introduction

A start signals the spring, blossom and shoots,
Vanishing cold, the appearance of fruits,
In bursts whisp'ring their smell, color, sweetness,
Awaiting the spring taste of that brightness.

Financial markets had been teetering for just over a year. It all started during the summer of 2007, when the first signs of a credit crunch had emerged. Traders had begun to air concerns about the US subprime mortgage market. All it needed was a trigger to evolve from nervousness to a full-blown crisis. The bankruptcy of Lehman Brothers, one of the largest US investment banks, in September 2008 proved to be the ominous spark that lit the flames of turmoil as though the market were covered in glistening gasoline.

Following the bankruptcy, equities were sold aggressively by investors, as were any assets perceived to be risky. The S&P500 moved from around 1,250 points, just before the bankruptcy, to a low below 700 points by March 2009. At the same time, safe haven assets rallied in a flight to safety (see Chapter 2 for our discussion of safe haven and risky assets). The US dollar rallied from $1.44 per euro to $1.25 in the space of a few weeks. The Federal Reserve and other major central banks slashed interest rates as a reaction to the crisis. When short-term rates could not be cut any further, the Federal Reserve embarked upon the policy of quantitative easing, effectively creating money to buy US Treasuries and other fixed income instruments in an effort to push down longer-term borrowing costs.

More worryingly, the turmoil quickly spilled over into the real economy, which globally went into recession. Unemployment in the US peaked at nearly 10% in October 2009 according to the Bureau of Labor Statistics. In the US, the recession ended up lasting one and a half years, from December 2007 to June 2009, according to the National Bureau of Economic Research (NBER). GDP fell by 5.1% during this period. This was the largest drop since the recession of

1

1945 after the end of World War II. Many books have been written about the financial crisis, covering its many different angles. I have read many over the years. One of my favorites is *Too Big to Fail* (Sorkin, 2010), which in its detailing of the crisis includes the myriad of deals done to save failing banks. Another book I can thoroughly recommend is *The Greatest Trade Ever* (Zuckerman, 2010), which tells the other side of the crisis, namely those few investors who shorted subprime and thus profited during the crisis. I was also lucky enough to hear Gregory Zuckerman speak at the Thalesians about his book.

However, this book does not purely analyze the financial crisis following Lehman's bankruptcy or tell the behind-the-scenes story using a myriad of secret sources. That story of the financial crisis of 2008 has already been excellently told, which negates the need for me to do so as well. I simply reel off all these statistics to reinforce a single fact: the events around the Lehman bankruptcy cannot be discounted as another "ordinary" risk event, the kind which seems to buffet markets every few months. It was a pivotal moment in the global economy.

Two weeks marched on from the bankruptcy. We had reached the end of September 2008. Those two weeks also constituted the last few days of my job at Lehman Brothers. I had not been made redundant at the time of bankruptcy. Instead, we had stayed in what seemed like a zombie company, working the hours we wanted (for we had no work to do) for this short period, whilst Lehman's administrators worked to find a buyer for our division. In the end, our entire European fixed income division, which included me, was made redundant on the last working day of September. I had always imagined being fired would somehow be done with more fanfare. I had expected to see the wave of a manager's finger, to hear the words "you're fired," which have been immortalized by Lord Sugar (and Donald Trump in the US) on his UK hit show *The Apprentice*. Instead, we had a bespectacled member of an accounting firm telling a crowded auditorium, in an extremely polite manner, to leave our desks one last time. Aside, from his glasses, I have little recollection of what he looked like.

However, I had few grounds on which to complain. My time without a job ended up being just several weeks. But it would be bending the facts to say that I had amassed a huge war chest of Lehman Brothers shares. Any number of these shares would be worth a similar amount to a single Zimbabwean dollar, post-Robert Mugabe's attempt at quantitative easing. For those who had held a large number of Lehman Brothers shares, the freefall in our stock price was especially painful. This was especially so given the knowledge that Lehman stock had peaked at around $85 per share... It is a strange paradox. It is one of the most basic rules of finance that some element of diversification is key to managing your investment portfolio. It is something that I have often discussed in my research and with clients. There is even an easy to recall cliché which can be used to describe it, namely "don't put all your eggs in one basket". Indeed, we shall discuss this subject in some detail in Chapter 4, discussing both diversification and also the concentration of risk within a portfolio. However, by working in an investment bank, it is always the policy of the firm to "put all your eggs in one basket", in any situation. For as you become more senior, you are rewarded more and more in that bank's stock, as opposed to cash, dramatically increasing your downside should the bank go into difficulties (the flipside is, of course, that should the bank do well, you also benefit from that). The argument is that owning stock makes traders behave in a more responsible manner. It was always lauded as an immensely worthy fact at Lehman Brothers, that the percentage of the company owned by its employees was one of the highest on Wall Street. Given Lehman Brothers went bankrupt, this idea of greater responsibility from greater share ownership clearly failed. It might actually have had the converse effect, at least judging by this example.

To occupy my time, after my non-Lord Sugar-style redundancy at Lehman Brothers, I joined the gym and idled aimlessly between job interviews. Sometimes, there would be a job, whilst on other occasions, it was merely an opportunity for competitors to comb my brain for knowledge. I remember on one occasion, one interviewer's shouts rang in my ears after I refused to divulge a very particular property of a trading model I had co-developed at Lehman Brothers called MarQCuS. (It stood for "Macro Quantitative Currency Strategies" and was pronounced like the name Marcus. It was a few years after the film *Gladiator* had been released.) During the same period, my friend and fellow ex-Lehmanite Paul Bilokon had an idea to use our new-found free time more effectively, which we shall discuss shortly. I had known Paul for many years, since our university days at Imperial College in London. I remember at one time, during his stay at Lehman Brothers, he had become relatively portly, which was exacerbated by his slight lack of height. We had entered what was called the "Fat Challenge" at work, which was essentially a contest to see who could lose the most weight over the coming weeks. Paul managed to put on the most weight of anyone in the competition. This was not precisely the object of the exercise. However, Paul was never one to admit defeat. Hence, it did not surprise me, that one day, several years later, I met a much thinner Paul. He then went on to tell me about his new weight-training regime, which involved waking up early most mornings to go to a gym. He described how some of the weights were so heavy that the gym's insurance stipulated a personal trainer had to be in attendance. Sometimes, I think the word "driven" probably had not been invented until Paul came along and needed a succinct word to describe him.

He had always been one of the smartest guys in our class. Such an accolade is tough in an institution such as Imperial College, which is such a microcosm of intellect in itself. I always hoped that I was considered as one of the smartest guys in our class as well. Expressing such a statement is always difficult, when the subject is you, given it is forever enveloped in an element of bias. Indeed, when have you ever heard someone saying the opposite, namely that his or her intellect is below average? It is not really up to anyone to judge whether he or she is smart or not. I would suggest that it is up to others to make that judgment, those who do not suffer from such a persistent bias.

Although I could never term my university days a roaring laugh, I did enjoy them. In particular, I made many good friends. My time at Imperial was a time of fulfillment, a time where the naivety of youth slowly began to fade. There is something tremendously satisfying about studying mathematics and its related fields. For hours, you may sit solving a problem without a hint of progress and then, miraculously, your mind finds the solution, that magical moment of eureka. For some of you, that previous sentence might not chime, for I admit that loving mathematics is unlikely to place me in the majority of humanity. Yet for the mathematicians amongst you, I do hope it has some resonance. Beauty is never in front of you, it is there to be found, to be striven for. In the same way, a mathematical solution of a hard problem is never "obvious." Most importantly, I believe Imperial nurtured our young minds to think in a mathematical way, a trait that would prove useful for the future, as opposed to teaching us simply to regurgitate information. Whilst knowledge is important, surely it is its application which provides value.

Following the bankruptcy, returning to the subject of free time, Paul wanted to start a group that would seek to discuss finance and related subjects in the fields of mathematics and computer science. He had already created a financial website, but this would be something more interactive. It would be our (very, very, very) small way of fostering understanding about finance, in particular the more quantitative aspects of the field. Amongst the many reasons which precipitated the Lehman crisis, it was clear that there was one critical element, namely the misunderstanding of risk, masked by mathematics. Mathematics ought to inform our understanding of finance, rather than complicate it. Mathematics is not a tool to prove ideas that you know to be untrue but would prefer to be true.

Together with another friend, Matthew Dixon, we would create the Thalesians, a quantitative finance group. Paul used the following words to describe the Thalesians:

> think tank of dedicated professionals with an interest in quantitative finance, economics, mathematics, physics and computer science, not necessarily in that order.

Indeed, it was those words which were emblazoned on the very first Thalesians business card I made.

At first, Paul's choice for the name of the group perplexed me. During my time at Lehman Brothers, I had worked with an intern named Thales Panza de

Paula, a jovial character from Brazil. He spent much of his time, whilst sitting on the desk beside me, teaching me all about Brazil. He made it sound like a magical land, describing how its coasts were littered with beautiful beaches, noting how it was filled with people who seemed to be forever happy and friendly (I have to admit I struggle to remember meeting a Brazilian whose outlook was not on the positive side of life). To this day, I have yet to visit Brazil, but I am keen to do so. If I do, I suspect it will largely be a result of Thales' efforts of preaching to me about his homeland. One day I had asked Thales about his first name. I had never met anyone called Thales before and was curious about the name's origin. He told me that he had been named after an ancient philosopher called Thales of Miletus. Miletus was in Asia Minor, in modern Turkey. As well as being a philosopher, Thales of Miletus was active in many fields, including politics and mathematics.

Indeed, I had a vague recollection of the name from the geometric theorem named after him. I knew little else until I read a biography of Thales entitled simply *Thales of Miletus* (O'Grady, 2002). So what did Thales of Miletus have to do with a twenty-first-century quantitative finance group? After all, Paul had named our group, the Thalesians, literally denoting us as the followers of Thales of Miletus. On the surface, the relationship between our group and Thales of Miletus seems tenuous, until we note that Thales of Miletus was actually one of the first people to trade derivatives. You know derivatives, those mysterious financial contacts built by people we used to call financial engineers, with letters such as PhD after their names, and prefixes such as professor. Admittedly, Thales of Miletus did not create such exotic financial instruments with funny names, such as CDO^2, whose complexity and unwieldiness ensured that investors would never quite understand them.

Instead, Thales of Miletus traded his derivatives on an underlying, which is still familiar to people who live around the Mediterranean today, namely olives or more precisely olive presses. He essentially bought options, which gave him the right (but not necessarily the obligation) to use olive presses at a pre-agreed price. In the *Politics*, Aristotle tells us the story of Thales and his olive presses:

> Thales...when they reviled him for his poverty, as if the study of philosophy was useless: for they say that he, perceiving by his skill in astrology that there would be great plenty of olives that year, while it was yet winter, having got a little money, he gave earnest for all the oil works that were in Miletus and Chios, which he hired at a low price, there being no one to bid against him; but when the season came for making oil, many persons wanting them, he all at once let them upon what terms he pleased; and raising a large sum of money by that means, convinced them that it was easy for philosophers to be rich if they chose it, but that was not what they aimed at; in this manner is Thales said to have shown his wisdom.
>
> (Aristotle & Ellis (trans), 1912)

Later, Aristotle notes that this is an example of a monopoly. The story told by Aristotle about Thales sparked a thought in my brain. My focus was not so much on the notion of a monopoly, something that could be construed as market manipulation in the current day or more specifically "cornering" the market. In any case, there are many examples where such behavior resulted in ruin for the protagonists, such as the Hunt brothers' attempt to corner the silver market in the 1970s. We could also argue that a sample of one trade is not sufficient to judge Thales' trading prowess (see Chapter 9 on examination of historical data).

Instead, I asked a more general question about whether Thales of Miletus could tell us something about modern financial markets. Is the way to succeed as a trader not to think purely about making money and instead to have other goals (see Chapter 5)? After all, Thales of Miletus was not primarily a trader. Aristotle tells us he merely used his intellect to prove that he could make money. The rationale is that if your primary objective is purely to make money from trading quickly, you can make decisions that perversely increase the likelihood of losing. In John Kay's book *Obliquity* (Kay, 2011), he keeps with this theme, arguing that goals are best achieved indirectly. He cites happiness, amongst his examples. He notes that those who are happiest rarely pursue it as a goal; instead it is a by-product of their circumstances. Bertrand Russell echoes these sentiments in the *Conquest of Happiness* (Russell, 1999 (reissue)). Forever thinking about happiness is not a way to find it, Russell suggests. Telling a girl you are madly in love with her upon first meeting her is unlikely to result in the reciprocation of that sentiment!

Could trading be viewed as one very specific example of the theory demonstrated by Thales of Miletus, and considering the indirect pursuit of goals as espoused by John Kay and Bertrand Russell? Are there other ways we can use examples from the ancient world to increase our understanding of markets today? Just as historians, such as Herodotus living in Ancient Greece, the "father of history," examine the past, can traders look at the past to learn something (see Chapter 9) to aid their trading? Can thinking across many different disciplines, like Thales of Miletus, who was active in so many fields, give traders more ideas about what will be a profitable trade (see Chapter 7)? Can we understand the risk in modern markets through the lens of the ancient world (see Chapter 2)? It is questions such as these which we will discuss more thoroughly in the rest of the book.

What does this book avoid? This book is not concerned with labeling every person who chooses to work in the field of finance as either a charlatan or a fool, even if some are undoubtedly one or both of these. It is not about belittling the skills of those investors who have throughout the years managed to create spectacular returns consistently. True, investors might be *fooled by randomness* on many occasions. An investor whose strategy is simply long stocks during a stock market boom is likely to have been helped by the market, even if he or she might not always admit it. Of course, luck can never be derided as being an important factor, which furnishes investors with success. One quotation by Mark Twain seems to sum this up in a manner far better than anything I might pen here, if we simply replace the word "inventors" with "investors" in his maxim, which is as follows: "Name the greatest of all inventors. Accident."

However, even if we take into account luck, repeated success when investing capital over an extended period, during different market regimes with a rigorous investment process, seems to be less a product of pure randomness, but instead a product of a profound understanding of markets. Is, for example, the success of Warren Buffett purely a function of luck? I doubt that. Skill also seems to have played a significant role in his success, as well as luck, judging from the longevity of his success and more crucially from observing his investment style. The last point is crucial: without understanding an investor's approach, it can indeed be very difficult to distinguish luck from skill.

This book is certainly not a diatribe against the ideas of Nassim Nicholas Taleb, who has popularized the notion of being *fooled by randomness* (Taleb, 2007), Black Swans (Taleb, 2008) and more recently the concept of antifragility (Taleb, 2013) in his books. I agree with many of his ideas (even if not all of them in their entirety). I have referred to his books on numerous occasions. Indeed, Paul and I have invited Taleb to speak at the Thalesians, and we hope that he will speak at one of our events in the future.

This book is full of opinions. I hope that some you will find illuminating, even if you do not agree with all of them. These words are merely a guide, not an instruction manual. Whatever I write here, I wish to stress that every trader needs to find their own path to a strategy which suits them. A strategy which might be advisable for one trader might be totally unsuitable for another (see Chapter 9).

So do you have a profound understanding of markets? That's a question for other Thalesians to answer!

2
The Basis of Everything Is Water: Understanding Risk in Markets

> With risk comes thrill, of whatever can will,
> Or could well be, as the future can see,
> One hopes reward, as fate could well afford,
> In place of loss, casting its path across.

Water as risk

Water covers much of the world's surface. Its ubiquity in many forms, in sea, in rain, in sweat and so on, perhaps explains why it has held such a fascination for mankind. Today, most of our lives are somewhat divorced from nature, in comparison with our forefathers who toiled the land or hunted their prey. Today over half the world's population inhabits cities. A minority lives in the countryside. However, even in cities, people are willing to pay a premium to have a view of a river or a sea. For humans, there is something appealing about water, aside from the obvious necessity that we need to drink it and the fact that our bodies are largely composed of water. Thales was particularly interested in water. One of the ideas that Thales is best known for is his philosophy about the importance of water. He believed that the principle of everything was water. Aristotle explains that:

> Most of the earliest philosophers conceived only of material principles as underlying all things. That of which all things consist, from which they first come and into which on their destruction they are ultimately resolved, of which the essence persists although modified by its affections – this, they say, is an element and principle of existing things.... Thales, the founder of this school of philosophy, says the permanent entity is water (which is why he also propounded that the earth floats on water). Presumably he derived this assumption from seeing that the nutriment of everything is moist, and that heat itself is generated from moisture and depends upon it for its existence (and that from which a thing is generated is always its

first principle). He derived his assumption, then, from this; and also from the fact that the seeds of everything have a moist nature, whereas water is the first principle of the nature of moist things.

(Aristotle & Tredennick (trans), 1933)

With the benefits of millennia of scientific progress, it is clear that Thales was wrong. Yes, water is a key prerequisite for life. Whilst this is the case, it is not as crucial as he believed for inanimate objects. Furthermore, water is not an element but a combination of both hydrogen and oxygen atoms. However, the principle that there are building blocks for everything is right. Today, we call these atoms, and there is also a whole host of subatomic particles. In the modern day, the verve with which physicists have searched for the Higgs boson illustrates that man's fascination with finding the single root of everything has not receded. This hunt is led today by physicists, who rely upon massive particle accelerators that collide particles with one another at speeds close to that of light, rather than philosophers such as Thales.

If we transpose this idea to the world of markets, namely Thales' notion of water, it can actually be closely related to the concept of risk. Make any investment and the idea of risk is at the basis of any decision, or is the principal element, in the same way that Thales believed water was central to everything. Higher-risk investments obviously promise higher returns, but the downside can also be more. Just as water can be the source of life, so it can be the element, which can be uncontrollable in abundance. The same is true of risk. Too little risk taken in any investment and we cannot expect a reasonable payoff. In the same way, if we drink too little water it will not be sufficient to quench our thirst.

The motivation to measure risk

Although our focus is on risk in the context of trading and investing, many decisions we make can be seen as taking risk for some element of reward. We shall ignore those decisions where both the risk and potential reward is very small. The decision whether to paint your living room white or magnolia sits in this category. Neither is likely to have significant upside (or downside) compared to the other, especially given that the cost of paint is likely to be very similar. This leaves those decisions where either the potential risk or reward is significant. Let us assume we decide to cross a road. This seems to fit in the latter category. The risk involved here is relatively binary. Our upside is reaching the other side, whilst our downside could be considerably worse. If we were to map this downside as a statistical distribution, we could see it would be seen as a tail risk. In other words, the probability of it is very small, but the payoff would be significantly negative. This contrasts to the probability of a positive outcome, which is very large. In this instance our positive payoff is not significant, since crossing a road successfully will not usually change your life. We can mitigate the downside by being cautious, using pedestrian crossings and generally taking care to both look and listen for oncoming traffic.

However, there are still risks that we cannot fully control, such as the driving skills of those motoring along the road. Other external factors include weather conditions and the impact they have on visibility and the slipperiness of the road. These would affect everyone crossing the road in the same area. Furthermore, in an unfamiliar environment, the method we have learnt to cross the road might itself be dangerous, even if usually we might think it cautious. For example, one of the most terrifying experiences I have faced is attempting to cross the wide road in Cairo which hugs the river Nile. Whilst I was waiting for the traffic to cease, I attempted to cross the road by running to avoid speeding cars. Locals adopted a different approach to crossing the road. They seemed to be perfectly at ease casually strolling across the road in between cars that were zooming past them. There seemed to be an implicit understanding between drivers and pedestrians, that this was the way you were expected to cross the road. By predictably walking across the road, pedestrians made it easier for drivers to judge where they were. This contrasts to pedestrians zipping between cars, using a combination of walking and running to create a seemingly random path. Ultimately, being cautious and adhering to local norms of crossing the road can ensure that throughout our lifetime we can escape the downsides of traversing roads.

In common with crossing roads, there are clearly some external risks we cannot control when it comes to making investment decisions. However, unlike with crossing roads, it seems folly to suggest we can go through a lifetime without experiencing some period of downside when investing if we choose to take anything more than a minimal level of risk. Admittedly, the downside of investing is rarely going to be as bad as the downside of crossing the road. Furthermore, the risks involved in crossing the road tend to be idiosyncratic rather than systemic, with obvious exceptions such as the weather. In the market, this is different; investors often face both these risks to varying degrees.

Hence, we should aim firstly to have a broad understanding of the types of risks we face whilst investing. We should also attempt to quantify these risks. Simply saying that every investment decision has binary risks to it but having little idea of the relative probability of each outcome is not sufficient. Furthermore, we need to understand the relative payoffs in these scenarios. When it comes to quantifying risks, it is important to estimate what the maximum potential downside could be in an investment. In Thales' case, his maximum downside was the deposit he put down for the use of olive presses. Unfortunately, the answer is not always as clear as this, without some further work.

Understanding risk in games

Before attempting to quantify financial risk using mathematical concepts, we briefly digress to the East to approach our discussion of risk from another angle. If there is a place which personifies the connected nature of the world, Istanbul must surely be one of them. Unlike other cities where trade is conducted mostly via intermittent electronic messages, in Istanbul trade largely remains a visible activity. There is of course the Grand Bazaar, which is filled with all sorts of traditional wares such as carpets and local specialties such as Turkish Delights. The shops seem invariably to be populated by experienced traders, who successfully give the illusion to tourists that their prices are indeed cheaper than the place next door. Elsewhere, a cursory glance at the Bosporus reveals a never-ending line of ships carrying freight, belching out thick black smoke from their aging diesel engines. Some are waiting to traverse the Bosporus to visit the Black Sea, whilst others are returning to Europe from Russia carrying copious amounts of crude oil, the blood of the modern age coursing through the veins of commerce. Alongside the Bosporus Bridge, which joins the European and Asian sides of Istanbul, is a relatively plush bar called Reina, which affords a panoramic view of the Bosporus and has apparently been a haunt of various celebrities. It certainly makes for a juxtaposition of two worlds. You turn to one side to see freighters chugging along in the middle of the Bosporus and turn to the other to catch sight of revelers partying in the open air and drinking raki, a devilishly potent spirit. By contrast, in many cities, waterways are underused and carry little other than the odd tourist boat.

I visited Istanbul several years ago. Just by my hotel there stood a traditional Turkish café, straddling a walkway meandering uphill. It cost a single Turkish lira for tea, which was served in a traditional tulip-shaped glass. In Turkish, the glass is called *ince belli*, which literally means "of a slim waist." For this solitary lira, I also got to sit on an immeasurably small wooden stool. I presume it was extremely small so I did not spend all day at the café.

Whilst waiting for my tea, I noticed a strange clicking noise, which seemed almost continuous. At first, I presumed this sound was the crackling of electricity. Instead, it was the sound of dice being rolled during the course of a backgammon game. I have to confess that the rules of backgammon were a mystery to me.

However, even though I continue to have little understanding of the game, it is clear that chance plays a crucial part of the outcome, through the rolling of dice. If we just focus on the die itself, the probability of throwing any single number is $1/6$, hardly a revelation. In giving this figure we are implicitly assuming that the die we roll is fair. Let us say we are offered an opportunity to play a game where you receive £1 if you roll any number other than six and it costs £1 to play the game. Would you take part? I certainly would not, because even if you win, your payoff only makes up for your participation. Then there is obviously the case that rolling a six results in the loss of £1. Clearly, in this game we can very easily calculate that the odds are against us, and hopefully we would decline to play it. Dr. Frank Berkshire from Imperial College has researched amongst other things the mathematics of gambling in particular games involving dice. I had the pleasure of hearing him speak at the Thalesians on this subject at one of our London seminars. He noted that in the vast majority of casino-style games the odds are invariably against the punter. One exception is blackjack as detailed by Thorp (1973).

Berkshire suggested that there are several ways to win when the odds are seemingly against you in a game. The simplest method is to actually run the game, rather than being a participant, which is what a casino owner would do. Another idea is simply to be lucky, which is somewhat difficult to engineer. Lastly, it is possible to cheat, although he did not recommend this. One point he raised is that subtle changes in games can sometimes severely skew odds. For example, in the case of dice, Berkshire has studied how shortening one side of a die can greatly skew the probability of throwing a particular number. Even shortening a side by several percent can skew the probability away from 1/6 quite considerably. So, even in a simple game, through small changes we can make it very difficult to calculate the odds. Whilst investing (or speculating) should not be viewed as a game, the idea behind gauging probabilities and their interplay with payoffs involved is key to financial decision-making. It is insufficient to look at only being right or wrong; it is how right and how wrong which ultimately matters.

Games such as backgammon were around in the ancient world. Bernstein (1996) notes that Pontius Pilate's guards cast lots for a chance to own Christ's robe. He also describes astragali, a game played in ancient Egypt that is similar to throwing dice. Hence, one might have expected that in the ancient world people would have attempted to quantify the risks associated with playing these games and also from gambling. Thales applied scientific thought to explain the world; for example, even venturing to predict astronomical events, such as eclipses, which we shall discuss later in Chapter 6 on Black Swans.

Why did the Ancient Greeks not apply a similar scientific approach to quantifying risk? Bernstein suggests that this was something which evaded the Ancient Greeks' grasp. For one thing, he notes that the Greeks' system of counting made it difficult to do many basic arithmetic calculations. He suggests that whilst the Ancient Greeks may have had ideas about probabilities (there is the word *eikos*, which means probable in Ancient Greek, for example), they were never about to accurately quantify them. It was only in more modern times that probabilities were studied in a more mathematical sense, for example by Pascal in the seventeenth century. A more profound explanation that Bernstein cites involves examining the attitude that Ancient Greeks held toward the future.

If the future is considered as something ordained by fate, then it might seem irrelevant to attempt to gauge the probabilities of multiple outcomes, especially in a more quantitative manner. I think that this explanation why the Ancient Greeks never strayed into the area of probability is probably the most plausible one.

Oracles rather than probabilities

Ancient Greeks preferred to consult oracles to gain an insight into the future rather than attempting to gauge the relative probabilities of forthcoming events. Although I had heard the term oracle and understood the meaning as defined by a dictionary, I had little idea what precisely oracles were in Ancient Greece, and was also unaware how they made their predictions. I thought, therefore, it would be a worthwhile exercise to delve into the subject by reading Broad (2007). Amongst the many oracles of Ancient Greece, the most well known was the Oracle of Delphi. The Oracle of Delphi was not a single person, but a series of people. Unlike other oracles of Ancient Greece, the Oracle of Delphi was always a woman. Apollo, a Greek god, was said to speak through the priestess. Amongst the many titles Apollo had, the title of god of prophesy was perhaps the most apt for his task. The Temple of Apollo was on Mount Parnassus near the Gulf of Corinth, where the Oracle of Delphi made her prophesies. The fame of the Oracle was so great that she was consulted on important matters. For example, she advised Solon, a politician from Athens, to advocate a policy of compromise with his critics as he sought to strengthen democracy. How the Oracle delivered her prophesies is told in detail by Broad (2007). He tells us how she breathed in sacred pneuma in preparation for channeling the wisdom of Apollo, as well as doing a series of purification exercises. Her pronouncements were delivered in a trance-like state.

One of the most famous stories concerning the various oracles of the Ancient Greek world is told by Herodotus, who has garnered the title of the "father of history." We shall learn more about Herodotus and his famous series of books, which are known in English as *The Histories* or *The History of Herodotus* (Herodotus & Macaulay (trans), 1890) in Chapter 9. In the meantime, we recount just one of the stories told by Herodotus. He tells of Croesus, King of the Lydians. Croesus sent his messengers to visit various oracles around the Ancient Greek world. Their task was to consult each of these oracles exactly 100 days after leaving Croesus, and they were to ask what Croesus was doing on that day. Herodotus does not recount what was said by all of the oracles, but he notes the reply from the Oracle of Delphi was as follows:

But the number of sand I know, and the measure of drops in the ocean;
The dumb man I understand, and I hear the speech of the speechless:

> And there hath come to my soul the smell of a strong-shelled tortoise
> Boiling in caldron of bronze, and the flesh of a lamb mingled with it;
> Under it bronze is laid, it hath bronze as a clothing upon it.
>
> (Herodotus & Macaulay (trans), 1890)

When his messengers returned, Croesus read each of the prophecies, which were delivered to him so he could assess their accuracy. What had he done on the day of the test? Something that would be extremely difficult for anyone to guess: namely, he was:

> cutting up a tortoise and a lamb he boiled them together himself in a caldron of bronze, laying a cover of bronze over them.
>
> (Herodotus & Macaulay (trans), 1890)

This was strikingly similar to the prophecy given by the Oracle of Delphi, and in recognition of this Croesus sent many gifts to the temple at Delphi. He also sacrificed many animals in honor of the gods. The purpose of the test was not purely academic. Indeed, the primary purpose was to understand which was the most accurate of the oracles, so that Croesus could ask far more important questions, notably those relating to whether he should fight the Persians.

It is difficult to say whether the test constitutes "proof" of the Oracle of Delphi's power for prophecy. Indeed, there are examples when her prophecies were either inaccurate or simply very vague and could be interpreted in a multitude of ways. However, it does illustrate that there was some effort to ascertain the accuracy of her predictions. In a sense we can draw a parallel with backtesting of trading strategies with historical data, in which we try to assess the robustness of a trading strategy by testing whether it has worked historically. When we are doing this with trading strategies, it is insufficient simply to show a strategy "works" historically; just as important is understanding the reason why it works. We shall discuss using historical data and how traders should look back at their performance in more detail in Chapter 9.

Modern analysis of the ruins of the temple and the geology underlying it has suggested that the pneuma which was inhaled was a mix of gases, which was likely to have had hallucinatory properties. Or as Broad puts it more succinctly, it may have helped the Oracle to get high. This might partially help to explain the workings of the Oracle, but perhaps not all.

In the modern day, drug-induced highs have been said to have "facilitated" the creative process for a number of songs and books. As an example, one of my favorite books, *On the Road* by Jack Kerouac (Kerouac, 2011 (reprint)), was said to have been written in a three-week-long drug-fuelled blitz on a single scroll of paper (Shea, 2007), which I was lucky enough to see on a visit to New York Public Library several years ago. Also, it has not been unheard of for trading to be conducted under the influence of nefarious substances. Indeed, in 2010, a broker bought $520m-worth of crude oil in the late evening after drinking a large amount of alcohol (Mason, 2010).

Following this discussion, we might think the notion of consulting an oracle today for trading advice would seem unusual, especially after our analysis of pneuma. However, to some extent the idea of inferring patterns in historical price action from technical analysis might seem similar, with technical analysts standing in for the Oracle of Delphi. Indeed, some market participants prefer to ignore the field of technical analysis. Historically, academia has been skeptical of the notion (I am skeptical of the skeptics!). Notably, the efficient market hypothesis postulates that all news is already in the price. However, there is a crucial difference between the observations made using technical analysis and the prophecies of an oracle; namely, that the profits from technical analysis have entirely plausible explanations.

One of the most important reasons why technical analysis is generally profitable is that it has an element of self-fulfillment. If many investors are trying to discern very similar patterns in price action and trade accordingly, they can help to perpetuate these patterns through their trading activity. The key to trading with trend-following strategies is to be the first rather than the last person in the queue identifying a trend. That is what separates profitable technical analysts from those who are not. Also, more deeply, there is a less obvious link between technical analysis and fundamentals, if we remember that there is a generally pronounced business cycle. If we think of price action as a reflection of fundamentals, then it should follow that the large trends in the economic growth during the business cycle should also be reflected as overarching trends within price action.

In Chapter 3, we discuss trend-following strategies in more detail, and note that at least in the currency markets a very generic version has historically been profitable. Lastly, what title do we bestow on one of the most famous investors today? The Oracle (of Omaha), namely Warren Buffett, whom we shall meet in Chapter 4 and have already briefly discussed in Chapter 1. The Oracle of Delphi has not been forgotten by investors.

Quantifying financial risk through volatility

If we speed forward to the modern world, in contrast to the Ancient Greeks and their oracles we have numerous ways in which to quantify risk. One of the simplest measures of risk is volatility, as it tends to be known in markets (but mainly as standard deviation in other contexts). The word volatility comes from the Latin *volere*, which means *to fly*. Despite spending years learning Latin at school, this point somehow evaded my notice until I read about its origin in *Antifragile* (Taleb, 2013). Indeed, this is also likely to be the root of the French verb *voler*, which can mean to fly or alternatively to steal. Please note, the following few lines might seem a tad pedantic for those of you who work in finance and are likely to be aware of how volatility is calculated (but do bear with me).

Before calculating volatility, we must first calculate the returns of an asset over time. Typically, for a stock, for example, this involves ascertaining the percentage returns over a period at regular intervals, which could for example be daily or weekly. Hence, if the stock is $100 today, and it goes up to $101 tomorrow, the daily percentage return over the day is +1%.

Following this, we calculate the average returns (or more precisely the mean) over the time period we wish to investigate. We also do the same thing with squared returns. Why would you want to do that, you might ask? Well, if the price action is relatively calm, not moving much away from the mean, then the squared returns would be pretty small. However, if the price action were very erratic, the squared returns would be very large. Clearly, simply looking at any average would not capture this dynamic of the price action. We than calculate the variance, which is the spread between the average of squared returns and the squared average returns (bear with me, the mathematical bit is nearly over – or skip ahead if this is too simple). The volatility is the square root of this spread, and it is usually annualized when used in finance. The relative riskiness of multiple assets can then be compared if we look at their various volatilities, which have been annualized. If we do not annualize our measure of volatility, it becomes difficult to compare volatilities measured over different time windows. The VaR (value at risk) calculation of a portfolio uses both volatilities of assets and the correlations of the assets within it. If a portfolio is full of assets which are highly correlated, then its risk is likely to be higher than a portfolio with uncorrelated assets. The rationale is that price swings would impact a correlated portfolio more.

The final output of a VaR calculation is a USD amount, which relates to the amount of money you might lose on one in 20 days. So, for example, if the VaR of your trading book is $500k, it means that on 5% of days losses could exceed $500k.

However, neither this volatility metric nor VaR, which uses it, is perfect. For one thing, what we have calculated is realized volatility (alternatively known as historical volatility). We have used a backward-looking window of data to do this. It does not require us to use the deductive capacity of Sherlock Holmes to ascertain a problem. Clearly, the issue is that whatever window we have used might not mirror the future period. We have nasty things called change of regimes where the previous pattern of volatility can suddenly alter. The calculation of historic correlations, which again is used by VaR, can be even more problematic. (We note that there are more complicated variations of VaR, which we shall very briefly touch upon later, which are designed to alleviate some of the concerns we have mentioned.)

Furthermore, we have made the assumption that we can regularly value our asset whilst we are holding it. This might be relatively easy for highly liquid assets, such as stocks, currencies or bonds. However, it is difficult for illiquid assets, which rarely trade. Take the example of a house which we own in the United States. We can estimate the approximate value of the house by looking at other similar properties in an area which have traded. However, if no similar properties have traded, than our estimate will be even more of a guess. If our estimate does not change significantly from month to month it implies that the volatility of our house price is close to zero. This implies that holding our house entails very low risk, which intuitively seems incorrect. A brief look at US nationwide house prices following the Lehman crisis (see Figure 2.1) would show that historically such an assumption is wrong. The main point is that estimates of the price would heavily impact our final volatility number.

In the ancient world, even if they had known a measure such as volatility, it would have been very difficult to calculate, given the difficulty to mark to market assets regularly, as in our house example. In Thales' case it would have required him to judge the market price for his olive press options at regular intervals. Options on olive presses were extremely unlikely to be sufficiently tradable in Ancient Greece; hence, such an exercise would be very difficult! Not only that, there would also have been the obvious difficulties of doing the large amounts of arithmetic manually at that time; perhaps less of a problem today. As an aside, the lack of Arabic numerals would have made it more difficult to undertake even what we consider to be mundane arithmetic calculations today. Greek and Roman numerals were useful for recording numbers, but only once a calculation had been done on an abacus, a contraption which was familiar

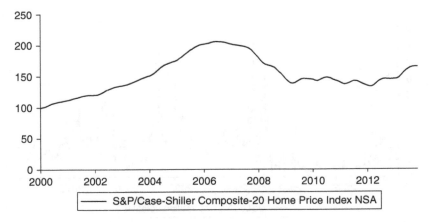

Figure 2.1 S&P/Case-Shiller Index of US house prices – a riskless asset does not drop this much!
Source: Thalesians, Bloomberg Finance L.P.

to many civilizations in the ancient world. The key point of these examples is that in the context of illiquid assets where valuation is difficult, measuring volatility is not always appropriate as the sole determinant of their risk, and it is challenging. However, it does not mean we should not trade illiquid assets since we cannot easily ascertain their volatility. That would mean we are implying there should not have been any commerce in the ancient world, in particular in assets which are not heavily traded, such as real estate: this seems like a ridiculous suggestion. It simply means that we need other ways of measuring risk when it comes to trading, rather than using volatility alone. Even when we can estimate volatility easily, we should utilize other risk metrics alongside it.

Structural breaks in volatility regimes

If we are able to calculate volatility for specific assets, we need to be aware that there can often be structural breaks in the volatility regime of an asset. This has occurred on numerous occasions in the world of currencies. The idea of a peg in currencies is relatively common within emerging market countries (see Figure 2.2), although less common with more developed market currencies. Broadly speaking, this involves a central bank keeping its own currency in a very tight range (usually against USD, EUR, or a basket of major currencies). In some cases, central banks might also institute capital controls, to prevent the free flow of capital to and from their country, in order to help keep control of their currency.

In the case of a peg, if for example the local currency appreciates, the central bank simply sells it and buys USD. If the currency loses value, the converse

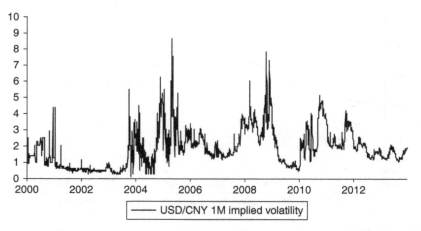

Figure 2.2   USD/CNY 1M implied volatility – jumps coincide with shifts in USD/CNY trading regime
Source: Thalesians, Bloomberg Finance L.P.

occurs and the central bank buys its local currency and sells USD. However, what happens if speculators lose confidence in the local currency and start to sell it repeatedly? At some stage, the central bank could run out of USD to sell to prop up their home currency. It is at this point, without the central bank to support the currency, that the local currency devalues and volatility explodes. Furthermore, whilst volatility may come off following the original devaluation, it may remain at significantly higher and more natural levels without further central bank intervention. This would signal a permanent shift in the volatility of that currency. Very often if a country has debt in foreign currencies, it is forced to default on it when its local currency devalues. Currency devaluations afflicted the ancient world, as noted by Winkler (1999). This example has also been cited by Reinhart & Rogoff (2011).

Winkler tells us of Dionysus of Syracuse, who was known as the tyrant of Syracuse. He borrowed from his citizens via promissory notes. When the time came to pay his citizens back, his government confiscated all the money in circulation. As his nickname might suggest, he instituted a rather hefty punishment for those citizens who did not adhere to his decree, namely death. The final step was to remint all the one drachma coins as two drachma coins. Hence, he was able to pay back his creditors by devaluing the currency and inflating away the debt. This devaluation "trick" has been repeatedly tried by rulers through the ages, in recent years most notably by Robert Mugabe in Zimbabwe, as discussed by Hawkinsin (2007).

Obviously, these days, if a government actively wants to devalue its currency it can do so by simply selling its local currency on the market, rather than physically changing the composition of coins. Coins no longer have intrinsic value and are merely placeholders, just as banknotes have always been. For example, on sterling banknotes there is the phrase "I promise to pay the bearer on demand." Unlike the case where a central bank is trying to defend its own currency selling USD, in this instance local currency is essentially in limitless supply. The only caveat is that it can drive up inflation, and also politically it can sometimes be difficult to weaken your own currency. Excessive currency weakness is also not always desirable.

These permanent shifts in volatility regimes are not restricted to managed currencies. Another notable example of a permanent shift in volatility has been seen in bonds of the Eurozone periphery. These countries are Portugal, Italy, Ireland, Greece, and Spain. Before the Eurozone debt crisis, which started in earnest in 2010, yields of the Eurozone periphery traded close to those of Germany. In other words, the bonds of these countries were trading at around the same price. This suggested that the creditworthiness of, for example, Greece was close to that of Germany. The rationale was that with European monetary union, there would be a convergence in how the sovereign debt of Eurozone members would trade. Obviously, with hindsight, this was incorrect: pegging currency rates between members was not the same thing as pegging sovereign debt yields (and by implication the prices of their bonds). Particularly following Greece's default during the Eurozone debt crisis, such a notion seems even more unlikely! Credit defaults are of course hardly a new concept, having been used for as long as humans have used debt as a financing tool. Indeed, Winkler (1999) notes that in Ancient Greece in the fourth century BC the case where 10 Greek municipalities out of the 13 which made up the Attic Maritime Association defaulted. Their single creditor was the temple of Delos, the mythical birthplace of Apollo, the Greek god whom we met earlier in the context of the Oracle of Delphi. Out of these, two municipalities completely defaulted, whilst eight were in a partial default. During the Eurozone debt crisis, the market repriced Eurozone peripheral yields a lot higher (so their bonds were a lot cheaper than those issued by Germany), and they began to trade with a lot more volatility. This illustrated that there was a structural break in the market. For background on the Eurozone debt crisis, I would recommend Jens Nordvig's book (Nordvig, 2013).

In the above cases we have described, any backward-looking volatility calculation will have been totally wrong. It would have been an inaccurate measure of the long-term riskiness of that asset. Essentially, when we have outsized market moves, realized volatility no longer becomes a reasonable estimate for the riskiness of an asset.

Risk sentiment and the impact on market volatility

In the earlier section we described a situation where there can be a structural break in the volatility of assets. However, on a short-term basis, volatility can itself change rapidly on a generalized market-wide basis (see Figure 2.3).

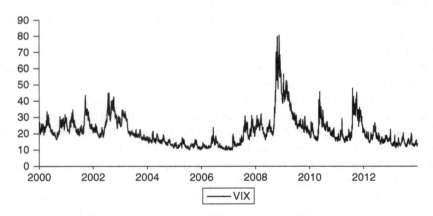

Figure 2.3   VIX (implied volatility of options on S&P500); spikes indicate times of market tensions
Source: Thalesians, Bloomberg Finance L.P.

Option traders call this property the volatility of volatility (or vol of vol, which is a touch easier to say). What would be the driver of temporary shifts in the volatility of assets across many markets, an acceleration in volatility of volatility? We can often find an answer if we look at changes in risk sentiment in the market. We can think of risk sentiment as the willingness of market participants to hold what are traditionally perceived as volatile assets. As we have noted, generally higher-risk assets will tend to offer a higher yield. Hence, we will get paid more to hold them. Conversely, lower-risk assets generally tend to offer lower yields, as we might expect. Risk is proportional to reward, after all.

During periods when investors have very strong risk appetite, markets are said to be in risk-seeking territory. In this type of environment, investors will be more prepared to both buy and also hold higher-yielding risky assets. In this scenario, volatility across the market tends to be lower and, generally, we might also expect higher-yielding assets to appreciate. Hence, we might observe that equities outperform bonds on a relative basis. Historically higher-yielding currencies, such as those in the emerging markets and the Australian dollar, are likely to be particularly bid. Measures of liquidity such as bid/ask spreads are probably going to be tighter, given that market makers do not need to take a lot of risk when they trade with their counterparties. When risk sentiment is more neutral in markets, investors may choose to reduce their exposure to risky assets, although they are still likely to be overweight. It can be a harbinger of worse times to come.

A major market risk event, such as the Lehman crisis, can push investors' risk appetite to the negative side, which is generally termed as risk aversion. We can think of a market crisis as a particularly brutal form of risk aversion. In this case, investors will seek to offload their holdings of higher-risk assets such as equities and will seek to buy safe haven assets, such as US Treasury bonds. In short, investors' priorities shift from seeking extra yield to preservation of capital. Liquidity is likely to worsen and bid/ask spreads will blow out, given that so many investors are seeking to liquidate their higher-risk trades. More simply, the cost of trading rises in such an environment. Market-realized volatility also blows up. Implied volatility explodes, as investors seek to buy options to protect against losses in the underlying assets they are holding. We shall discuss implied volatility in more detail soon and how it differs from realized volatility.

Correlations can also be highly unstable and are liable to flipping. They can be brutal at times of risk aversion and in particular during market crises. In ordinary times, a portfolio might appear to be full of totally uncorrelated assets. However, during times of market crisis, there can be widespread liquidation of many investors' portfolios, as they seek to come up with cash to pay for margin calls. As a result, seemingly uncorrelated assets can suddenly behave like one another. So investors are faced with two issues at times of crisis: spiking volatility and also an undiversified portfolio.

Can we predict shifts in market risk sentiment? We can try . . .

Attempting to detect shifts in risk sentiment before they occur is extremely difficult. One approach can be to monitor risk factors, which are those contracts which are particularly susceptible to changes in risk appetite. Hence, for example, this could be the implied volatility on various risky assets, which we mentioned above. However, which assets in particular should we be examining for clues about shifts in market risk sentiment?

One of the difficulties is that major market crises can emanate from many different areas. If we take a look at the Lehman crisis in 2008, some of the first elements of stress appeared in the credit markets before spreading to the rest of the market. In the decade leading up to the Lehman crisis, many of the crises observed were those afflicting emerging markets, such as the devaluation of the Turkish lira in 2001 or the Argentinian peso in 2002. Hence, if we had been using the template of recent crises to detect changes in the market before Lehman, we would be obsessed by risk factors associated with emerging markets. Our efforts would have been futile in trying to detect the Lehman crisis. Emerging markets did sell off, but only after the initial shock of the collapse of Lehman Brothers.

One solution is to look at a wide array of risk factors across many markets, rather than purely focusing on one or two. Alternatively, if we are looking at trading a specific asset class, we can look at risk factors specifically related to that asset class. So, for example, if we are interested in trading FX carry (buying higher-yielding currencies funded by selling lower-yielding currencies), then we might choose to look at price changes in FX options (which is essentially implied volatility), to gauge whether risk aversion is impacting the FX market. There is unfortunately no right answer. However, doing diligent backtesting using historical data can help inform us of a "better" or "worse" way, if we are careful with our approach and avoid doing excessive data mining. In Chapter 9, we look at using historical data when trading in more detail.

Aside from monitoring price changes within markets, we can also examine fundamental data, such as the unemployment rate, to estimate when risk sentiment is turning sour. The rationale behind looking at fundamental data is that moves in markets can be seen as a reaction to it. There are certain factors that are very difficult to measure, such as politics and civil strife, which can often be a trigger for shifts in market risk sentiment. During the Eurozone debt crisis, the market essentially swung on the constant trickle of news flow from negotiations between the various Eurozone countries. Elsewhere in this chapter we also discuss the particular notion of risk on/risk off markets.

In practice, the best we can expect from the methods I have discussed is that they will help us detect market crises and shifts in risk sentiment as they happen. It seems unlikely they will enable us to predict them repeatedly. At worst they tell us about a market crisis once it has happened. In our section

Figure 2.4   The cycle of price action during a crisis
Source: Thalesians, Bloomberg Finance L.P.

concerning risk on/risk off markets, we discuss the problems with late identification of the risk regime. To some extent, the difficulty in trying to predict market risk sentiment is that price action can end up being circular. This can especially be the case during market crises. Worsening market turmoil can make investors' risk appetite poor, which can in turn exacerbate the market selloff and so on. This vicious cycle does eventually break, once investors have finished the (often forced) liquidation of all their positions. However, this point of utter capitulation is precisely the time when it is mentally the most challenging to get back into the market (see Figure 2.4).

RORO your investment boat

The term risk on/risk off (RORO for short) has become popularized in recent years. In such a market, risk sentiment is the overriding factor driving asset prices, as opposed to idiosyncratic factors. As the acronym would suggest, the market continually oscillates between risk aversion and more benign risk sentiment. In a risk on/risk off market, the correlation between assets of a similar risk profile is generally higher than it would ordinarily be. It is often the case that the driver for risk on/risk off markets is a single overriding theme of critical importance impacting risk sentiment. In recent years, the clearest examples of these singular risk drivers have been the financial crisis of 2008 and also the Eurozone debt crisis, which started in earnest in 2010. In such a scenario, it is likely that investors will also consider using risk sentiment as one of the primary factors in their decision-making process.

Just as we characterized different risk environments by referring to changes in various risk factors, so we can use the approach to think about risk on/risk off-style markets. Generally, during risk on/risk off-style markets, risk factors such as FX implied volatility will maintain some element of elevation. The explanation is that even when we have "risk on" style price action in such markets, with, for example, equities rallying aggressively (see Figure 2.6), fundamentally, investors are still wary about the potential negative impacts from the background risk driver. Hence, they are still prepared to buy "insurance" as a hedge, resulting in elevated implied volatility (see Figure 2.5).

So how should investors approach a risk on/risk off market? Earlier, we gave some ideas which we can use (to some extent!) to estimate changes in risk sentiment. We noted that it is incredibly difficult to predict shifts in risk sentiment. In practice, one of the issues we stressed is that being able to identify the

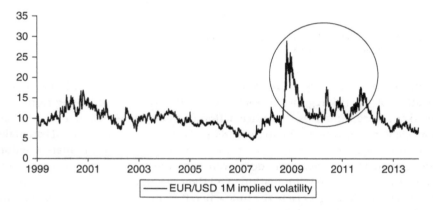

Figure 2.5   EUR/USD FX implied volatility was elevated for many years, whilst the market was buffered by both the fallout from the subprime crisis and the Eurozone debt crisis
Source: Thalesians, Bloomberg Finance L.P.

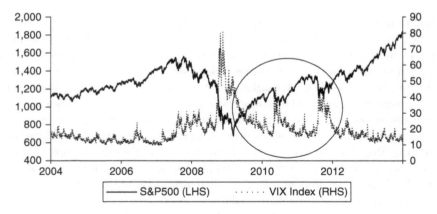

Figure 2.6   Even with heightened market volatility (VIX) and more vol of VIX, risky assets (S&P500) can still rally in risk on/risk off environments
Source: Thalesians, Bloomberg Finance L.P.

current state of risk sentiment falls short of predicting it. At worst, we can end up identifying the previous incarnation of risk sentiment. The difficulty with risk on/risk off markets is that the oscillation between states of risk sentiment can be very rapid. If investors repeatedly identify the previous state of risk sentiment, they can also be repeatedly caught on the wrong side of the market, given that the states last for a very short amount of time. We can draw a parallel when attempting to follow trends if the market is trading within a range. This results in what is commonly called a whipsaw signal. In such a situation, the difficulty in timing can result in investors buying during short-term tops and selling when there are short-term lows in price action. Buying at the high and selling at the low is hardly a recipe for successful trading. This also relates to our later point about how the frequency of trading can be related to the risk of a strategy.

What should investors do in a risk on/risk off market? Sometimes it can simply be better, when there are very rapid changes in risk sentiment, to stick to a fundamental view (or being flat) rather than constantly switching exposure. This might well entail taking smaller positions given elevated market volatility and the likelihood of increased drawdowns during risk off periods. Indeed, in the years following Lehman, despite the market turbulence, S&P500 eventually managed to rally (see Figure 2.6). The problem is that repeatedly being on the wrong side of the market is a tail risk that can also afflict higher-frequency traders. We shall write about this subject later in this chapter.

Although the term risk on/risk off has become popular, technically speaking the term is incorrect. We should note that whenever investors hold some sort of investment, there is some element of risk in your portfolio. This is regardless of whether or not the investor has invested in what is perceived as a safe haven asset or a high-risk asset. Even if investors simply hold cash, that does not mean they hold no risk (think back to the holders of coins during the time of Dionysus of Syracuse). However, readers should be informed about the term, given it has appeared so often in the financial press following the financial crisis.

Furthermore, whilst the idea of a risk on/risk off market is a characteristic of markets in flux following crises, the more ordinary state of a market is to be driven more by a mix of idiosyncratic factors and broader market sentiment. Whilst shifts in risk sentiment are still a feature of more ordinary markets, they are not the persistent overriding factor that they are in a risk on/risk off-style market.

Understanding implied versus realized volatility

We have briefly talked about implied and realized volatility without describing how they differ. Before discussing this difference, we must first delve into the world of options. For options traders the next few lines are likely to be a touch trivial, so please feel free to skip them.

The simplest options are calls and puts. A call gives you the right to buy an asset for a certain price in the future, which is known as the strike price. Conversely, a put gives you the right to sell an asset for this predefined strike price. One use of options is of course to hedge exposure to an underlying asset. For example, investors might be long FTSE 100. To hedge their exposure through the options market, they can buy put options on FTSE 100. In Chapter 4, we discuss the idea of hedging and insurance within the context of a portfolio. The other use of options is to take an outright speculative view. This is what Thales did. Thales effectively bought call options on olive presses.

The valuation of the option depends on many factors such as the tenor of the option. The larger the time window, the more expensive it is likely to be. Similarly, if the strike price is far from the current price (known as out-of-the-money) it will generally be cheaper. Several factors can be input into an option-pricing model to output an option price. One key factor for the option price is the volatility of asset and this is the basis of the Black-Scholes option-pricing model. Indeed, options traders often speculate not on the direction of an asset, but specifically on how volatility will behave. As a result options traders are interchangeably known as volatility traders in banks. But which volatility can we use to value an option? After all, realized volatility is a backward-looking estimate and we have already discussed the various problems with that. So rather than using realized volatility, we can use implied volatility, which is an estimate from market traders for future realized volatility. In practice, implied volatility will often end up being higher than what is observed as realized volatility over the same period (see Figure 2.7). Why is

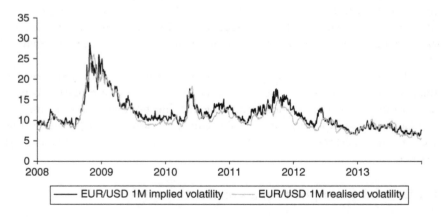

Figure 2.7 Implied volatility is generally higher than realized because of the risk premium (EUR/USD 1M implied versus realized)
Source: Thalesians, Bloomberg Finance L.P.

this the case? Given that implied volatility is basically an estimation of a hitherto unknown quantity, there is usually a risk premium embedded into it to compensate traders who are selling it. However, the key point with implied volatility is that it has at least some forward-looking aspect.

Hence, it should react to what are perceived as important forthcoming scheduled events (such as a central bank meeting to set interest rates). We note that implied volatility is still not a perfect predictor when it comes to identifying the likelihood of risk events, even if it is better than using realized volatility. In these scenarios, implied volatility tends to spike repricing the riskiness of the market, but usually only after a risk event has occurred. In my experience, implied volatility tends to be one of the best (of the simple) measures for future expectations of volatility, in particular when compared to realized volatility. Options in asset classes such as FX and equities are often very liquid assets themselves and traded widely, so the measure is unlikely to suffer from being "stale," which can afflict less traded markets. There are some subtle touches we can use by combining the various elements of both realized and implied volatility to create a better forward-looking measure of future volatility. Whilst I was working at Nomura, one of my colleagues Will Johns, an options trader, had a brainstorm to create such a combined measure. We found that in general it was indeed a better predictor of future volatility compared to either implied or realized volatility. Another important property of market volatility is that it tends to be mean-reverting, which helps us to forecast it. Hence, high volatility is likely to be followed by levels of low volatility and vice versa. There are of course countless methods for forecasting volatility, which are beyond the scope of our discussion.

One of the major deficiencies with the Black-Scholes option-pricing model is that for whatever strike of an option or tenor it assumes the same implied volatility. Generally, implied volatility is proportional to the option price. Even without reference to any mathematics or formulas, such a notion seems like an inaccurate reflection of the market. Let us take options sold on S&P500. Say we are given a call option which has a very high strike and a put which has a very low strike. Which one is likely to have a higher implied volatility? Which type of price action is likely to frighten market participants the most? It seems the put with a very low strike is likely to be more expensive. Generally, investors are long stocks; hence, to protect their exposure, they are likely to want to hedge against big falls in the stock market rather than big rises in stocks. After all, they would profit from rises in stocks, if they are already long the underlying asset. As a result, in most cases the demand is likely to be more for downside equity options than for upside. Black-Scholes assumes that price action follows geometric Brownian motion. This would imply a normal distribution of returns which is symmetric for both gains and losses. In practice this is not the case for stocks, because of the way large losses skew the distribution, and results in a fat tail in the distribution toward losses. In Figure 2.8, we illustrate this with

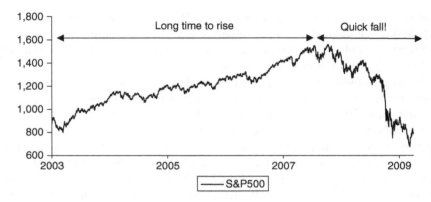

Figure 2.8   S&P500: the way down is quicker than the way up
Source: Thalesians, Bloomberg Finance L.P.

S&P500, where we note that the big falls in S&P500 generally happen quicker than moves higher.

More generally, Black-Scholes also has a tendency to underprice very heavily out-of-the-money options, given its assumption that the implied volatility surface is flat. This is particularly the case for those options which are used to hedge blow-up risk, such as downside equity options, which we have noted. In recent years and particularly following the financial crisis, options market makers are much more likely to place a large premium on these types of options. In some cases they might simply refuse to sell them to clients because of the difficulties in pricing them. In practice these days, at least for liquid assets, traders will mark many points on a volatility surface for a large selection of both tenors and strikes. They no longer assume a single implied volatility for every strike and tenor combination.

This is not to say that the options models used today are perfect. It is up to the trader to put what he or she believes are reasonable parameters into an option-pricing model, taking into account the various deficiencies of the model. If totally unrepresentative parameters are inserted into a model, then the price output will be totally out of line with the market and the result. There are arguments by Taleb (2013) that before the advent of option-pricing models such as Black-Scholes, traders traded options by looking mostly at relative supply and demand. This is indeed the usual way in which we would expect prices are made in a market. Using option-price models, whilst adopting some common sense when interpreting the output, is a compromise between the two approaches. A more mathematical way of saying this is that the emphasis should be on calibrating a model to the observed market, rather than trying to fit the market to the model. There needs to be willingness to skew the pricing if it feels wrong to a trader. At this point, it is probably worth recalling a few words from my friend Iain Clark. Iain humorously described implied vol in the following way: "implied vol is the wrong vol to put into the wrong model to get the wrong price for the wrong product for the wrong client."

Trading risk directly through options

We have touched upon the vagaries of the options market, in particular the way in which it can be used to express directional views (or hedge directional views) through calls and puts. Indeed, if we think back to Thales, he was buying olive press calls, taking a directional view. As we noted, however, it is perhaps less well understood that options can be used directly to trade risk or more accurately to take a view on the future path of volatility. As a result, we noted options traders are often interchangeably known as volatility traders. The simplest way to get exposure to rising volatility is to purchase a straddle, which involves buying a call and put at the same time, both with the same strikes. A large directional move in either direction will see the investor making a profit. Conversely, if the price does not change much, the investor will lose money on the premium paid for the straddle. If we want to take an even more nuanced volatility view, we can do this by delta hedging the option.

Delta hedging involves doing additional trades in the cash market to cancel out our risk from directional moves in the asset price, whilst still also having option exposure in the underlying. If we are long a straddle and the asset price goes up, in order to delta hedge we would generally need to sell the underlying asset. Conversely, if the asset price goes down, we would have to buy the underlying to delta hedge. Our payoff from such a strategy will be based upon the difference between implied and realized volatility (the precise payoff is slightly more complicated than this in practice). In Figures 2.9 and 2.10, we illustrate the types of scenarios from future asset prices that will result in profits and losses for a strategy which involves buying a straddle and delta hedging. In other words, we are taking a view that current implied volatility will turn out to be lower than future realized volatility. More simply, we think that the market is pricing implied too cheaply. Generally, if spot goes back and forth across the strike, we would make money from delta hedging a long straddle position. If the option expires and spot is very far from the strike, we would also make money on the underlying straddle position.

Rather than going through the complexity of trading straddles and delta hedging in the underlying cash market, we can use products such as volatility swaps, whose payoff is directly the difference between implied and realized volatility. There are also options contracts, which allow us to speculate on changes in implied volatility such as forward volatility agreements. The key to all these instruments, though, is understanding them before trading, which is a point that we shall reiterate in Chapter 3.

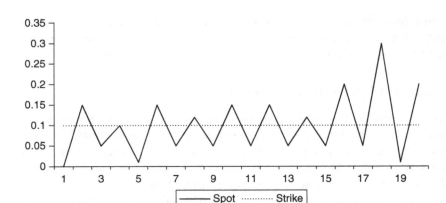

Figure 2.9   A good scenario if you are long straddle and delta hedged
Source: Thalesians.

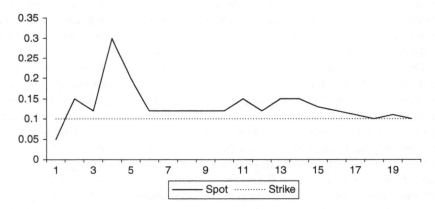

Figure 2.10   A bad scenario if you are long straddle and delta hedged
Source: Thalesians.

As we noted earlier, generally implied volatility tends to be higher than realized volatility (the so-called volatility risk premium). It is generally profitable to be short volatility, for example by selling straddles, albeit with some crucial caveats. Indeed, Morris, Balakrishnan, Rushton, Aggarwal, & Rajendran (2013) discuss the long-term characteristics of selling volatility in various fixed income markets and also provide historical results. The major caveat is that given that selling volatility is basically an example of collecting risk premium, it can be subject to severe drawdowns when risk aversion shakes markets. We have noted that at such times market volatility explodes. Hence, managing risk around a short volatility strategy is crucial. In some circumstances, the risks outweigh any possible awards, such as when repeatedly selling heavily out-of-the-money options (see Chapter 6) without hedging any of this exposure. We can view this as a highly leveraged form of collecting risk premium. Indeed, we need to be aware that selling parts of the volatility surface can be more "dangerous" than others. For example, longer dated contracts can be exposed to larger blow-up risk. Hence, it is for that reason that funds often employ long/short volatility strategies, picking up risk premium for shorter dated contracts, whilst buying longer dated contracts. There are still risks to doing this, notably curve inversion of vol. The market might panic about shorter-term events. Hence, shorter dated implied vol might go up more than longer dated implied vol.

It is difficult to argue that those in the ancient world would be able to trade such sophisticated options strategies. However, the idea of transferring risk premium is something which was part of the ancient world. Indeed, if we think about insurance, that is very much built upon the idea of collecting risk premium by one party from another. As we shall note in Chapter 4, the rise of trade helped to sow the seed of the insurance industry. Hence, the notion of a short volatility trade is not new.

Classifying groups of investors by their attitude to risk

Thus far, we have assumed that all investors have similar attitudes when it comes to risk-taking. In the real world, this assumption seems hopelessly inaccurate! Let us take skydiving as a simple example. There are some people who are prepared to take the risk which is associated with such an activity, whilst there are those people who would not. I belong to the latter group. In practice, the financial world is no different. Investors have different attitudes to taking risk, as we might expect. Indeed, we can classify groups of investors by their approach to risk-taking. Even in heavily risk-seeking markets, there can be a large divergence between the risk appetites of investors. Equally, when risk aversion comes to markets, the degree to which investors will be impacted can vary. If we think of pension funds, they are by their nature more conservative. The time horizon of their trades is very long term, and they tend to have much lower levels of risk appetite. This should not be surprising. The idea of investing in a pension is to provide a regular income in old age. It is not to use as funding for casino-style investments!

At the other end of the spectrum we have speculators. In general, they are willing to take more leverage when they trade. More simply, they are prepared to borrow more, thus taking greater risk when they trade. Higher levels of leverage imply that the size of any possible reward is greater. At the same time, it means that potential losses could be higher. In particular, during swings in risk sentiment, their higher leverage could mean that they are more likely to liquidate exposure because of losses. The result is that the volatility of a speculator's returns is likely to be much higher than those of a pension fund. Also, speculators have fewer restrictions when they trade. For example, very conservative investors will tend to have a far smaller group of assets which they are authorized to trade. In many cases, they might avoid derivatives or at least the ability to write options, where potential losses can be unlimited, compared to potential gains. At the same time, they might have restrictions on the direction in which they can take exposure. For example, more conservative institutions might be authorized to be long stocks but not short stocks. Taking a short position in stocks would be profitable if stocks fall. We discuss how investment mandates impact traders in Chapter 5.

Does the time horizon of a trading strategy correlate with how risky it might be?

The time horizon of investors and the typical holding period of their trades can have a relationship with the riskiness of their strategy. Simply having a short-term horizon can sometimes increase risks, if we consider worst-case scenarios. If we repeatedly trade and are unlucky enough to be on the wrong side of a trade in most cases, seemingly sane markets can still result in heavy losses. Say a certain stock market has generally risen at most 10% a year, but the worst annual losses have been 10%. Over the course of a week we assume that stocks can rise or fall around 2%. Although we cannot assume that future performance will be bounded by previous high and lows, it can at least give us some sort of guideline. Let us assume that some investors take an annual view on this stock market, buying and holding it for a year. Other investors might trade on a weekly basis, either long or short. If this second group repeatedly misjudges the direction of stocks every few days, their losses could easily exceed those from the first group. Admittedly, this is a manufactured example, but it still illustrates that we need to consider carefully many different possible scenarios for whichever investment strategy we employ.

Also, in my experience, higher-frequency trading strategies can have more of a tendency to break quickly, which is essentially a latent risk, a property which is difficult to observe. Whilst high-frequency strategies are "working," typically their risk-adjusted returns will be better than lower-frequency strategies. Again, this tells us little about a possible breaking point. Obviously, very high-frequency trading is something which is more a characteristic of today's markets, rather than during ancient times, or even markets 20 years ago. The reason that such higher-frequency strategies can suddenly break is that the certain market behaviors they seek to leverage can often disappear if a large number of investors attempt to trade them. In a high-frequency trading strategy, typically investors will be trying to capture only a few basis points of profit, a fraction of a percent (or possibly less). This is such a small amount that it does not take much for transaction costs to eclipse any of the potential gain. If a large group of traders is attempting to seek out market liquidity at the same time to execute a similar strategy, it is likely that transaction costs will significantly eat into the strategy's profits.

This effect, which can negatively impact the returns of a strategy, is known as crowding. In some ways, we can make a parallel to the situation we discussed earlier: the breaking of currency pegs and the sudden associated change with currency volatility regimes. Crowding can still impact longer-term strategies. This is something which we can see with the most generic forms of trend-following strategies traded within FX. I discussed this point in a paper (Amen, 2013). Essentially, I examined a generic trend-following strategy in FX, using data going back to the 1970s. For the first 20 years, the strategy performed very well. However, over the past ten years, crowding from a large number of funds adopting a similar style have resulted in this strategy becoming less profitable, save for the period in 2008, during the post-Lehman market liquidation. In recent years, it has required additional bells and whistles on trend-following strategies to make them profitable. In a sense, for trend-following strategies, there is an element where you want some crowding, but not too much. One of the reasons given for the success of trend-follow strategies is the element that they can be self-fulfilling. This is a point which we shall come back to in Chapter 3 and which we noted earlier in this chapter. However, we do not want too much crowding, such that other investors get into the trade before you, pushing the price away from your entry point.

Although we have cited an example of a long-term strategy which was crowded out, it took a long time for this generic trend-following strategy to become loss-making. With high-frequency strategies, it is likely we might observe crowding out over a much shorter period of time for the reasons we mentioned earlier. Furthermore, the capacity of the market to absorb longer-term strategies is likely to be far higher. In the case of longer-term strategies, often the key is understanding the type of market that is most suitable for a particular strategy. For example, if markets go through extended periods of risk aversion, strategies which attempt to harvest risk premium are unlikely to be profitable. This does not always mean that these strategies are "broken." A more amenable market environment for such a strategy could come. We give the example of being long S&P500. Whilst a passive buy and hold strategy has endured considerable periods of drawdown, over the longer term it has nevertheless been a profitable strategy despite this (see Figure 2.11). In Chapter 9, we discuss the importance of testing strategies in different market regimes.

Understanding risk through the use of scenarios

We have discussed many dynamics of understanding risk when it comes to trading. We have noted that one particularly important risk metric is being able to estimate the most likely largest loss you could face on a trade. Expanding upon

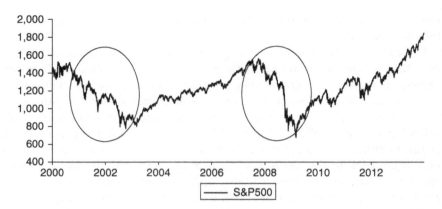

Figure 2.11 Simply because long S&P500 has lost money for extended periods has not prevented it from being profitable in the longer term
Source: Thalesians, Bloomberg Finance L.P.

this topic, when placing any trade it is useful to contemplate the probabilities of various outcomes and payoffs associated with them. If at any point you are not comfortable with any of the outcomes, it is probably a sign that you do not have enough confidence in the trade! Also, trying to understand the sensitivity of a trade to a possible change in expected market conditions is crucial.

Let us consider a trade where we buy EUR and sell USD, so we expect EUR to appreciate versus USD over a period of several weeks. More succinctly, those in the currency markets would refer to this trade as long EUR/USD. This terminology confused me no end when I started working in currency markets many years ago! When we put on this trade, we will probably have our base case of likely events which we think would be favorable for our trade.

We digress briefly to the world of currencies to run through some typical reasoning for our trade. Our rationale for placing this trade could be that we think US economic data is likely to be weak compared with Eurozone economic data in the short term. As a result, we would conjecture that a shift in relative interest rate expectations would be bullish for EUR and bearish for USD. Generally, relative interest rate expectations tend to be related to relative growth expectations. Higher economic growth is generally accompanied by high inflation. Central banks tend to hike rates (hawkish monetary policy) to keep inflation in check. We make an exception for the times when inflation is out of control and there is little or no growth. An extreme case of this would lead to the debasement of a currency. Conversely, weaker growth and low inflation will often encourage central banks to cut rates (dovish monetary policy) to foster growth and to keep inflation within a target range. FX often reacts to shifts in these relative interest rate expectations. At least for developed markets, hawkish monetary policy tends to be positive for currencies, whilst dovish monetary policy is generally negative. Although our example presents a rationale based on relative interest rates, this is of course not the only strategy for trading currencies. Very often in practice, there will be several factors behind an investor's decision to place a trade.

We have gone through the rationale behind our hypothetical long EUR/USD trade. However, our mental checklist should also go through possible events which would be detrimental for the trade. In the case of Thales, the most obvious negative scenario would be if the olive harvest came out poor. In that case, the demand for olive presses would be weak and it is likely that his olive press options would expire worthless. In the example of this currency trade, there are several factors which are likely to have a negative impact. We will brainstorm a few possible negative scenarios for our long EUR/USD trade:

- Federal Reserve adopts more hawkish monetary for the US – bullish USD
- European Central Bank becomes more dovish – bearish EUR
- Equities fall, dragging down risk sentiment – bullish USD, which is considered a safe haven

For each of these scenarios, we also need to understand the probabilities and to be able to estimate the likely losses. Clearly, none of this estimation process is easy, but we should never go into a trade blinkered as to the possible scenarios which would present downside risks. If we feel the probability of any of these negative event risks is too much (and their associated losses would be too great), we should reassess our original trade. There will of course be scenarios which we would never have been able to envisage before a trade. This is the reason why we should be comfortable with a maximum estimated loss.

Branson (2011) goes through his experience of creating many businesses under the umbrella of his Virgin brand. Whilst the book is not specifically about trading in financial markets, one point he repeatedly reiterates is that when taking any risk it is crucial to limit the downside, emphasizing the above point I have made. Perhaps, as an entrepreneur creating businesses, this point is easier to contemplate for Branson than it is for investors in financial markets, where gains and losses appear to be numbers on a screen, rather than tangible assets. However, the lack of visibility of profits and losses should not be an excuse for investors. After all, making money on an investment is just as much about reducing losses as it is about making gains.

How can we estimate our maximum possible loss? Using stop losses and take profits is one way

We have reasoned that one of the most important risk metrics is the maximum possible loss on a trade. For some illiquid assets this might be particularly tricky. However, for the case of liquid assets, such as large cap stocks, equity indices, US Treasuries, and currencies, to name a few examples, this is somewhat simpler. Typically, traders will place stop losses and take profits on their positions. A stop loss level is placed away from the entry point, such that if the level is reached a trader will be taken out of their position for a loss. By contrast a take profit level is designed to protect profits. At which level should you place your stop loss? The general market intuition is to place stops closer than take profits. The rationale is that we want to let our winning trades run for longer, but cut our losses relatively quickly. Certainly, I have found this to be the case with trend-following strategies within FX.

We must note that in practice the precise levels of stop loss orders are rarely guaranteed, because the market can gap between prices (in other words jump). Let us say you are long gold and have a stop at $1,500. Gold is currently trading at $1,510. After an important economic data release comes out, the price in gold gaps from $1,510 to $1,490. In this instance, your stop loss would be executed at $1490. Clearly, during more turbulent markets the likelihood of such slippage increases (Figure 2.12).

A trickier question is how we should place our stops and take profit levels when we trade. Specifically, should we place it on an individual trade or on a specific strategy, or even on our whole portfolio? My take on this question is that it depends. For discretionary trading, where the decision-maker is a human rather than a systematic trading model, it seems to make sense to place them on individual trades. This is in part to provide some discipline over a trade decision, which we cannot backtest. When trading on a discretionary basis, experience is the closest thing we have to a backtest. Although experience in trading

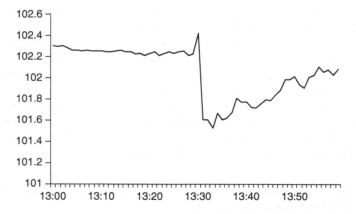

Figure 2.12   Gapping price action causes slippage in stop loss execution (USD/JPY during US employment data release in February 2014 in LDN afternoon)
Source: Thalesians, Bloomberg Finance L.P.

can of course be considered as some form of backtesting (and what we might wish to call gut instinct), it might not cover the precise strategy we are trading.

However, if we are running a specific strategy, we have the benefit of a historical backtest for that strategy in addition to our experience. In this case, we might actually find it more effective to place stops and take profits on an entire strategy rather than an individual trade. In Chapter 9, we shall discuss analyzing the historical behavior of a strategy.

Should we even bother to quantify risk if it's difficult? Yes!

Given all the problems with the relatively simple methods of quantifying risk that we have discussed, some readers might think that it is a worthless exercise using measures such as volatility and VaR, given they cannot capture changes of regime. They can also downplay the riskiness of a portfolio. Also, in the case of illiquid assets we noted that using volatility is sometimes inappropriate given that we cannot estimate the value of illiquid assets easily at regular intervals. However, we think that throwing away such metrics is not the answer. Instead, when using them some careful thought needs to be applied.

As an example, say we are holding an asset (or indeed a portfolio) which appears to have a low VaR. We need to be conscious that this scenario may not persist forever. Also, we need to be able to understand the reasons why an asset has a low VaR. In the case of a currency, which is being managed heavily by a central bank, thus dampening volatility, we need to consider how likely it is that their policy could change, thereby initiating a structural break.

In addition, we have advocated the use of implied volatility to measure the riskiness of assets, as opposed to simply using realized volatility, which is by its nature a backward-looking measure. Whilst implied volatility will still jump (too late) following unpredicted risk events, it will nevertheless price in the possibility of increased risks around scheduled events in the future. This is something that realized volatility does not do. Also, in many asset classes the options market is very liquid, so implied volatility quotes are unlikely to be "stale."

Furthermore, we discussed the importance of going through the various scenarios that could negatively impact a trade, and also to be able to estimate the likely probabilities of these multiple outcomes. Even more important, we should try to understand what our possible losses are in each case. Often it can be tempting for investors to focus more on the positive scenarios rather than the negative ones. Yet it is the losses which a trader endures that will ultimately cause him or her to stop trading, not profits.

In summary, I think that such risk metrics are still useful, provided we have a deep understanding of their deficiencies and do not simply take their output as a "truth." Furthermore, traders should not attempt to game our measures of risk. Just because we have a certain VaR limit, we should not stuff our portfolio to the limit with what appear to be low-risk assets, but which we know could easily suffer from structural breaks in their volatility regimes. We should also try to monitor many different measures of risk at the same time, such as combining volatility with an estimate of what our largest loss might be.

In a sense, our estimate of the largest potential loss is the most important. It is this measure which will force us to stop trading, rather than momentarily hitting a VaR limit. From a pure computational perspective, estimating our maximum loss can often be simpler than trying to construct an estimate of VaR or other metrics such as volatility that at the very least need a spreadsheet or laborious calculator work. For liquid assets, we have noted that stop losses can help us enforce a maximum loss on specific trades (or sometimes more appropriately on strategies). To illustrate the differences between these risk measures, let us go back to Thales! Consider if you had asked Thales what the maximum loss on his olive press option trade would have been. His answer would have been simple: it was the margin he paid. Later in the book, we shall reacquaint ourselves with the various measures of risk, to ask ourselves which metrics investors should target (see Chapter 5) when they make their investment decisions.

3
Harvesting Olives: Alpha and Beta Strategies

> So bathed in black and green, so soaked in Greece,
> A taste bitter yet bold, its branch of peace,
> In the smoothness of its oil's decadence,
> Imbued is each age's lack of prudence.

Olives, presses and Ancient Greece

Before we delve into the depths of finance, discussing the alpha and beta strategies which are the primary subject of this chapter, we digress to the olive. Why olives? As we noted in Chapter 1 and numerous times since, it was in the olive market that Thales did the first recorded option trade. Hence, it seems like an appropriate place to start our story. Greek cuisine has become very popular worldwide. If there is a food which seems to embody Greece and its cuisine, it would likely be the olive. The very slightly bitter taste of the olive is incredibly distinctive, and a flavor which is instantly memorable. For those who have grown up surrounded by olives, it is a taste which reminds them of home. For the rest of us, it is a taste which whispers to us from the shores of the Mediterranean.

I last visited Greece over a decade ago. Aside from the various ancient monuments I saw, such as the Acropolis grasping a high hill above Athens, one of my clearest memories is the many groves of olive trees hugging the hills of islands such as Poros and Hydra, surrounded by the deep blue Aegean Sea. Their branches were close enough to the ground that I could grasp them by simply raising my hands. Even in the middle of Athens, olive trees seemed to be omnipresent, occupying small spaces in the bustling streets. The ubiquity of olives and their trees tallies with the idea that they remain a prominent part of life in that region of the world. In Ancient Greece, the olive was also a significant part of life, according to Foxhall (2007). The olive permeates Greek and Mediterranean culture over the ages. You can find it on Ancient Greek pottery, its immortalization in the medium of ceramics affirming its importance in the ancient world. Foxhall's book carefully details the nature of olive cultivation in Ancient Greece. It also discusses the Ancient Greek olive market in some detail, including many numeric estimates.

The olive tree is a native of the Mediterranean region. Today, the largest producers of olives are still concentrated around the Mediterranean, in, for example, Spain, Italy, Greece, and Turkey. However, the olive tree has been successfully replanted in many other areas of the world, including in areas as far from the Mediterranean as Australia and the USA. Foxhall estimates that the olive tree was domesticated for the production of olives nearly 6,500 years ago. At first, it was likely that olives were used for animal feed, given that they are not edible by humans without treatment. As olive trees have been domesticated for a relatively long time, Foxhall suggests that it is difficult to consider any of them to be wild today. They cope well with semi-arid environments and can live for a long time. Generally they grow wood in one year and fruit the next, following a biennial pattern. However, Foxhall points out that this pattern can be impacted in particular by negative external conditions, such as droughts. Although it might impact the fruiting cycle, in general olive trees themselves can withstand a lack of water. As we might expect, external factors such as the type of soil, availability of water and light are crucial for cultivating olive trees and increasing the chances of a good crop.

Whilst table olives were a relatively cheap commodity in Ancient Greece, olive oil was highly prized. The creation of the oil required a considerable amount of labor and the use of machinery, which was generally costly. Foxhall suggests that the relative value which Ancient Greeks gave to olive oil was likely to be related to these costs of production. She conjectures that this was the case even for those parts of the production process where the improvement in the final product was unclear or more symbolic. For example, she notes the existence of sacred olive trees in Attica. Sacred oil from these trees held particular value and was given to winners in the Panathenaic games. Green olives generally yielded less oil than black olives, and this scarcity factor increased their perceived value; it was also reflected in the perceived nutritional value of food. Ancient Greeks placed a greater value on the nutritional value of green olives compared to black olives, which required less processing (and were hence cheaper). In practice, we now know that black olives have more nutritional value in terms of their calorie count and the amount of protein they contain. We might argue that consumer behavior today is not much different from that of ancient times. Consumers value products which are scarcer and hence have a premium attached to them, regardless of whether they are intrinsically better. As an example, consider the specific toy which becomes a must-have item around Christmas every year (Newcomb, 2011). We can also relate the same type of concept to financial markets. In a sense, this notion of scarcity is often also a driver for price action in financial markets, particularly during market turmoil, when the emphasis switches from capturing risk premium to safeguarding capital. During times of risk aversion, risky assets flood the market as investors seek to unwind their holdings. By contrast, safe haven assets are scarce during risk aversion, and hence increase in price.

In her book, Foxhall carefully details the creation of olive oil in Ancient Greece. This required several steps. The olives had to be made into a pulp, usually using a rotary mill that consisted of two millstones, which crushed the olives at the center when it was spun. The resulting olive pulp was placed in a press, which used a combination of levers and stone weights to apply the pressure necessary for fluid extraction. In later times, the Romans used a screw-press mechanism. The pressing would occur more than once, and hot water would be used in an attempt to extract the oil. The resulting liquid from the pressing process would consist of not only oil but also water and juice. This was left to rest in very large tanks, where the oil would float to the top – given that it was the least dense substance of the mixture. The preparation of table olives involved a far simpler process: they were pickled (soaked in water and salt).

Today, we tend to think of olive oil as a food ingredient. However, in Ancient Greece the use of olive oil in rich households was not restricted in this way, but was also used for purposes that we would rarely consider today. It was used for lighting in oil lamps, and for bathing as well as for ceremonial purposes, such as the example given earlier about sacred olive oil in Attica. Foxhall estimates a household used 200–330kg of olive oil per year, which is a substantial amount. The majority of this would have been in food, with most of the rest used in lighting and a far smaller amount in bathing.

In practice, Foxhall suggests that despite the significance of olive oil from a value (and cultural) perspective, it could have been the case that most olives went into the production of table olives rather than into oil. Regardless of the precise split, it would be difficult to downplay the industrial scale of the olive industry in Ancient Greece. Indeed, the importance of olives in Ancient Greece explains why Thales was attracted to trading in the olive market. Later, we shall return to the humble olive, after a short digression to the Olympic Games.

The ancient Olympic Games, the unusual olive trade of Thales, and following your strengths

We have briefly mentioned the Panathenaic games of Ancient Greece, which were similar to the ancient Olympic Games. One event which featured at ancient Olympic Games was the ancient pentathlon, which is described by Smith (1875). It featured five events: long jump, javelin throw, discus throw, foot race, and wrestling. It was relatively easy to crown athletes as winners if they won all five events, or at least three of them. However, this was not always the case, and it was difficult for the Ancient Greeks to decide a clear winner in such a scenario.

The ancient pentathlon inspired modern Olympic events, such as the modern pentathlon, which also consists of five events. These are somewhat different to the ancient version and include swimming and pistol shooting. The decathlon which is staged at the modern Olympics does share many of its track and field events with the ancient pentathlon, though, with the obvious exception of wrestling. Unlike in Ancient Greece, in the modern decathlon there is a points system to score competitors, related to the time taken by athletes to complete track events and the distances they achieve in field events. The points system makes the winner unambiguous once all ten events have been completed, unlike in the ancient pentathlon. If we look at the world records of specialists in the various events, comparing them to decathlete bests (Wikipedia, 2013), we notice a fairly obvious pattern. In nearly every case, the world records of specialist athletes outperform the best results from decathletes. We can take the 100m sprint as an example, which is run both as a separate event and also as part of the decathlon. The world record is currently held by Usain Bolt at 9.59s. The decathlete best time, held by Ashton Eaton, is somewhat slower at 10.21s. By the same token, though, it would be debatable that an athlete such as Bolt could outperform Eaton at the ten events which make up the decathlon on aggregate. Ashton Eaton holds the world record for the highest decathlon score. Both athletes are clearly consummate professionals when it comes to their events. However, in this example of the 100m sprint, it seems clear that the specialist has the advantage, as we might expect. Usain Bolt can dedicate all his training time to sprinting, whilst Ashton Eaton needs to split his energies across all ten events.

So whilst on aggregate Ashton Eaton might be the best track and field athlete, at specific events he is unlikely to overcome a specialist. Whilst this is only one example, the lesson is that superior performance in a specific area can be gained if it is our specialty. However, we cannot simply infer that a large amount of training will ever make us sprint like Usain Bolt!

We can also illustrate this point that following our strengths or specialties can improve results if we return to Thales and Ancient Greece once more. Let us pretend for a moment that we live in the time of Thales. We have noted the importance of the olive and in particular the high value of olive oil in Ancient Greece. If we wanted to gain exposure to the price of olive oil, the most obvious way to do this would be to own an olive grove. We could grow olives and harvest them. During the harvest, we could either sell olives or, more likely, go through the laborious process to press them into olive oil. We would have to weigh the cost of either approach. It would be likely that the returns we would generate would be similar to other olive growers in the region. Our assumption would be that nearby olive growers would be exposed to similar weather, and hence their harvest yield would be similar to ours. Indeed, in practice, olives within the same region tend to have similar fruiting patterns.

Of course, from what Aristotle tells us, Thales did not attempt to grow olives or even press them. As we have explained, such a process is relatively laborious and costly, not only in terms of having the right conditions to grow olives but also in the extraction of the oil. As a philosopher, Thales' expertise was unlikely to have been in the subtleties of growing olives or the various stages of the process by which you make olive oil. Hence, it seems likely that even if he had tried to grow olives, he might not have been as successful as experienced olive farmers. We draw a parallel with our athletics case: it seems unlikely that Usain Bolt could outperform Ashton Eaton on aggregate in the decathlon, even if Bolt could beat Eaton in the 100m.

Although, if we believe Aristotle, Thales did have some understanding of the likely conditions which might facilitate a good harvest. We may conjecture that his ability to foretell the harvest was related to his desire to use scientific thought to understand the world, which may have been superior to a farmer's predictions about the harvest.

However, within financial markets today, very often market participants do not follow this approach of trying to stick to their strengths or specialties and using them in their trading decisions. Rather than sticking to their area of expertise, they can be tempted to trade markets or assets which they do not fully understand. Remember those exotic collaterized debt obligation (CDO) contracts we mentioned in Chapter 1? How many CDO investors really understood them before the Lehman crisis? They might have understood the potential upside involved in holding a CDO, but were unsure about the potential pitfalls. This is not a diatribe against trading exotic options or assets which have an element of complexity, or indeed markets in which you have little experience trading. Instead, it is merely a suggestion that should investors stray from a part of the market that they understand thoroughly to a relatively novel area, they should do a significant amount of research.

Alternatively, if investors are not experts in a specific asset class, they might instead turn their thoughts to the question of allocating capital to those funds or broad-based indices which will probably be best to articulate their views in that asset class. Their time will then be spent assessing the relative differences between similar funds and indices, rather than trying to ascertain the precise microstructure of the market.

An example of differences between supposedly simple cash markets

We can illustrate the idea that supposedly simple markets can be very different with the example of an investor who wishes to trade two cash markets.

Let us take an investor who is used to trading domestic equities and wishes to trade currency spot markets for speculative purposes, as opposed to doing it for hedging purposes. Both markets are cash markets, so we might expect some similarities. The products are the basic building blocks of financial markets. Indeed, they are so "vanilla", that they have been traded throughout history. In Ancient Greece, each city state would mint its own coins, effectively resulting in multiple currencies. Adkins & Adkins (1998) tell us that for those who travelled between the various Greek city states, money changers would offer the service of exchanging coins, essentially acting like modern foreign exchange traders. The idea of stocks is also something which was present in ancient times. In Ancient Rome, there was a concept similar to that of the modern notion of equity. Goetzmann & Rouwenhorst (2005) give us several instances where Cicero described the concept of *partes*, which can be literally translated into English as shares. They also give us examples from Cicero's speeches, which indicated that there were owners of these shares, giving rise to the idea of a shareholders. Furthermore these *partes* were transferable, indicating that they were tradable. Cicero discussed how *partes* were high in price at one point, suggesting that their price could change, just as in modern markets, where volatility is an important characteristic of price action.

Hence, both equity and currency markets are very well established, having been around for thousands of years, albeit in much simpler forms. Whilst we can hardly term these markets as exotic, the dynamics of how they trade are very different today. If we think about the market today (or even since the dollar floated in the 1970s, when currency markets developed in their modern form), we can identify many differences between these supposedly simple markets.

Let us take the idea of market liquidity, which is a broad term to describe how easy it is to execute a trade within the markets, something we mentioned in Chapter 2 when we discussed risk sentiment. Liquidity can also refer to a company's ability to meet its payment obligations. Our focus here will mainly be on the first meaning. Liquidity for stocks in a single company, known as single stocks for short, is very different compared to that in foreign exchange. Hence, the cost of trading is much lower in foreign exchange, in particular for the most liquid currency pairs, both in terms of the actual spread between bid and ask prices, but also in terms of market impact. We shall elaborate upon these two issues.

The cost of the spread is relatively simple to measure and is not something unique to the financial markets. Typically in financial markets, market makers will display bid and ask prices to their clients. Clients have to buy at the ask price, whilst they sell at the bid price. The market maker makes a profit on this spread. Indeed, this is no different to a shop, whose profitability rests on its ability to buy merchandise at a lower price than it sells to customers. However, this is not "free" money for the market maker (or our real-world shop example), because often they will take risk to facilitate the transaction, as it might not always be possible to match up buyers with sellers. Hence, the spread between the bid and ask prices can be seen as proportional to the risk which market makers take. The reason is that market makers will have to hold the trade on their own trading book as inventory, regardless of their view of the potential price movements of that trade, if they cannot find another market participant willing to take the trade. Whilst they hold that trade, they are clearly exposed to risk given that the price can change. During risk aversion, which we described in detail in Chapter 2, typically the spread between the bid and ask prices will widen. Why is this the case? Essentially, market participants will demand liquidity and the ability to trade to get out of their positions. Hence, the cost of liquidity will go up, which is reflected in widening spreads. We can think of market makers as those who give liquidity to the market and their clients as traders who take liquidity.

Aside from the spread between the bid and ask prices, the market impact from a trade will differ. This is another factor we use to assess market liquidity. In currency markets, given they are far larger than many other markets, generally trades of a similar size are likely to have a different market impact compared with one in equities. For example, say a trader wishes to buy 100mm (i.e. million) USD worth of stock in a company, whose market capitalization is 2bn USD and at the same time wishes to buy EUR and sell USD in around 100mm USD of notional. It is likely that the stock price will move a larger amount during the transaction, given that the supply of stock is so constricted and we are trying to purchase 5% of the company's stock. In currency markets, whilst 100mm USD in EUR/USD is a reasonable sized trade ticket, it is unlikely the market impact will be as great as trading our single company stock. Hence, if we wish to transfer a trading strategy from the currency market to trade single name equities, we need to be very careful how we scale the size of the strategies we can employ, given the relative differences in liquidity. Given the difference in liquidity, higher-frequency strategies can be employed in currency markets than those that can be used in single stocks, for similar-sized notionals. Hence, the universe of strategies that can be used may differ between asset classes (or the relative capacity of the strategies can be different).

Setting aside the topic of liquidity, we need to be aware that market events impact currencies and single stocks differently. If we look at large market-wide events, which impact many assets, the way in which they might manifest themselves can be different. For example, during a market risk event, equities typically sell off. However, in currency space, we cannot say all currencies sell off. The nature of the market is that to buy one currency you must sell another. Looking at more idiosyncratic events, typically in currency space, the earnings of companies rarely impact markets, unless it is for very large bellwether companies; whilst for single stocks, earning releases are clearly of great significance. Indeed, many of the various idiosyncratic drivers are very different!

The difference in terms of the various drivers is also reflected in the fact that participants in the various markets can be very different. In currency markets, contrary to what might be the perception of those who do not trade in them, many participants are not simply speculators, even if the speculators do form a reasonable proportion. Many people trading in currency markets are doing so as a by-product of other activities. A company which is doing business abroad needs to trade currencies as part of its everyday business. Central banks trading currencies do so to manage their reserves and often to reduce volatility in their own currency. Their primary objective is not to generate profits. Portfolio managers trading foreign bonds and equities will also trade in currency markets, but simply because they need to do so in order to transact in foreign markets. Hence, many transactions executed in currency markets are a by-product of other objectives, rather than purely speculative trades. The objective of a central bank trading in currency markets is clearly not to generate profits and behave like a hedge fund. If we think about the equities markets, generally most participants will be investors seeking to generate profits from their investments. It would be difficult to characterize most equity investors as market participants who do not seek to profit from their investments. Amongst equity investors, the degree to which they seek profits is likely to vary, with some preferring wealth preservation as opposed to (riskier) large profits. On the other side of equity markets, there will also be companies seeking to raise capital through equity markets to help grow their businesses. However, even in these cases, companies will be trying to maximize the capital they can raise on their equity issuance.

We have seen that even in supposedly simple markets, which have existed in some form since ancient times, there can be many differences in how they trade. These include: the liquidity, the drivers of price action, and the make-up of the investor community. This list is of course not complete. Most of all, when trading a different market or an unusual asset, investors should be aware of the type of risks associated with that investment. Hence, it can be the case that strategies that can be employed in one market might not be totally replicable in another, without some element of modification which takes into account market-specific factors such as liquidity. This might be the case even if they draw upon a common factor that is a driver for many markets (such as trends).

The ideas of alpha and beta in the present day

As we saw in Chapter 1, Thales merely purchased options for the use of olive presses, which he later sold for a profit. So whilst he traded in the olive market, he did not do the "obvious trade," which involved buying an olive grove and collecting profits from its harvest and cultivation.

Within financial markets, the same concept is applicable. The "obvious strategy," which represents most market participants' returns, would be akin to owning an olive grove in Ancient Greece and harvesting it. This is referred to as a beta trade (for a moment we'll ignore localized conditions, which would make the harvest slightly uneven across the whole of Ancient Greece). Given how interconnected the various markets are, beta trades can often be correlated across the asset classes. The Thales-type strategy, where your returns are less correlated to the broader markets and which is more "unusual," is known as alpha.

I could tell you that the reason we use the letters alpha and beta to denote these two strategies, the first two letters of the Greek alphabet, is related to Thales. Whilst it would be a fantastic story, it would also be totally untrue! Instead, the concepts of alpha and beta come from the CAPM (Capital Asset Pricing Model), which was introduced in the 1960s to help decompose the risks which impacted an asset into generalized market risk (beta) and risk specific to that asset (alpha).

If we think of stocks as opposed to olives and bring our analysis to the present day, let us think about the S&P500, an index which we have already met on many occasions. This equity index is based around the 500 biggest publicly traded US companies by market capitalization. Hence, it gives us a good proxy for the returns of investing in the US equity market. Also, given it consists of the largest stocks by market capitalization, its underlying constituents are relatively liquid. Very often many investors might have investments in assets which directly track the performance of market beta too. Indeed, many investors have investments which passively follow S&P500. We can consider S&P500 as a proxy for the broader market beta.

Other strategies, which exhibit little correlation to S&P500 and trade equities, can be thought of as alpha. Each market will generally have its own specific beta, which captures the typical investor returns in that market. For example, for bonds a market beta could be one of the world bond indices produced by major banks, such as the Barclays Global Aggregate index. As with S&P500, in fixed income markets many investors passively follow such bond indices. We need to be aware that betas in different markets can also display some element of correlation.

For some other markets, our choice of beta is not an obvious index as it is for equities or bonds. One such market is that of currencies. In FX markets, there is not an obvious trade that an investor will generally place. For example, are investors usually long or short USD, which is the most heavily traded currency? We can look at positioning data. This gives us a snapshot of the exposures which traders have across the market; hence, it can help answer this question. Positioning data suggests that there has not always been a historical asymmetry in how speculators have positioned in EUR/USD, which is the most liquid currency pair (see Figure 3.1). In some currencies, there can be some sort of

Figure 3.1   Net long EUR/USD positions – speculators are not always long or short
Source: Thalesians, Bloomberg Finance L.P.

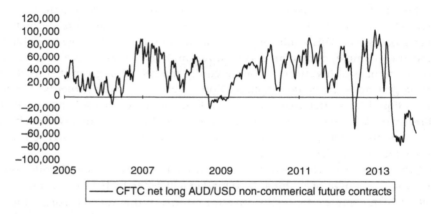

Figure 3.2   Net long AUD/USD positions – speculators tend to be net long
Source: Thalesians, Bloomberg Finance L.P.

asymmetry in positioning (see Figure 3.2). However, in many currency pairs, it is difficult to say on average whether on aggregate traders tend to be either long or short USD.

What if there's no obvious market beta?

So what can investors do in this scenario, when we cannot immediately conjure up an obvious market beta for that specific asset class? In such a situation, one approach is to proxy what investors' typical returns are using alternative methods. We can attempt to come up with generic strategies which illustrate how a typical inventor trades in that asset class. First, we need to work out a shortlist of typical factors which we think impact that market and are typically followed by investors. In foreign exchange markets, some of the most popular strategies employed by investors are those ideas such as carry, trend, and value, which we shall explain. In Chapter 2, we alluded to the idea of carry, when we were discussing risk sentiment. We noted that generally during risk-seeking markets higher yielding assets (which have more risk premium associated with them) tend to do well. This contrasts to risk-averse markets, where investors are more concerned with preserving their capital than seeking yield.

A carry strategy within FX is based on this idea of capturing higher yield (the risk premium). Essentially a typical generic carry strategy is long the highest yielding currencies in G10 (the developed market currencies) against selling the lowest yielding currencies in G10. As we might expect, such a strategy does best during risk-seeking markets. The reason why there appears to be an asymmetry in AUD/USD positioning, which we saw earlier (see Figure 3.2), is likely to be a result of the carry trade within FX. Australian interest rates have generally been higher than US interest rates throughout history. As a result, investors have tended on average to be long AUD/USD as a by-product of the carry trade. The carry trade is not simply a phenomenon that is practiced within FX. It is also a strategy which can be seen in other markets, even if the term tends to be associated most with FX.

A large part of banks' historical profits have been as a result of undertaking the carry trade in the rates market. They offer loans to customers with a long tenor, for example lending on consumer mortgages. These longer-term loans are funded by the banks via shorter-dated instruments. Since longer-dated yields are higher in general than shorter-dated yields, banks can profit from this differential. The risks are, of course, when there is an inversion in the yield curve, so short-term funding becomes very expensive or is simply unavailable. A recent example of this was seen in the crisis which afflicted Northern Rock in 2008. It was heavily reliant on short-term funding to fund loan-term loans. When short-term funding dried up, it had to be bailed out by the British government. Funding crises are not unique to modern times and impacted the ancient world too. Both Roberts (2011) and Durant (1944 (reprint 1994)) recount the financial crisis of 33 AD. Durant discusses the economic policies of Tiberius. He had wanted to save money by reducing public spending in an austerity drive, following the reign of Augustus. Unlike Tiberius, Augustus had spent heavily, increased the money supply, and pushed down interest rates, causing inflation on the premise that such policies would encourage economic growth. Tiberius did the opposite, restricting the supply of coins to the markets; he kept a large amount of money saved in the government coffers. The curtailing of the money supply had a severe impact. Creditors foreclosed on their loans. Interest rates rose, as the supply of debt was constricted. The Senate imposed a policy similar to the introduction of capital controls. Essentially, senators were forced to keep a large proportion of their net worth in Italian land. This was intended to reduce the outflow of capital eastwards for the purchase of luxury items such as silk (does this sound familiar, running up a large deficit to fund the purchase of Chinese exports?). In Chapter 8, we shall discuss the Silk Road in some detail, through which silk travelled westwards. We have a parallel for these policies in modern times. Following the Asian crisis in 1998, many emerging market economies in the Far East enacted capital controls to prevent the flight of capital abroad, which had already caused severe devaluation of their domestic currencies.

The net result of these measures in Ancient Rome was further pressure on the supply of credit. A toxic storm of bank runs ensued, which was exacerbated by rumors. In the modern age, television pictures of people queuing outside banks to withdraw their savings has had similar impact. In the end, the vicious circle was brought to a close when Tiberius supported banks with interest-free loans. He also suspended the requirement for senators to have a significant amount of investment in Italian land. The credit crunch and the ensuing financial crisis of 2008, nearly 2,000 years after Tiberius' ancient credit crunch, suggests that time has not prevented a repeat of such events.

Aside from carry, trend following is also a popular strategy for trading currencies, as it is for many other asset classes. Unlike idiosyncratic factors which might differ between asset classes, trend as an idea transcends many markets, which we have discussed earlier in Chapter 2. Among the most well known of trend-following investors were the Turtle Traders. Faith (2007) explains the story of the Turtles. The premise was that traders could be grown (or at least taught) like turtles. By following an array of trend-following rules and ideas in money management, in the 1980s Richard Dennis and William Eckhardt turned a team of 23 trading trainees, which included Curtis Faith, into largely profitable traders. Although time has passed since then, trend following remains a popular strategy for trading markets today.

There is also the concept of long-term value in trading. Again the idea of value is not uniquely an idea which is traded by market participants in FX, although the precise measures of ascertaining what value is does differ from asset class to asset class. Generally, for currencies, we can use a long-term measure of value, such as PPP to estimate the long term. The acronym refers to purchasing power parity. The best-known version of PPP (although certainly not the most sophisticated!) is the Big Mac index, published by the *Economist* magazine. The idea of the Big Mac index is relatively simple. The price of a Big Mac is converted from local currency to USD terms in a variety of different currencies. Where the USD value of a Big Mac in a specific country is very expensive, it implies that local currency is overvalued. Conversely, when the USD value of a Big Mac in a particular country is very low, it implies that the currency of that country is relatively cheap. However, Big Macs are not easily transferable between countries and would incur transaction costs (as well as getting cold). In practice, more sophisticated PPP indices use a basket of goods and

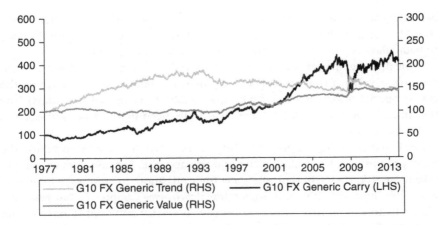

Figure 3.3 Generic FX strategies (carry, trend, and value) have been profitable over the long term
Source: Thalesians, Bloomberg Finance L.P.

services, rather than a single item. It is important to understand that currencies can remain under- or overvalued for significant periods of time, although over the long term they are generally mean-reverting. Hence, any value-based trading approach needs to have a very long-term time horizon. There are of course other metrics we use to decide value in currency space, many of which seem to have amusing acronyms, such as FEER and BEER.

I discuss the idea of FX beta in significant detail in Amen (2013), going through ways of constructing generic carry, trend, and value strategies in a systematic fashion. Furthermore, the paper shows they have been historically profitable (see Figure 3.3). Later in the paper, it is shown that it is possible to replicate an index of FX fund returns, using a mixture of carry and trend strategies. Hence, the approach of using these generic strategies as a proxy for FX beta is a reasonable approach, given that it seems to proxy the returns of investors using FX as an asset class.

Allocating between different market betas

In this chapter we have mainly talked about stocks, bonds, and currencies (and olives, of course) in isolation, when it comes to the idea of beta. Obviously, there are many other markets aside from these. In each market there is also often an index which might constitute beta, which we have noted, or at the very least generic strategies akin to beta, such as in currencies. If we had gone through all the various asset classes, we would see many different betas. Each one of these betas would represent the returns of a typical investor in that specific asset class. The question therefore arises, if we are allocating for market beta, how should we allocate between the various asset betas? In other words, should we mainly invest in equity beta or bond beta, and what about FX beta, or beta related to EM assets, property, commodities, and so on.

Typically, the answer for broad-based portfolio managers has been to concentrate largely on the mix between equities and bonds (we are ignoring the case of specialist asset managers who specifically focus on one asset class). The traditional proportions which have historically been used are 60% in equities and 40% in bonds.

Asset managers have some flexibility within that framework to adjust the exact proportions, given their views and risk appetite. For investors wishing to take more risk, they will typically skew their mix more to equities, which tend to exhibit more volatility and higher drawdowns (see Chapter 2), but generally higher historical returns. More conservative investors will tend to have higher bond holdings in their portfolios, which are typically less volatile, and as a result tend to have lower returns over the long term. Furthermore, sometimes it is within the investment mandate of asset managers to allocate to other asset classes betas such as commodities to help diversify the mix.

Typically, a more active investor will allocate exposure to the various market betas according to his or her views about the economy. Investors expecting strong growth would want to have more exposure to equities as an asset class. However, strong growth is likely to be accompanied by higher yields, as central banks hike rates to combat inflation. Hence, at the same time they might consider reducing exposure to bonds. Although this is a somewhat simplistic example, it does illustrate the thought process behind the vagaries of asset allocation. Later, we have a chapter dedicated to diversifying investments that builds on this theme, and also to hedging risk within a portfolio (see Chapter 4).

Ancient Greek maritime traders, grain, timber, olives, and alternative beta

Up to this point, we have talked about asset allocation in the context of deciding how much to allocate between betas. We noted that the classical question facing many portfolio managers is deciding how to split their allocation between bond and equity betas. However, is there another way we can allocate our beta, which uses some element of active trading but does not quite stretch to trading alpha? Yes, there is!

Let us return to the ancient world for a moment. We have already talked about the olive market in Ancient Greece. We noted that the most likely way of gaining exposure to "olive" beta was to own an olive grove, to harvest the olives which we have grown, and then to sell this harvest in the market. At the same time, olives could be pressed into oil to provide further income, if we wanted to get exposure to "olive oil" beta. Despite our discussion around olives, they were not the most important part of the Ancient Greek diet. Grain was of special importance and provided the staple of the Ancient Greek food intake through bread. Reed (1999) discusses the nature of maritime trade in the Ancient Greek world. In particular, he notes the particular importance of the grain trade in the city-state of Athens. It was no longer self-sufficient in grain as it became wealthier and its population expanded. Indeed, he notes that by the fourth century BC, food shortages forced the authorities to organize the importation of grain in a systematic manner. However, grain was not the only commodity imported into Athens by maritime traders. Timber was also of particular importance, primarily for use in the city's fleet of ships, which was used to project military power. Rather more ominously, the slave trade relied on maritime traders, as it did later between Africa and the Americas. In later Roman times, olive oil was also a significant export from Spain and North Africa (Foxhall, 2007), which was facilitated by maritime trade. Foxhall also notes that olive oil was exported from Attica in Ancient Greece, the historical region which encompassed Athens.

Amongst those involved in maritime trade in Ancient Greece were *emporoi* and *naukleroi*. They can be loosely thought of as traders and ship-owners respectively (although Reed (1999) notes that this is a bit of an over-simplification). He writes that *emporoi* did not tend to produce the goods they carried, although they usually owned the goods they purchased. In a sense, they could be considered to be like modern market makers in financial markets, who are willing to take risk to facilitate transactions. Indeed, this seems to be the most generic description of what a trader typically does.

Discussing maritime trade in Ancient Greece might seem unusual in the context of describing alpha and beta. However, the reason we are discussing maritime trading in Ancient Greece is that it was a key part of the importation of many crucial goods, including grain and timber. In a sense, we can think of maritime trading in Ancient Greece as an industry which cut across the various commodity markets. Hence, maritime traders in Ancient Greece were exposed to all the different underlying markets of the goods they were carrying, but clearly to a differing extent to the farmers. Rephrasing this argument, but this time with our financial terminology, an olive farmer had direct exposure to the olive market beta. However, a maritime trader had indirect exposure to both olive and grain market betas, since both olives and grain would be amongst his or her cargo. At the same time, some profits associated with maritime trading would be impacted by factors largely unrelated to the price of the underlying goods being transported, such as the sea winds, the availability of seafarers, and so on. We can think of the profits of maritime trading in Ancient Greece as being a form of alternative beta, using a term which has gained popularity in finance. Similarly, we can think of a farmer, who grows many different types of food, as having exposure to the general activity of farming. Farming could be considered as another form of alternative beta.

More simply, we can think of alternative beta as an exposure to a particular style of trading across many different assets. So rather than allocating capital to a particular type of asset beta (say olives or equities), we instead allocate capital to a particular style of trading (such as maritime trading in a variety of different commodities in Ancient Greece or trend-following strategies in the modern day), which cuts across many different markets.

Earlier, we noted that there was no obvious market beta in FX markets. In FX, we noted that historically investors are not always long USD or short USD, for example. This contrasts with equities and bonds, where most investors tend to be long only and often tend to have exposure to well-known beta indices, such as S&P500 in equities or Barclays Global Aggregate index in bonds. In FX, our solution was to create generic trading strategies for currencies which followed popular trading styles, such as carry, trend, and value. We noted that we could actually use a mixture of carry and trend strategies to explain a large amount of the returns from FX funds. At the same time, we suggested that whilst the precise expression of these styles in different asset classes might differ, these generic (and somewhat commoditized) styles could be applicable in other asset classes. More simply, our focus in this process is not on those types of strategies which are very particular to a specific asset class or on alpha-based trading approaches. The value of generic and relatively simple strategies is that investors can understand them well. If a strategy is very profitable, but investors have no idea how it generates returns, they are more likely to turn it off at the first signs of losses. I, for one, would never run capital in a strategy where I could not really understand why I was putting on a specific trade! It is a theme which we shall repeat on many occasions.

When using an alternative beta approach, we can allocate capital to a trend-following strategy, which trades across many markets, such as currencies, equities, and bonds. Another part of our portfolio could be dedicated to carry across these assets. So, rather than deciding what mix of our allocation should go in equities versus bonds, as classical asset allocation might suggest, we instead try to decide the mix between the various styles, such as trend and carry. Whilst applying equal weighting of the various styles is the easiest approach, clearly the value added by a portfolio manager will (hopefully) come from picking a winner amongst the various styles. Just as with classical asset allocation, where longer-term fundamental views might impact the relative mix between equities and bonds, a similar approach can be used with styles. Hence, if our view is of strong growth, we might be inclined to overweight carry. However, if we think that there might be significant market turbulence, we might consider increasing our allocation to trend-following strategies, which can capture large market moves in whichever direction they occur.

We should note that unlike the traditional view of beta, alternative beta often requires a larger element of active and more involved trading, compared with passively holding beta. The promise of alternative beta is to offer something akin to the returns from hedge funds (I shall leave it up to the reader to decide whether this promise is fulfilled). At least in FX, we noted how generic beta strategies can be used to proxy FX fund returns.

There is another way to attempt to mimic hedge fund returns, which we touched upon earlier in the context of FX funds. We can try to replicate these returns by using a factor-based technique, by looking at the relationship between hedge fund returns and various factors (such as various market beta, including S&P500). This approach requires us to extrapolate the weights of the various factors over time and invest in them accordingly. In a sense, we can characterize the factor-based approach as a top-down way of replicating hedge fund returns. This contrasts to our bottom-up approach, which we have largely focused on, coming up with trading styles (such as trend, carry, and value) and using them as the basis of our portfolio to mimic hedge funds.

To some extent, we can think of alternative beta as being halfway between alpha-style strategies and traditional passive beta strategies. It should be noted that alternative beta strategies might also use derivatives or some elements of short selling (Jaeger, 2008). The topic of alternative beta has been discussed in the financial press, so it is something that has evolved from the purely academic to usage in the real world (Jenkins, 2013). Indeed, just as there are passive index following funds which follow market betas such as S&P500, we have seen the evolution of mass-market products such as ETFs, which follow specific trading styles. These prepackaged products allow investors to have exposure to alternative beta, without having to trade that actively themselves if they do not have the manpower.

A practitioner's thoughts on alternative beta, alpha, and beta

I was keen to ask Patrick Burns about the idea of alternative beta (or smart beta as it is known in some circles). Hailing from the West Coast of the United States, Pat is somewhat laid back and very approachable. His hair is a mix of white and black and, for as long as I have known him, he has sported a beard, which seems to add to his air of friendliness. Much of the time, our discussions center on anything but finance. Indeed, Pat's knowledge of American literature is very detailed and it has always been great to chat with him about this. The last time we spoke, we discussed the literature of Truman Capote. Admittedly, I have only read one of his books, which hardly makes me an expert, but Pat had read a large number of them and was thus able to make many valid comparisons between them. However, the reason I wished to ask Pat about smart or alternative beta is that he is also a very accomplished financial statistician.

Pat was one of the lead developers on S Plus in the earlier days, a popular software application which most statisticians will probably have used at one point or another in their careers. These days he leads his own firm, Burns Statistics. Currently, much of the work he does is in the area of random portfolios, a subject which he has spoken about at the Thalesians on several occasions. The idea of random portfolios is to create a statistical test to show that a trading strategy is performing better than chance (Burns, 2006).

Whilst the focus of our discussion was smart or alternative beta, Pat felt compelled to start by commenting on the definitions of alpha and beta. He suggested that although alpha and beta are derived from a model, as I have noted earlier in this chapter, the ideas seem to have hardened in people's minds into something quite tangible, which he described as the *Truth* (my emphasis). In his opinion, they are best thought as useful concepts, rather than things that exist. Indeed this tallies with the earlier point I made, where I noted that in some markets such as foreign exchange there is often no obvious beta. Furthermore, the types of strategies that could conceivably qualify as alpha are very broad.

Pat also gave another view on what could define alpha and beta, without recourse to mathematics or acronyms such as CAPM. He said that another way to think about alpha and beta was in terms of their cost with respect to the time and effort used in constructing them. Alpha takes a lot of effort, whilst beta strategies, he noted, require close to no effort. This is especially the case when there is an "obvious" proxy for market beta such as S&P500. Alternative beta roughly falls between the two. The aim of alternative beta is to get some alpha but with minimal work.

One of the implicit features of beta is diversification, Pat said. Alternative beta strategies that do not address diversification are the ones that he thinks will cause anguish amongst investors. The alternative beta strategies that never seriously underperform fungible strategies are likely to survive.

Pat stressed that the key issue is that the market is dynamic. Beta strategies are meant to invest in the "market," hence they cannot underperform the market. Pat flagged the point that the "market" is another idea that really is ephemeral, yet is specific in many people's minds. By contrast alpha strategies are dynamic and try to adjust to changing market dynamics. As a final point he added, alternative beta strategies are basically static and hence have the potential to be problematic if they are not constructed carefully. In the latter parts of the chapter, we shall build on some of Pat's points.

Alpha is not always better than beta

Let us think about an investment strategy for which we have lots of data, over 70 years, which is far longer, than most investors (or funds) would be active for. This strategy has been profitable in 67% of the years since 1920s. The strategy has been hit by some large drawdowns, but has nevertheless managed to recover. This strategy is buying and holding S&P500 since the 1920s. I have somewhat simplified my calculations, and have not included dividends or the cost of capital. In addition, past performance is also not a guarantee of strong future performance as a disclaimer. However, it does illustrate that just following the market can be profitable over extended periods of time, without any fancy investment strategy. So whilst the buzzwords amongst every investor seem to be "beating the market," simply trading with the market (or being exposed to beta) can actually result in perfectly respectable returns from the perspective of a long-term investor historically. The investment fees associated with such strategies are also comparatively low, at least in more recent years, a period when S&P500 has become more widely traded as an asset through futures and ETFs. We recognize that trading S&P500 in the distant past would likely have been considerably more expensive (Figure 3.4).

This leads to the question whether any investor should even try to deviate from traditional beta strategies, at least in equities. We have already mentioned alternative beta strategies, which can be seen as the first step away from traditional beta strategies and have become commoditized. Furthermore, we have touched upon the idea of alpha. Generally alpha is supposed to outperform beta and should generally be uncorrelated to beta strategies. Hence, when stock markets are collapsing, it should not mean that true alpha strategies also lose money. Investors who seek to gain exposure to alpha strategies, for example through hedge funds, will typically pay much higher fees, which often consist of a 2% management fee and a 20% performance fee. This is generally much higher than the fees associated with passive beta tracking funds or alternative beta strategies offered to investors. More succinctly, alpha costs more whichever metric you use, whether it is time and effort or investment fees.

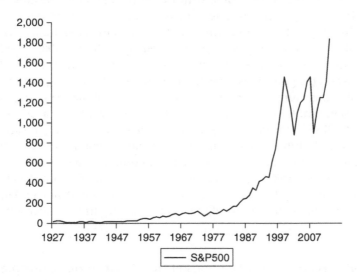

Figure 3.4 S&P500 over the past 70 years
Source: Thalesians, Bloomberg Finance L.P.

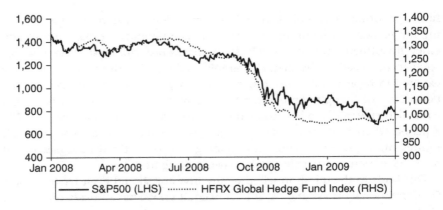

Figure 3.5   Hedge fund performance in 2008 versus S&P500
Source: Thalesians, Bloomberg Finance L.P.

The problem is that in the recent crisis of 2008, hedge funds, which are all about generating alpha, lost money on aggregate just as the broader market did, if we look at broad hedge fund indices (see Figure 3.5). This is despite the fact that hedge fund professionals are working full time on their port-folios and in many cases are extremely experienced. The underperformance of hedge funds in 2008 has to some extent helped to popularize the idea of alternative beta, which we have noted is a cheaper way of improving upon simpler beta strategies, compared with capturing alpha by investing in hedge funds. Some hedge funds managed to make money in 2008 (Barr, 2010), of course. Notably, CTA (commodities trading advisor)-based funds, which use trend-following strategies, performed extremely well in 2008. Despite hav-ing "commodities" in the acronym, these days CTAs trade many different asset classes. This point illustrates the importance of spending time to choose the right hedge fund manager, who can capture alpha. This decision still requires significant work on the side of the investor. Just because we are not directly trading on a day-to-day basis ourselves, it does not mean we can abstain from decision-making. Indeed, capturing alpha does not come easily. The whole exercise does underline that sometimes, broadly speaking, beta is not always worse than alpha. Pat noted that one of the properties of beta is that by following the market, by implication it should not underperform the market. This contrasts to alpha, which can at times underperform the market.

Do retail investors beat the market beta? Not in our examples

If we think of typical retail investors, the time they can spend both analyzing and trading the market is far more limited compared with the hours that a professional investor can dedicate to the market. We can think of trading in the financial markets as a product of many factors, notably capital, but also importantly time spent honing a strategy and interpreting the market, echoing Pat's sentiments about the differences between alpha and beta. As we have already noted, professional investors will be flush with both of these assets, so are already at an advantage compared to retail investors, before a single trade has been executed.

It might not be surprising that research into retail investors such as Clare & Motson (2010) shows that they can be on the wrong side of the market during their attempts to "beat the market" and to "capture alpha" by timing their investments. Their paper shows that in general UK equity retail investment flows follow good performance and try to anticipate poorer performance. Hence, UK equity retail investors end up buying on the highs and selling on the lows. The authors note that on average retail investors underperformed by 1.2% compared to institutional investors over the 18 years of the study. The authors write that flows of institutional investments into equity mutual funds were likely to be more stable over time. Hence, these flows were less influenced by judgment on timing. In other words, in this instance, retail investors who tried to time their investments underperformed when compared with a long only equity investment. Hence, whatever attempt which was made in capturing alpha, the outcome was worse than beta.

Another simple observation can be made in currency markets, along the same lines, where it is possible to obtain data for Japanese retail FX positioning. We can use this as a broad proxy for current exposures of FX retail traders. If we were to compare AUD/JPY spot against the positions that were held by Japanese retail FX traders historically, we tend to see when they were accumulating large long positions (hoping for the Australian dollar to appreciate against Japanese yen), spot often did the opposite. The pattern is a near mirror, with some exceptions during the period around the Lehman crisis (Zurawski & D'Arcy, 2009). Indeed, adding credence to this point, Nekritin & Peters (2012) argue that most clients of retail FX brokers lose money. One culprit is also likely to be the excessive leverage which retail FX traders can take (Murphy, 2012). The result is that even if they do happen to be right, they will often be forced to stop out of their position, because of underlying market volatility. As a result, Nekritin & Peters (2012) note that retail foreign exchange brokers can sometimes under-hedge their exposure to retail client trading activity, rather than immediately hedging out the risk to the markets. This can be the case even when there is sufficient liquidity to do so. In this instance, if a client loses money, the broker is on (at least partially) the other side of the trade and profits. Hence, the example we have cited in the UK equity retail market does not seem to be unique, but could be applicable to other asset classes, such as the foreign exchange market. So in summary, whilst attempting to capture alpha, as a group it seems that retail investors can underperform a passive beta strategy.

Should investors trade alpha or beta?

Our comments might seem to imply that retail investors should never try to trade actively and capture alpha. I am not saying this! It is just that typically retail investors perform worse than the beta benchmark. From that perspective, if most active equity retail investors had instead been passive investors simply having passive exposure to FTSE, as an example, they would have made more money. The lesson is only try to beat the market, if you have the time to do it and can use that time to research the market sufficiently. We have also discussed the idea of using alternative beta, which can be seen as an interesting strategy which fits in between alpha and traditional beta. Very often alternative beta strategies are pre-packaged in ETFs or similar wrappers, making it easier for investors to gain exposure to them without the necessity of doing the underlying trades themselves. Even from an institutional perspective, investors might feel it better value to migrate to trading alternative beta than attempting to capture alpha. Although, as Pat noted, alternative beta strategies are generally static, they hence have a potential to be problematic if they are not constructed carefully. I would have to agree with this point. A hybrid approach might also be applicable sometimes, farming out some style exposure to hedge funds, whilst using alternative beta products to gain exposure to other investment styles. For those wishing to understand more about "styles"-based trading, I would thoroughly recommend Antti Ilmanen's book *Expected Returns: An Investor's Guide to Harvesting Market Rewards* (Ilmanen, 2011).

The lesson is that, sometimes, just following the market and being exposed to beta will be good enough, and on some occasions trying to "beat the market" can end up with investors being "beaten by the market." Not everyone is Thales!

4
The Code of Hammurabi: Reducing Risk

> In codes of law it is that men are made,
> That men are they, not beasts so weighed,
> Solely by thirst, hunger and their urges,
> But by justice, right and truth which surges.

The origins of insurance and Hammurabi

When I was young, which I must add was not that many years ago, I went on my first holiday abroad. I think I must have been around eight years old. As well as being my first trip abroad, it was also my very first encounter with air travel. We took a flight on a now defunct airline from London to Paris. I clearly remember the sensation of the take-off. I continue to find this the most exciting point of a flight, although, admittedly, ear popping does somewhat impact the whole take-off experience and is perhaps one of the less pleasant aspects of air travel. This was also the age when traveling by plane had an element of bling to it, even in my economy class seat. There was not the endless queuing which plagues busy airports today or the litany of additional add-on costs you have to incur. Indeed, I find it amusing today that airline companies charge extra for minuscule portions of disgusting food (where disgusting is perhaps over-complimentary).

Paris was then and is forever for me a place as enchanted as it is wonderful. The romanticism of the river Seine; a city where the buildings seem alive, breathing through lights; a city where simply walking down the street is an experience: Paris is all of these things. My visit included the usual tourist checklist such as the Arc de Triomphe and the Eiffel Tower, the French equivalents of the hamburger in New York or red phone boxes in London, quintessential ambassadors for their country. In addition, it was the one (and only) time when I visited the Louvre, Paris' most famous museum. I remember little of it, save for the funky glass pyramid and possibly the world's most famous painting, the

Mona Lisa. I saw little of this, as my view was mostly interrupted by tourists (such as myself) fawning around it. I have to say for an eight year old, as I was then, I failed to see what was so amazing about this painting. Maybe it was the expression, neither smiling nor frowning, which puzzled me, as it has generations of onlookers. As for the other exhibits in the Louvre, I do not remember anything at all. Fast forward over 20 years to the present day, and I wish I had taken at least a few minutes to examine another exhibit, rather than being part of the rugby scrum surrounding the Mona Lisa.

The other exhibit, which still stands in the Louvre, is made from diorite, an igneous rock that is a type of rock made from volcanic activity. This stone (or stele, to be more exact) is 2.25 meters high and 0.65 meters wide, giving it the profile of a finger. Two figures are etched on the upper part of one side, or on the "finger nail" portion. The rest of the stele is etched in cuneiform script in Akkadian, a language spoken in Ancient Mesopotamia. Cuneiform script has at its core wedge-like shapes. Mieroop (2004) discusses the content of the text in some detail. Collectively, it is known as the Code of Hammurabi. Hammurabi was King of Babylon, ruling from 1792 BC to 1750 BC. Much of Hammurabi's fame stems from the famous code and his status as a lawgiver to his citizens and, more generally, to mankind, rather than as a conqueror, a role that he pursued for much of his rule. Indeed, Hammurabi refers to himself as the king of justice. Hammurabi's stature contrasts with that of other ancient kings of Babylon, whose fame was more a result of their military conquests.

Mieroop thinks that terming the text as a law code is likely to be inaccurate. He believes it was unlikely to have been designed as a law template for citizens of a new state to follow, unlike the well-known Code Napoléon in nineteenth-century France. Indeed, he notes that many areas of law are missing from the text, and there is little evidence that legal decisions of the time referenced the code.

In amongst the text there are 275–300 laws. Mieroop notes that the precise number is unknown, as some were erased from the stele. They generally consist of "if" clauses followed by a consequence. Mieroop notes that the concept that punishment for a physical injury committed by one person on another should be of the same nature is present. Indeed, he notes that this idea is perhaps one of the most famous of the laws (which can be more succinctly be thought of as an eye for an eye and a tooth for a tooth, a concept that is also in various religious texts). I would guess that many people are familiar with this notion (including me), but are unaware that it appears in the Code of Hammurabi.

The laws in the text which we shall focus on first are those related to merchandising, which are laws 100–105. Trenerry (2010 reprint) notes that Babylon imported a large amount of raw materials for use in manufactured goods that were then exported. This presented several problems. In particular, the difficulty lay in those situations where traders were robbed of the goods that they were due to sell. In such a scenario, without some form of insurance, they were liable to pay the merchants who had advanced these goods. In cases where they were unable to repay there were grave consequences, which would result in them becoming slaves of the creditor. The risks seemed to outweigh the possible rewards.

In such an environment, where the downside is so great, would you want to become a trader? The answer is probably no. More generally, if trading proved to be an unattractive occupation, then the pool of traders would be diminished. As a result, we might conjecture that the cost of trading from a merchant's point of view would become much more expensive. How could merchants reduce the risk for individual traders?

One solution to this problem was mentioned in the Code of Hammurabi; it was a simple version of a bottomry loan. Merchants gave a loan to traders, which was either money or merchandise to be sold. The traders then undertook a land crossing, usually in large caravans, given that Babylon was landlocked. The loan and the interest were forgiven if traders were robbed on their journey. Hence, there was a transfer of risk from the trader to the merchant. In a sense, we can therefore view this contract as a very simple form of insurance. We could also view the contract as a form of put option held by the trader; this put option would effectively pay out in the event of the trader being robbed. From a purely theoretical point of view, the cost of the put option is embedded in the interest payable on the loan.

Today, we also have debt instruments with embedded optionality. Most common is the idea of a callable bond. Unlike in the Babylonian case, it is the creditor rather than the debtor who holds an option which could potentially be of value. The issuer of the bond has the option to redeem the debt earlier than the original maturity of a bond, but not necessarily the obligation. If interest rates fall significantly, this option becomes valuable, as the issuer is able to exercise the option and redeem the debt. The issuer can then go out into the market to refinance the debt at a lower interest rate. Obviously, if interest rates rose, the option would not be exercised. In the event of higher rates, it would not be in the issuer's interest to refinance the debt in the market, when he or she is already servicing a debt with lower rates.

Other parts of the Code of Hammurabi describe similar insurance-like contracts related to loans, but in different contexts. Whaley (2006) discusses the contents of law 48, which examines the conditions under which interest on a loan should be forgiven. Whaley notes that the law seems to relate to farmers who used their harvest as a means to pay interest on loans, which were likely to be related to property. It states that a creditor should forgive the interest paid in a year when the harvest fails or is very poor owing to a lack of water. Whaley argues that as a result of this, by implication the farmer holds a put option on interest, similar to our trader's loan example earlier. Should the harvest be successful, the put option becomes worthless, since interest would need to be paid in such a scenario. However, in the event of a poor harvest, the put would expire in-the-money for the farmer (and clearly out-of-the-money for the creditor, on the other side of the trade, who would not receive any interest that year).

Trenerry (2010 reprint) suggests that the idea of the bottomry contract later spread from the Babylonians to the Phoenicians and then to the Greeks, who adapted it for the purposes of maritime trade. Unlike the Babylonians, both the Phoenicians and the Greeks conducted a large amount of trade via the sea, perhaps unsurprisingly, given the very different geographies they inhabited. Reed (1999) notes that Ancient Greek bottomry loans probably first appeared in the fifth century BC. When conducting trade by sea, the risks were far greater than on land. Of course ships could be robbed by pirates, just as land traders could be robbed. However, the risk of accidents was much greater at sea compared to voyages on land by camel. In these cases, if ships sank, bottomry loans would be forgiven. Reed notes that even those wealthier *emporoi* (loosely translated as traders) might prefer to take bottomry loans to fund their voyages, given it essentially took risk off their hands and transferred it to another party. In this instance, the benefits of the insurance offered by the loan would offset the interest paid. However, sometimes the prospect of not having to pay back a loan was too appealing. Reed points out several cases in Ancient Greece where Greek traders tried to scuttle their ships to avoid paying back their loans, or others who simply lied to their creditors. Insurance fraud is not a new phenomenon! Other than bottomry loans, other forms of insurance were also present in the ancient world. Trenerry discusses life insurance in Ancient Rome, for example.

However, the idea of insurance is not purely a matter which is related to the cases we have discussed in the ancient world. Indeed, insurance has spread today to offer individuals and companies a way to transfer risk in all sorts of scenarios, rather than purely those relating to trade or life insurance. If we step back and look at insurance in the context of investments, the idea seems very appealing. After all, if we can somehow insure (or hedge, as it is more commonly described in the context of investments) against some losses, we can reduce the risks associated with investments. The first point is that there are several ways we can "insure" our portfolio to reduce certain risks. Some methods involve changing the composition of our portfolio, whilst others involve paying a premium to purchase derivatives, which we shall discuss in more detail.

The first method we can use to reduce risk within our portfolio is to find optimal exposures using mathematical techniques such as portfolio optimization. The primary objective of the exercise is to diversify our portfolio. However, we shall show that simple forms of portfolio optimization can have drawbacks. Alternatively, we can do something more akin to taking out insurance: this can involve purchasing options to hedge the risks in our portfolio. Furthermore, we could enter into positions in the opposing direction with assets which we believe have similar behavior. This idea is essentially a proxy hedge. We shall discuss why we would sometimes prefer to apply a proxy hedge as opposed to a more direct hedge.

One important point is that it is difficult and often not desirable to hedge out every risk in a portfolio. After all, if you are exposed to no risk at all, there can be no potential return from an investment. Simply making no investment would be the easiest approach to having no risk! It would also suggest we are very risk averse. If we wish to hedge an extremely large number of risks within our portfolio, we should consider investing in less risky assets. Hence, we should always view the ideas of diversification and hedging a portfolio as ways of reducing our risk, but not entirely eliminating them.

The concept of diversification when investing

The idea of diversification is something which is practiced not only in finance. Indeed, if we think of the various sayings that we accumulate in our very earliest years, surely the idiom that we do not put all our eggs in one basket is a saying that comes to mind. If you do put your eggs in one basket, dropping that basket is likely to break all of them. Outside finance, it can of course be difficult to follow this idiom. We are very often faced with decisions which require us to put all our eggs in one basket. Let us take the example of managing our time amongst a plethora of jobs. Splitting our time amongst many jobs, where the skill sets required are totally different rather than complimentary, will result in less expertise in any specific area. Whilst this might be necessary for a manager overseeing a large business, such diversification is unlikely to be beneficial for an employee tasked with a very specialized project.

However, in terms of financial investments, it is easier to apply the concept of diversification. Capital can be more easily split than our time. Of course, there will still be some cost in terms of time by diversifying a portfolio, when it comes to understanding the various markets where our capital will be invested. To some extent we could argue that there is a crossover in the skills that are required to assess investments in different assets classes. I discussed the idea of diversification with one of my friends, Steve Zymler. I know him from the time he was studying at Imperial College in the year below Paul and me. His English is tinged with a Belgian accent, which has softened over the years.

I have not had many opportunities to go to Belgium. However, if I do end up there and find everyone there is as courteous and friendly as Steve, my visit will be very enjoyable. Aside from being Imperial graduates, the other thing that Steve and I share is that we both value the idea of a perfect steak. Indeed, I think that on most occasions we have met in recent years we have dined at

Hawksmoor, which can possibly lay claim to the best steak in London. There is something incredibly satisfying about having a fantastic steak, which is precisely the opposite of having a tough, overcooked and rubbery steak, something that is most definitely an affront to the taste buds!

As well as having an appreciation of a great steak, Steve also happens to be very smart, and has an in-depth knowledge of optimization, a mathematical subject which is intrinsic to the creation of diversified portfolios. After completing an undergraduate degree at Imperial in Computer Science, he later went on to do a PhD, also at Imperial, in optimization. Indeed, Steve spoke to the Thalesians in 2009 on improvements to VaR, namely WCPVaR (worst case value at risk) and WCQVaR (worst case quadratic value at risk), which attempt to alleviate some of the concerns I voiced about VaR in Chapter 2. The subject of Steve's talk is detailed in a paper he co-wrote (Zymler, Kuhn, & Rustem, 2012). Following his post-graduate studies, he went into the world of developing systematic trading models, like me; but it should be said that the financial services industry does not appear to have stressed him as much as it has me, as evidenced by his full head of black hair, versus my relatively sparse excuse for hair which occupies a relatively small area of my head!

When Steve heard that I was writing this book, he immediately brought to my attention an ancient reference to financial diversification in the Talmud. A little further investigation of the topic showed that this reference has been discussed in many books and articles on diversification that are floating around the Internet. Although the precise translation seems to differ slightly from source to source, the general principle appears to be the same. Dubnov (1968) notes that in the Talmud (Bava Metzia 42a) it is advised that the rich split their capital into thirds. One third is to be used in commerce. One third is to be in a liquid asset such as cash. One third is to be placed in land.

Although the approach is relatively simple, it makes intuitive sense to always keep some liquid assets in your portfolio. After all, when your portfolio has large losses, if you have no cash or liquid assets to sell to come up with cash to cover those losses, you would be forced to liquidate your portfolio. Furthermore, the idea of splitting up investments into different areas (here commerce and land) helps to cushion the portfolio in the instance of underperformance in either, even if our objective is to profit from all these areas. The one problem with diversification is that it relies upon having assets which are relatively uncorrelated in a portfolio. If assets are all heavily correlated in a portfolio, it makes a mockery of the objective of diversification. Another issue we discussed in Chapter 2, on risk, is that correlations are themselves volatile. Hence, what might appear to be a well-diversified portfolio when risk sentiment is very strong can suddenly behave like a single asset during risk aversion. During these periods, high beta assets become much more heavily correlated with one another. One of the most obvious examples can be seen in stock markets. Investing in every stock market in the world might seem to

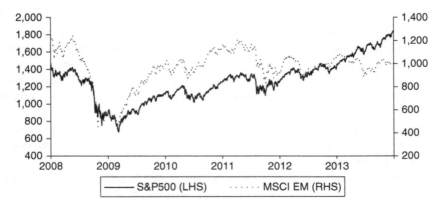

Figure 4.1   S&P500 and MSCI EM
Source: Thalesians, Bloomberg Finance L.P.

offer some element of correlation, when markets are focused on idiosyncratic events. In that instance, there might be some independence in the price action. However, when there is a massive risk event, correlations are suddenly heightened and it is likely that such an investor would face losses in many parts of his or her equity portfolio. So-called diversification from this sort of portfolio is therefore not a persistent reduction in risk and is diminished during periods of significant risk aversion. Unfortunately, these are precisely the periods when diversification is needed most.

In Figure 4.1 we illustrate this by plotting S&P500 against a large basket of stocks in emerging markets (MSCI EM). For a lot of the time, we can see quite different performance from each of these indices. However, during particular periods of market turbulence both indices experience drawdowns. So whilst investing in both would provide some element of diversification, compared to just one, diversification would not always help during the drawdowns.

The mathematical way to diversify: The good, the bad and the super-leveraged portfolio

We have discussed a very simple suggestion for diversifying a portfolio into cash, commerce, and land, and the rationale behind it. We also gave the simple case of splitting a stock investment into both S&P500 and emerging market stocks. This has provided some element of diversification in the past, but it has not eliminated large drawdowns during times of particular market turbulence, such as during the Lehman crisis.

Today, we are not limited to investing in a small number of assets. Indeed, the number of assets to choose from is bewildering, thus complicating the investment process. This is not just the case with investment decisions: when there are a large number of choices in any decision, it increases the time which is necessary to investigate the problem. If we think back to the ancient world and Chapter 3, we discussed the diet of people in Ancient Greece. For the most part it was a relatively simple affair, with bread providing the staple, as well as other foods we associate with the Mediterranean, such as the olive. Today, by contrast, the choice of foods available is huge. In London there are so many types of food that there are times in the supermarket when I see fruits which I have trouble naming. Trying to make a decision about buying different types of food for the creation of a sandwich opens up a massive permutation of possibilities, just as when we are try to select assets in a portfolio (even if we restrict ourselves to a single asset class).

Given the abundance of computing power today, it might therefore make some sense to try automating the process of diversification. Furthermore, a mathematical model might give us possible suggestions on the makeup of a portfolio which we might not have had the inspiration to pick up ourselves without a hint.

Is there a way to do this? More precisely, can we mathematically construct a portfolio to optimize the amount of risk we wish to take versus our potential reward? In the early 1950s, Harry Markowitz developed a method to do this (Markowitz, 1959). The story behind his original idea is told in Bernstein (1996).

In more mathematical language this is known as mean-variance optimization. Although we will not go into the vagaries of how this process words, we shall endeavor to discuss the general principle. I remember having to solve optimization problems by hand at university and it was extremely painful, but going through such an exercise makes it much clearer about what is going on in the algorithm. In practice these days, an investor wishing to solve such a problem would use a computer rather than a pen and paper! Indeed, without a computer it would be difficult to solve the problem for all but the simplest of portfolios.

By understanding the correlations between various assets (and their volatilities) and estimating the potential returns of these various assets, mean-variance optimization comes up with optimal weights for the amount of exposure for each asset in the portfolio. If we repeat this process many times we can come up with weights for a large array of portfolios, each with the lowest risk for a potential reward according to the model. When we plot these portfolios on a graph, they create what is termed an efficient frontier, with volatility on one axis of the graph and returns on the other. We plot a typical efficient frontier in Figure 4.2. So far, finding the best possible portfolio for whatever risk we wish to take seems like a great idea.

However, there are many problems associated with the method, as noted by Bernstein (1996), amongst others. In particular, let us consider the inputs we used for the model. Let us first consider the correlations and volatilities of the

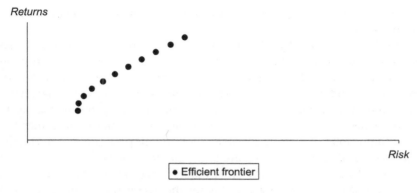

Figure 4.2 The efficient frontier between risk and reward
Source: Thalesians.

various assets. We have already mentioned in Chapter 2 that these are difficult to estimate, in particular when we use realized volatility and correlation: these do not take into account structural breaks in markets. Indeed, this was one of the problems with VaR which we mentioned, its reliance on historical correlations and volatilities. Furthermore, these correlations, which we are attempting to estimate, are volatile in themselves.

There is also the question of which precise risk we are attempting to optimize during this exercise. As we noted in Chapter 2, volatility is one way of looking at risk, and in this instance we are optimizing for that. However, there are many other measures of risk which are just as crucial (or perhaps more so). We could examine drawdowns, in other words the most an investor could possibly lose. We shall give an example to illustrate that minimizing portfolio volatility is unfortunately not always the same thing as reducing drawdowns.

Say, for example, that our historical correlation suggests that two assets are heavily correlated. Our optimization might then tell us to take large positions in opposite directions in these assets, given that their risk should theoretically be cancelled out. I have observed this in the instance of creating an FX carry portfolio using this method. This might be fine when the correlations are working as planned in our long-term historical sample. However, what happens when there is an idiosyncratic event and suddenly the correlations flip? We are faced with a super-leveraged portfolio, which has large positions in a multitude of different assets that are behaving in a very similar way! When assessing the output from our portfolio optimization problem, we should have considered asking several important questions.

In particular, we should have asked what our likely loss could be in the case of an adverse scenario. If we had asked such a question, we would have refrained from building up a massively leveraged portfolio, even if superficially the risks appeared to cancel themselves out judging by the "optimal" output of our optimization.

Taleb (2013) is especially critical of Markowitz. I take a more sanguine view, acknowledging some of the drawbacks of portfolio optimization whilst noting some of the various benefits. Rather than saying we should never use this approach, I would instead advocate what I would term as cautious usage. Hence, when we see the output of such a portfolio optimization problem, we need to consider whether the weights make intuitive sense. Is the result a massively leveraged portfolio? Can we understand why certain positions are much larger than others? Is there an excessive amount of capital allocated to a specific asset? Just as with Black-Scholes or any other model, financial or otherwise, we need to interpret its output! Having a feeling for the data is just as important, even if we might not fully understand the precise mechanics of the algorithm.

Furthermore, we should note that many of these questions can be "included" in the model. For example, it is possible to put lots of extra conditions on the model to prevent leverage from exploding, as well as specifying maximum weights for every asset. We can also pose more complicated optimization problems, which involve trying to solve multiple objectives such as volatility and drawdowns. These do not solve deficiencies created by imperfect volatility and correlation data, but they do prevent some of the more problematic issues of the model, which we have discussed.

Admittedly, once all these additional conditions have been placed on your portfolio, you might actually end up with something you could have obtained more easily by another simpler method! Also, adding complexity can sometimes make it more difficult to understand why the model has chosen specific weights for each asset. The only way in which to make a true judgment on the effectiveness of this portfolio optimization approach is to try applying it to your own portfolio, and to add the various conditions which seem to result in reasonable output.

Alliances amongst Ancient Greek *poleis*: Hedging specific risks

In the ancient world, people also hedged risks: we have already seen that ideas such as insurance were present then. We can also observe instances of hedging risks in the ancient world when we consider how various conflicts were conducted.

For part of its history, Ancient Greece was made up of independent city states, or *poleis* to give them their Greek name, which we have mentioned already on several occasions. The dominance of the idea of city states was current until the Hellenistic period, which started in 323 BC, the end of the wars of Alexander the Great. Later, Ancient Greece was subsumed into the Roman Empire.

Amongst the various Ancient Greek city states were Sparta and Athens. Whilst the city states often fought one another, when there was the specter of a greater enemy, such as Persia, they were willing to enter into alliances. In a sense, we can think of such alliances as hedges against the risks of defending foreign invasions. However, there was some cost to this hedge. In particular, entering into alliances could be seen as reducing the relative independence of the various city states. Furthermore, there was also a military cost to aiding fellow city states in their hour of need. Of course, avoiding alliances would not always mean that a city state did not need to fight; it would simply result in facing a foreign foe alone at a later time. As soon as the foreign threat passed, city states "unwound" their hedge and broke up their alliances.

Hedging specific risks in a portfolio: A financial viewpoint

So whilst we can think of hedges in the context of ancient alliances, or in more conventional settings such as insurance, we can also apply the same hedging principals to investing. We have seen how portfolio optimization can help us to give us optimal portfolios for our predetermined level of risk. Unfortunately, such an approach is subject to the deficiencies in our estimates which are input into the model. There is also the issue that the simple case of portfolio optimization we have presented is attempting to reduce volatility for a specific return. This is not the same thing as optimizing for other metrics of risk such as drawdowns, even if there is some link between volatility and drawdowns. Furthermore, the portfolio generated by such an optimization exercise may not tally with an investor's preferences. Hence, any output which is generated from such an approach needs to be understood fully and, if necessary, adjusted, rather than being applied blindly.

As well as using a mathematical model to diversify a portfolio in order to reduce risk, investors can also place hedges which are specifically targeted to their portfolio. In a way, we can draw a parallel with Ancient Greeks entering into alliances for those times when they wanted to "hedge" the risk of an external foe. The idea of placing specific hedges is slightly different to diversifying the composition of a portfolio in an effort to reduce risk (although the end result of a hedge should also be to reduce risk in the portfolio). Also, hedges do not need to be instituted on a continuous basis, just like the various alliances amongst the Ancient Greek city states, which were intermittent.

We can think about the subtle difference between actively hedging a portfolio and diversification in the context of our Talmud example. That discussed splitting wealth into thirds, with one third in commerce, one third in land, and one third in cash. The income from commerce and land (notably agriculture) is unlikely to be 100% correlated, whether in the ancient world or today. After all, it is likely that income from land would be influenced by different factors, such as the weather, which has a huge impact on the harvest. This contrasts to income from commerce, which is likely to be impacted more considerably by the general growth environment rather than the weather. As a result, there would be some diversity in our income stream.

Our combined income stream is likely to be more stable, compared with the scenario where we invest all our capital in only one industry. However, we should not think of either the income from commerce or land as a pure hedge for the other income. Indeed, our long-term objective for investing in both commerce and land would be to gain a profit in both cases. At the same time there are benefits from diversification in terms of reducing the volatility of our overall income over a long period.

The idea of a hedge is to reduce the underlying risk in our portfolio, whilst at the same time not curtailing the upside significantly. The main motivation for using a specific hedge is not to make money on it. Any position which is primarily intended to generate returns is a speculative investment and should not be thought of as a hedge to the portfolio. We can easily make this distinction between a hedge and the rest of our portfolio. If our hedge is likely to make money, in what we consider to be the most likely scenario for the market, then it is difficult to call it a hedge.

In Chapter 2, we discussed the idea of running through various scenarios which could negatively impact a portfolio. We might wish to buy hedges to reduce the risk from these possible scenarios. However, which risks are the most important for us to hedge? The main objective of a hedge is that it can be used by investors to guard against a scenario which could have a considerable negative impact on their portfolio, in particular those which are judged to have a higher probability of occurring. Multiple hedges can be used if there are many potential scenarios which concern an investor.

Illustrating hedging with an example

Thus far, we have broadly outlined the definition of a hedge. In particular, leveraging our base case is not a hedge! The next step is to illustrate it with an example. Let us say that we have a large long stock position in, for example, the basket of stocks which make up S&P500. What types of scenarios might we wish to guard against? The most obvious risk is a large-scale position unwind in stocks. As discussed in Chapter 2, during periods of risk aversion risky assets such as stocks are prone to large losses. It is these large losses which give the characteristic fat tail in the distributions of risky assets. It is these drawdowns which are the most painful part of being long risky assets. On the flipside, without these large losses there would be much lower risk premium and, as such, risky assets would not yield as much. As ever, the returns we can potentially gain from an investment are proportional to the underlying risk. When the returns on an investment seem totally disjointed from the risk, we must be very cautious.

One way to hedge this tail-risk-style scenario is via puts on S&P500 or similar instruments, such as VIX futures. As we noted in Chapter 2, buying a put option gives an investor the right, but not the obligation, to sell an asset at a predefined price in the future. So if stocks fell, our put would become valuable. If stocks rose, our put would expire worthless. However, the purchase of such a hedge is of course not free. Whilst it is possible to create zero cost options structures, these are often funded by selling options, which could potentially increase the risk of our portfolio significantly in an adverse scenario. Hence, the lack of a premium has a potential consequence and we should not view it as a free hedge. As such, we need to make several decisions before we institute our hedge. We need to weigh up the cost against the potential benefits in terms of reducing some of the risks of our portfolio, as well as understanding what any losses could be from our hedge.

Before even considering the precise type of hedge, we need to ask when we would like to institute our hedge. If we would like a continual hedge over time through options, it will be more costly. The difficulty with tail-risk-type scenarios is that they can be virtually impossible to predict in terms of their timing, so this might be the only way to protect ourselves against these. A selective hedge that we only institute at specific times would be cheaper, but it might end up missing these risk blow outs.

Furthermore, if we choose to use an option hedge, we need to work out what strike of the option we wish to purchase. A strike which is very close to where S&P500 is currently trading would protect us even against very small falls in the stock market. However, the cost of continually rolling such a put option over an extended period would be very costly. Hence, in all likelihood we would need to buy puts with strikes which are further away from where spot is trading (so called out-of-the-money strikes), which would be somewhat cheaper. Whilst such out-of-the-money options would not protect against small falls in stocks, they would help to protect us in the case of very large downside moves in stocks. This fits in with the original risk we wanted to hedge, namely large unwinds in stocks. Of course, during benign times, our returns would be reduced by the cost of our put hedge expiring worthless. Importantly, during severe risk aversion our drawdowns would be less. In Chapter 6, we shall return to the subject of tail risks and hedging them in a discussion about Black Swan events.

As we have repeatedly noted, understanding the maximum potential downside from a trade is a very important consideration! It is this figure which helps to guide investors to scale the size of their trades. The crucial point of a hedge is that whilst it might help reduce some risks such as potential drawdowns, hedges are not designed to make a portfolio profitable when the portfolio has expressed a view which turns out to be totally wrong. If a hedge repeatedly makes a portfolio profitable, when the "wrong" view ends up happening it would be difficult to call this position a hedge, even if its profits might be welcome! This would suggest that the relative leverage of the portfolio versus the hedge is somehow mismatched. It would be a case of the tail (hedge) wagging the dog (portfolio).

Aside from directly hedging our portfolio, we might also wish to hedge against other risks which could negatively impact our long S&P500 position, such as rising interest rates. These risks can be hedged using interest rate futures or interest rate options, as an example.

Simply hedging every conceivable risk we could be exposed to is likely to be very costly, and would call into question why we placed our original investment. It also suggests that we should cut our position to a size which is more consistent with the level of risk we are willing to take.

For times illiquid: A proxy hedge

The most obvious "hedge" we can employ to reduce our risk is simply to cut the size of our investment. If we have $100 invested in a stock, selling $50 immediately cuts our risk in half. Admittedly, under the definition of a "hedge" this would be a relatively aggressive trade and would also have a large impact on the potential upside. It is nevertheless the case that we might want to do this on occasions, when our focus switches from collecting yield to preserving our capital, such as during risk aversion. However, there are times when attempting to reduce or entirely exit an investment might be difficult. Let us assume that we were invested in real estate during the financial crisis of 2008. Whilst our long-term view was that real estate prices would be stable, in the short term we were concerned with falling property prices. In such a situation, we might think it prudent to reduce some of our investment, just in case.

We could reduce our exposure to real estate by selling part of our portfolio and buying it back later. However, attempting to sell a highly illiquid asset such as real estate when house prices are falling would probably have been very difficult. We might even have been unable to find any buyers. So what can investors do in such a scenario, when they are forced to hold illiquid positions they wish to reduce but cannot find any buyers? One answer is hope, and ask the Oracle of Delphi when the market will pick up!

A more prudent approach to calling on the Oracle of Delphi would be to use a proxy hedge. This involves buying a hedge in a fairly liquid instrument which would act as a proxy for falling housing prices. So even if we were losing money on our real estate investment, our hedge would become more valuable, offsetting it. We could, for example, use short positions in S&P500 as a hedge for exposure to real estate. So as stock markets fell, our hedge would become more

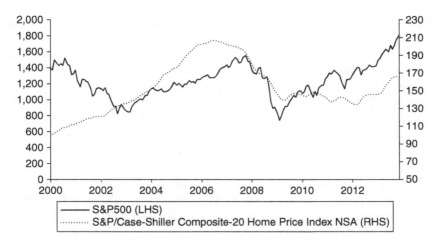

Figure 4.3   S&P/Case-Shiller index of US house prices against S&P500
Source: Thalesians, Bloomberg Finance L.P.

valuable, offsetting the loss from our original investment. In Figure 4.3, we plot US house prices against S&P500. The relationship between the two indices is not perfect throughout the history, but it would have been an effective hedge at the very least in 2008.

Whilst I have presented a favorable case for proxy hedges, there are obvious downsides. Primarily, the assumption we make when putting on a proxy hedge is that there is a reasonable relationship between our proxy and the underlying asset. Unfortunately, correlations between assets are themselves volatile, as discussed in Chapter 2 and alluded to in Figure 4.3. If correlations manage to flip between our proxy and the underlying asset, we could be faced with a scenario where we lose money both on our underlying investment and also on our proxy hedge. On the flipside, shifting correlations are not always a downside risk, as they can also result in both our investment and the hedge making money. Whilst an obvious positive, this is not the original idea of a proxy hedge.

We can also use an option to proxy hedge a portfolio. When buying an option, our losses on our proxy hedge are limited to the premium paid. Let us take the case of an investment in a highly illiquid emerging markets (EM) bond. As with the case of real estate, trying to get rid of this asset from our trading book would be exceedingly difficult during times of risk aversion. This necessitates another approach to reducing our exposure during these periods. One choice would be to go short a high beta asset such as S&P500 futures, which is still relatively liquid at times of risk aversion. Admittedly, if risk aversion was serious enough, it might still be difficult to execute even this trade in large sizes.

It is likely that it would be an imperfect hedge, but even so it would be better than hemorrhaging cash from our illiquid EM bond exposure during market turmoil. As with any trade, we would need to consider potential risks from placing our hedge. By shorting S&P500 or another liquid equity index in the cash market, we could open ourselves up to large losses if there was an unexpected change in the correlation between S&P500 and our underlying EM bond position. For example, what if S&P500 rallied significantly and our EM bond continued to lose value? This would result in losing money both on our hedge and the underlying position. Hence, we would have made the situation worse!

We could express the view via put options on S&P500 and also probably on the local EM currency. As noted earlier, the advantage of buying options is that we have a cap on how much we can lose on our options hedge. Indeed, this is what Thales did when he bought call options on olives (although in his case he bought options to express a view, so it could not be called a hedge). There is still the risk that our option hedge will not work, as with doing the trade in cash. However, at least we are not faced with the potential for large losses in our hedge, which is capped.

Furthermore, in general EM currencies tend to be more liquid than other EM assets. Hence, there is very often a developed options market in most EM currencies. The same is unlikely to be the case for the illiquid EM bond in our example. Also, proxy hedging via a put option on the local EM currency would likely provide a better fit than simply using S&P500 options, in terms of the fundamental linkages between the markets. If liquidity is not good enough for the amount we wish to transact in the local EM currency options market, we could always resort to a basket of options. The lesson is that even if we invest in illiquid assets, a proxy hedge provides the possibility of hedging against adverse market moves, even if we cannot get out of our underlying exposure.

Is diversification always a good thing? Is concentration always a bad thing?

We have written about using diversification as a method of reducing risks within a portfolio. There are of course some problems to this. Notably, we suggested that during the hairiest of market risk events, the benefits from diversification are unlikely to be as useful, given that correlations between assets tend to heighten. What were previously uncorrelated assets suddenly behave as though they were very similar.

However, the idea of some element of diversification is still popular amongst investors, in particular because of the way it can help reduce idiosyncratic risks. When does too much diversification actually start to have a large negative effect on a portfolio? In particular, do we reach a point where the supposed benefits of reducing risk end up severely curtailing the upside? Or should we go the other way and attempt to concentrate risk? Is this a better way to approach investing?

Warren Buffett's mastery of the financial markets has been legendary and he has been elevated to near rock star status. Over the past 50 years, his investment vehicle has been Berkshire Hathaway, which was originally a textile company. The annual shareholder meetings of his company have become huge events: the 2013 meeting was attended by over 35,000 people (Stempel & Ablan, 2013), eager to hear from Buffett himself. His story is told in some detail in Schroeder (2009).

If we look at Berkshire Hathaway stock price changes over time, we can gauge precisely how successful Buffett has been in his investment career. Berkshire Hathaway stock was trading at around $7 when Buffet first bought it in 1962. At present Berkshire Hathaway's A shares, which have never split (and have also never paid a dividend) are trading at nearly $175,000, which is quite a return. In 1962, S&P500 was trading between at between 50–60 points compared with over 1,700 in 2013. If we were to take into account dividends, we have seen an even higher return from S&P500. However, it would still be far smaller than the return you would have accrued from owning Berkshire Hathaway stock. Indeed, in Buffett's 2012 letter to investors (Buffett, 2012) noted that the company had an average annual increase of 19.6% over the previous 48 years, compared to 9.4% for S&P500 including dividends. A triumph of alpha over beta? (Figure 4.4).

Admittedly, it would be easy to outperform S&P500 if we simply leveraged our investment considerably (which would increase return volatility), but Buffett has not done this. In Chapter 5, we examine other measures of investment performance rather than purely looking at annualized returns.

The reason why I am bringing up Warren Buffett is not purely because he is one of the world's most famous investors and his investment record has been exceptional. I am mentioning him because he has been particularly scathing about the whole principle of diversification as part of the investment process.

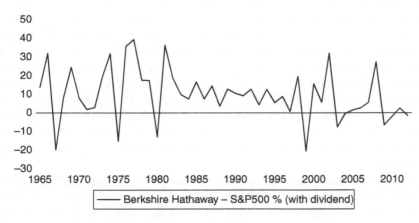

Figure 4.4 Berkshire Hathaway outperformance versus S&P500 YoY
Source: Thalesians, Berkshire Hathaway, Bloomberg Finance L.P.

Schroeder notes how Buffett's approach throughout his long history of investing has been more a matter of concentrating risk and placing confidence in his own abilities to spot a winner. Rather than spreading risk amongst countless assets, Buffett instead places them only in those stocks he thinks present the best opportunities. I would hardly place my abilities to spot market opportunities in the same league as Buffett: that would be somewhat facetious! However, I do wish to highlight a few points from my personal experience, limited though it is compared with Warren Buffett's time in finance. In my career, I have studied numerous trading strategies both in FX and in other markets, such as precious metals, and also to some extent in equities. However, in practice, I would say that after thorough investigating only a relatively small number of them have represented trading opportunities that I would take further. The difficulty is that it is only possible to make a decision after spending a significant amount of time investigating a particular idea.

My discussions with traders seem to tally with this point as well: the number of truly good trading opportunities are relatively difficult to find, whether we look at markets on a discretionary or systematic trading basis. Intuitively, this makes some sense. If successful trading strategies or particularly good trading opportunities were so easy to find, then surely many more investors would be outperforming the market.

Indeed, this is the gist of Buffett's message: that real opportunities are rare, but, most importantly, once found they need to be valued highly. As Schroeder notes, he would literally put all his eggs in one basket in accordance with this method. This contrasted to the approach of his mentor Benjamin Graham, Schroeder writes. Graham would identify a large number of stocks which he would call "cigar butts." As the name seems to imply, "cigar butts" were not desirable stocks. Indeed, they were cheap and largely ignored by market participants, which could potentially present a trading opportunity. In general, these companies were trading below the price of their working capital, and inevitably, some of them would prove to be duds. Depressed stock prices were justified in those latter instances, but in many other cases there would be some value to be extracted by a canny investor. Graham did not think it was worth trying to investigate which ones would turn out to be duds from the many stocks he had screened. Instead, he simply invested a small amount in a very large number of these "cigar butt" stocks. If some did indeed turn out to be duds, then it would not matter much, given that on average the rest of the "cigar butts" would be profitable.

This is the same approach I use when developing a specific trading strategy. If on average I estimate that just over 50% of the trades are likely to make money, but just under 50% are likely to lose money, then that will be sufficient for the strategy to be profitable as a whole. Obviously, the skew of returns is also of significant importance, with the preference being to have winning trades earning more on average compared with the losing trades! For strategies where the vast majority of trades are likely to be profitable, unfortunately the skew of returns can be the "wrong way." In other words, winning trades, whilst more numerous, tend to yield less. Losing trades are rarer, but tend to exhibit larger losses. This type of return profile is characteristic of high-risk trades. This would include trades that repeatedly capture risk premium, with selling options being a prime example. These can be problematic to risk-management (a polite way of saying that there is a chance a large loss could bankrupt you, if you are not careful).

Schroeder notes that Buffett's approach was to look at the opportunity cost of one investment versus using that capital in another investment. If for example you are placing capital in one stock, which is not amongst your favorite bets, it would imply that you have less capital to place in another stock which you prefer more. Putting myself in a Warren Buffett frame of mind, I am sure he would ask why you should invest in a stock you do not like as much and with less likely upside. The approach of investing in countless "cigar butts" is at total odds to Buffett's approach.

The tangible benefit from investing in more stocks might be reducing a possible downside from such diversification. However, it is also likely that the upside will be reduced simultaneously. If we were to repeat this process hundreds of times, there would be further dilution of our initial portfolio. We would probably be holding stocks that, were it not for diversification, we would not otherwise wish to hold. The result of the whole exercise could be a portfolio that does not represent our strongest views or only expresses them in a relatively tangential manner.

It is difficult to fault Buffett's argument if we only consider his record, which has been so incredible throughout his investing career. Clearly, concentrating risk in a fewer number of stocks, which represents his strongest views, has been very successful for him. However, the crucial point is that not everyone has been as successful in their investment judgment as Warren Buffett. Furthermore, being able to undertake the painstaking analysis of identifying trading opportunities is not particularly easy. Indeed, in Chapter 3 we noted that the characteristic of alpha strategies is that they are hard work.

For every Warren Buffett, there are likely to have been countless investors who have placed a significant amount of their net worth in a single stock (or an extremely small basket of stocks) seeking alpha, only to see that company go bankrupt, wiping away a large chunk of their net worth. Whether it is through a lack of judgment or circumstances which could never have been foreseen seems irrelevant. Employees who squirreled away their savings into a company share scheme which later went bankrupt come to mind, as do those investors who have had massively concentrated risk which went wrong. Not only did they work in a company, which provided them with a salary, they also invested their wealth in the same institution (or in some cases it was invested for them, regardless of their preferences).

Furthermore, we could argue that Warren Buffett's approach to investing has often revolved around placing large stakes in big corporates, such as Coca-Cola. These in general tend to be less risky than many of the smaller cap stocks which are traded; although we note that, admittedly, large corporates have gone bankrupt in the past. Furthermore, his time horizon of investing has been very long term. As such, short-term gyrations in the stock price of his holdings would be less of a concern for him, and this is dampened by a modicum of diversification.

There is evidently a middle ground between putting all your eggs in one basket, as Warren Buffett might suggest, and excessive diversification, which ends up diluting an investor's view to such an extent that it becomes unrecognizable.

What about other choices an investor could make? One alternative to just using diversification is decreasing the leverage of a portfolio: as we have said earlier, this is the easiest way to reduce risk. A combination of the two, some element of diversification and also deleveraging, might prove to be more satisfactory, rather than one or the other. Let us take an investor who has an extremely strong positive view in two or three specific stocks. This investor has $100,000 in cash to invest. One approach could be to put all that cash into those two or three stocks as well as a multitude of other stocks, purely to engender some element of diversification.

However, an alternative would be to leave some of the capital in cash and only use a proportion of it to invest in those two or three stocks. Indeed, Warren Buffett has often kept a large cash pile as part of his holdings. There is some loss of opportunity by not using all the cash, but at least the investor is not faced with investing in assets he or she has no view on or does not like. Furthermore, should the portfolio lose money, the investor still has cash to cover losses, rather than being forced to liquidate stock to cover losses. If we think back to our example from the Talmud, this approach seems familiar, namely to split your wealth into three parts: one third in commerce, one third in land, and one third in cash.

We have spoken purely about the case of stocks, but we could also apply the same principle when deciding how much capital to place in various trading strategies. Hence, we could allocate more capital to a trading strategy which we like more, even if it might reduce the diversification of the portfolio. There might be a multitude of reasons why we would want to do this. We could judge that market liquidity is of a sufficient quantity to absorb this strategy in a reasonable size. Furthermore, we might wish to take advantage of the strategy with a larger amount of capital to maximize profits until that point when the strategy begins to break down. At the same time, I would not advocate putting every ounce of capital you have in a particular trading strategy, no matter how much you like it (again, recall that very few of us are Warren Buffett!). In a sense, I would summarize my view as one which occupies a middle ground between Graham's style of diversification and Buffett's idea of concentrating risk in the best bets.

As always, each case is different, but it is nevertheless a reasonable point to make that excessive diversification can at some point dilute an investor's view significantly. In that instance, we might as well just consider trying to capture beta, as it will be somewhat quicker and cheaper to achieve (in terms of time).

Diversification in a hedged world

We started this chapter by discussing the idea of insurance, which was mentioned in the ancient world in the Code of Hammurabi in the form of bottomry loans for trade and also loans for farmers. We elaborated on the topic of insurance, discussing how we could "insure" against certain risks. In our section on diversification, we noted that splitting our investment into multiple assets can help reduce risk. Mathematical ways of solving the problem of diversification have their benefits, but we need to be cautious about the output generated by these models. In many cases, we may need to add additional conditions to have more reasonable portfolios.

We discussed the idea of using specific hedges to reduce the impact of potential scenarios, relating it to the idea of alliances amongst the Ancient Greek city states at times of external threat. We noted that instituting a hedge is often not free, because of hedging our exposure through options, for example. Hence, we need to carefully consider the particular hedge we wish to use. Furthermore, we need to consider whether our hedge needs to persist over time or whether we should simply institute it on a more active basis. If we want to have a more active approach to hedging, then timing will be crucial. We primarily looked at using options as a relatively direct way of expressing a hedge.

When dealing with a more illiquid investment, it might be difficult to hedge specific risks directly. Often an options market might not exist, and simply exiting our position during risk aversion might be difficult or impossible (the most obvious way to reduce risk is unfortunately not possible!). Later, we delved into the world of the proxy hedge, which aims to solve this problem. The idea is to use a related (more liquid) asset as a hedge, either via the options or cash market. Whilst diversification or directly hedging risks should not be seen as methods of creating a profitable portfolio, as they merely try to distribute the downside, these concepts are nevertheless something to consider carefully when investing.

We rounded off our study by looking at Buffett's approach of concentrating risk, which runs at odds to the idea of diversification. Whilst this approach might work if you are relatively confident (and most importantly successful) in your views, for the rest of us with a less stellar record it might be a more difficult approach to adopt. We could also note that today the holdings of Berkshire Hathaway are actually in quite a large number of companies, which gives some element of diversification. So today, perhaps Buffett is less concentrated then you might expect. This is also representative of the fact that the company has so much cash to invest.

What Buffett's original notion of concentrating risk does highlight, though, is that we should ask questions about the level of diversification we wish to use in a portfolio. Diversification taken to an extreme might end up severely impacting the upside potential of a portfolio. If we are so intent on using a significant amount of diversification, we might instead consider investing in beta, which is much cheaper.

5
Not What They Care About: Having Targets Other than Returns

> Waltzing to leap, our hands reach high above,
> Seeking to grasp that which to be proud of,
> Yet what is that we seek, we think we want,
> A path so difficult it starts to daunt.

How did Thales' motivation to trade differ from the investors of today?

When Thales undertook one of the earliest recorded option trades, Aristotle tells us his primary motivation was not to make a large sum of money. Instead, he merely wished to prove that he could use his intellect to do so, after he was mocked about being a poor philosopher (see Chapter 1).

As a philosopher and scientist, Thales' experience of market has parallels with many modern traders. Today, trained mathematicians often trade markets alongside more traditional traders who use their own discretion to trade. Trading the markets using mathematical models is not necessarily a better approach. It is merely a different way of predicting the future path of asset prices. For certain people of a more mathematical background, this approach seems more amenable (including myself). More broadly certain trading strategies will suit different traders. In Chapter 9, during our discussion of analyzing historical trading returns, we shall delve into the idea of how different trading strategies can be more suitable for some traders than others.

The argument against just using a mathematical trading style is that there are (a small number of) investors who are very successful discretionary traders. Indeed, there are also times when as a whole systematic traders have done worse than the discretionary community (as well as vice versa). If anything, this suggests that a mixture of the two approaches would be ideal. Indeed, it is the case that many investors adopt a combination of quantitative techniques to identify trades but use discretion later, when deciding which trades to execute. We could also argue that systematic trading does have some element of discretion around it, notably in the creation of the initial trading model. The assumptions used when creating the trading rule are in effect applied each day a model is running. In addition, there is always discretion around precisely how much money is invested in a model. I would not be comfortable with a model automatically taking money out of my bank account and "optimally" investing it, no matter how smart it was. A comment I once heard was that the best traders are those who know precisely when not to put on a trade.

Another point we can draw from the case of Thales is that even today, people might transact in financial markets for reasons other than maximizing their trading returns. This is the theme of this chapter. In Thales' case it was to prove that he could use his intellect to make money, in an effort to disprove those who doubted the worth of being a philosopher. Like Thales, companies whose primary business is not financial trade markets for reasons other than speculation. For example, as we noted earlier in Chapter 3, a company might transact across different countries and would need to trade currencies to facilitate this. For that company, trading might be seen as a distraction from its underlying business. The paradox is that investing too little time in trading can end up reducing the profits made from the underlying business. I am not saying that corporates should be wildly speculating in financial markets; it is more a case of corporates thinking about the trades they have to make and trying to optimize those trades as best as they can.

For financial institutions and individual investors without some secondary business motivation, their primary objective is clearly some sort of financial gain from their investments. So from that perspective, most of today's investors are unlikely to be like Thales. Hence, there have to be some targets for their investment portfolios.

The key is to understand how we should set such an investment target. Should there be a single target or should we have multiple targets? Furthermore, how should we calculate these targets? Investors need to note that the nature of how they create targets can vastly impact whether they actually end up realizing returns from their investments or not. The target can set off a virtuous circle of investing behavior. Alternatively, if it is not constructed properly it can trigger a vicious trading circle, which is most commonly the result of excessive risk-taking. Indeed, as an example, simply targeting returns by themselves can often be counterproductive, even though returns are by far the most obvious of investment targets. We shall discuss how this can be the case in the next section. Like Thales, we sometimes need to have other objectives when we trade, rather than purely maximizing returns.

The problem with only targeting returns

Let us take a first step back and think of several metrics for understanding (and also targeting) an investment's performance. Whatever return statistics we use for our investment target could also be used to examine the historical performance of a portfolio or our expectations for our strategy. The most obvious metric is the one that everyone knows, namely percentage returns on an annualized basis, which we have touched upon already. However, this comes with the problem that it can encourage excessive risk-taking, as we noted earlier. Let us present a very simple example. We can assume that returns are 100% on an annualized basis over the past 20 years. Hence, if we put in $1,000 to fund the trade, we can make $1,000 over the course of the year. That sounds like a great investment at a superficial level if we are not given any other information; although whenever I hear very large percentage returns like that, I am always suspicious about the sustainability of the trading strategy.

Annualized returns fail to tell us the risk entailed in the investment. They clearly only tell us the reward. Somewhat stating the obvious, whenever considering an investment we need to understand the risks involved, just as much as the returns. As we discussed in Chapter 2, there are ways of measuring risk associated with the market. In particular we discussed the idea of volatility, and we also noted the benefits of other forms of risk measurement. Chief amongst these was the notion of the maximum possible drawdown or, more simply, trying to quantify the largest amount it is likely you would lose in the event of the investment going against you.

Let us revisit our original hypothetical investment armed with figures for both these measures of risk. Rather than purely examining the annualized returns, let us also consider performance in some of the best and worst years, which can give an idea of the potential drawdowns. Historical performance is a useful measure, but it is rarely a perfect predicator of future performance. The key point is to use a bit of common sense when looking at historical returns, and we shall endeavor to do so here. We shall discuss ways in which we can interpret and analyze historical investment performance in more detail in Chapter 9.

In our mock example, we find that in some years returns were 300%, even better than the long-term average, which sounds like a phenomenal return. However, somewhat disconcertingly, in some years returns have been as bad as –200%. So potentially, if we invested $1,000 in one year, we could have lost that $1,000 and been forced to come up with another $1,000 to cover our losses, which we would probably have needed to borrow. If this was the very first year of our investment, it seems likely that we would have been forced to exit the trade, and we would have never realized the upside. This might sound like a heavily manufactured example, but we could just as easily come up with a less ludicrous example. If we invested in a long position in S&P500 with ten times the leverage (every $1 we use as margin to borrow $10, placing all our borrowed cash in a long S&P500 investment). Since 1980, our investment would have an annualized return of around 100% (excluding borrowing costs and dividends). For the full sample, it is around 75%. Both of these numbers

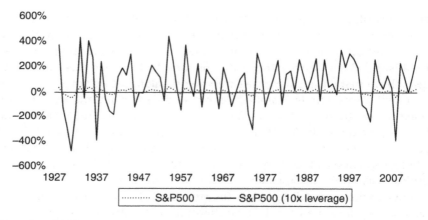

Figure 5.1   S&P500 year-on-year returns with ten times leverage (and without)
Source: Thalesians, Bloomberg Finance L.P.

seem appealing. In Figure 5.1, we plot year-on-year returns of this investment. We note how some of the yearly negative returns have been sufficiently large to completely wipe out our margin. As in our first example, this would mean that it would be unlikely we could hold onto our investment during periods of poor performance without finding extra cash to cover our losses. By chasing after a high return, we could perversely end up much worse off on a returns basis. Targeting a very high annualized return by its nature means taking on higher levels of risk and often having to endure higher drawdowns. Leverage is not always wrong, but traders need to be aware of the risks entailed. As we noted earlier, Thales did not target high returns when he traded. He was simply trying to show that he could use his intellect to generate a profitable trade. For him the profits were a useful by-product of his trade.

Furthermore, we have not even ventured into the question of the volatility of our investment, which is ten times the amount of the unleveraged index. Hence, it is ten times more risky, as measured by volatility. This comes on top of the very large drawdowns (Figure 5.2).

The lesson is that when we make a judgment about an investment, we need to examine several metrics, not purely annualized returns but also multiple measures of risk. Whilst it is easy to be seduced by annualized returns figures alone, this is not sufficient to make a rational investment decision. This might seem obvious, but it is not something that every investor considers. Indeed, while writing this book I discussed this matter with a friend who manages a medium-size systematic fund. The most common question he receives from potential investors concerns returns, rather than risk-adjusted returns.

If we look at annualized returns in isolation, it is very difficult to understand whether they are simply the product of huge leverage (as reflected by large

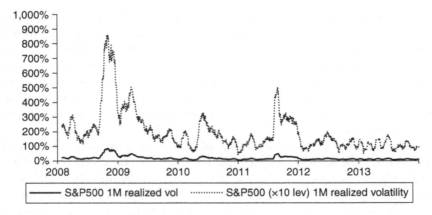

Figure 5.2 S&P500 ten times leveraged 1M realized volatility versus S&P500 1M realized volatility
Source: Thalesians, Bloomberg Finance L.P.

drawdowns and huge amounts of volatility) or shrewd investment decisions. Indeed, we can actually end up with higher returns over an extended period if we are prepared to take less risk for lower returns. In such a scenario, we are more able to hold onto trades over periods of bad performance, without being forced to exit them (we discussed the idea of stop losses in some detail in Chapter 2). Of course, you might be "lucky" in that when you enter a trade it will be profitable at first, creating a cushion, which you can fall back upon in the case of drawdowns. However, pinning the sustainability of your investment purely on an early lucky run to avoid an initial drawdown seems less like investing and more like gambling. What it suggests is that you have excessive leverage, precisely the situation when large drawdowns need to be avoided most.

What about purely targeting risk within a limit?

So instead of targeting percentage returns, what about a totally different angle? What if we attempt to create a target for an investment or analyze its historical performance purely from a risk perspective? Indeed, traders have very firm risk limits in terms of VaR, which they can sometimes end up using like a target, as we noted in Chapter 2. Trying to max out your risk limit is unfortunately not the point of having one. Indeed, placing a priority on reaching a certain risk limit, without understanding the potential returns of a strategy, might result in putting too much risk at stake. There might be times when it is prudent to cut risk and trade far below your risk limit, particularly when you have no clear views on the market, rather than artificially trying to maintain a high level of risk.

If you were to ask sell-side traders about risk limits, they will tell you several things. They will note that they have a strict risk limit. They should also have a realization of where their VaR limit lies. Even before the Lehman crisis, this was likely to have been the case, even though risk limits might not have been enforced as strictly. They should also know what the current profit and loss of their portfolio is in USD, even if they might be reticent when it comes to telling you. Sometimes you do not even need to ask: body language can also give this away, from experience.

However, if you ask about a measure of risk-adjusted returns of their portfolio, they will not always know. After all, they will often have a profit target for a year set by management in terms of an actual USD amount. Indeed, this seems little different from many other businesses, where monetary targets might also be set for individuals in terms of sales or profit targets. The main difference between banks and other businesses is the way in which risk is taken. Within other companies, there is obviously some level of risk involved in their operation. However, it is not general practice for a large number of employees to leverage their company's balance sheet by taking out large loans on the company's behalf. By contrast, individual traders within banks do this. They directly take reasonable amounts of risk on the company's balance sheet to generate returns.

Targets are often not set on a risk-adjusted returns basis for individual traders in sell-side banks. Hence, it is not surprising that the focus on risk-adjusted returns is not as great as you would expect amongst sell-side bank traders. After all, compensation is more related to the pure USD amount they generate. This means that traders could potentially place relatively large and somewhat risky highly leveraged bets, and if they are successful they could improve their compensation. This is despite the potential for such a trade to cause significant losses. The potential drawdown from a trade which has gone awry is obviously a lot higher for the bank than it is for the individual trader. For the trader, the drawdown is losing his or her job. This downside, whilst unpalatable, has a clearly defined limit. As a result, to some extent we can think of the trader as owning a put option on any risks he or she takes, where the premium of the option is loss of employment. If traders invest only their own personal assets (or have skin in the game, to use a popular industry term which is often used by Taleb), they clearly do not benefit from such a put option. We might conjecture that the presence of such a pseudo-put option impacts the type of trades that a trader is willing to undertake, given the downside is rather more serious: personal insolvency rather than losing a job.

A tale of two traders

We can illustrate our point about the problems with setting targets for individual traders purely based on returns. We shall tell "A Tale of Two Traders," our little homage to Charles Dickens. Let us say that two traders in a specific sell-side bank have each made $12mm. If we were purely compensating them for the size of their profits, this fact suggests that both traders should have the same pay. However, let us delve into precisely how they made these profits. One trader made around $1mm a month, give or take $100–200k, during a particular financial year. The other trader made $5mm in the first month, consecutively lost $1mm on several months and then had a month making $5mm, before being flat at the end of the year. We have noted that if their targets were based purely on returns, their compensation would be identical. However, this seems somewhat unfair. Whilst the first trader has generated relatively stable returns, which are preferable, the second trader appears to have adopted a double or quits (or double or nothing) strategy, given the scale of losses he or she has incurred. Such an approach seems more akin to playing poker than to trading financial markets.

Hence, it seems as though the identical compensation each has received ignores the fact that the second trader is likely to have taken much larger risks to achieve the same objective. Whilst I acknowledge that this is a manufactured example, it does illustrate the problems with setting targets based on returns alone. Also, in practice, we would hope that a risk-manager at the bank would raise concerns about the erratic profits of the second trader.

Ancient incentives to change trader behavior

So what sort of targets could we use if returns on their own or risk objectives seem suboptimal? We need a target to solve the problem of compensating the two traders we gave in our example. One candidate we can use as a target is risk-adjusted returns. If more traders had targets for risk-adjusted returns, then it could engender a different sort of behavior. Indeed, it would essentially penalize very large wild bets of the type we discussed in the previous section. At the same time it would reward more prudent trading, helping to keep volatility in check. It goes back to our earlier point that targets themselves can heavily influence the type of trading that is undertaken.

In the ancient world, there were instances where punishment would be administered in the course of business as a way of preventing excessive risk-taking and to change behavior. Taleb (2013) discusses a particular instance mentioned in the Code of Hammurabi, which we talked about at length in Chapter 4. He notes a law which relates to the builders of Ancient Babylon. This details the consequences of shoddy workmanship in building houses. In particular, if a house collapsed killing its owner, the builder who built that house would be put to death. It goes on to describe other similar punishments which could be administered if the homeowner's son were to die in a house collapse. I suspect you can probably guess what the punishment would be in that instance.

It would be difficult to call this sort of law an "incentive" for Ancient Babylonian builders to place a priority on good workmanship, as traders might be incentivized for generating large profits today. Instead, it clearly exposed them to a very unpalatable downside risk should they fail. So what would the solution be for Ancient Babylonian builders wishing to comply with the law? Clearly, it would be the case that they would not take any risks in the construction of the house, given the potential punishment. Instead, they would make doubly sure that the house was of a solid construction to reduce as much as possible the chances of the house collapsing. Even without such a punishment, you would have hoped that they would not take any risks in building a house, but the presence of such a law seems to suggest that in the past builders did take such risks. Alternatively, builders might simply give up building houses altogether, given the potential risks involved, thereby causing a shortage of housing.

On a purely personal note, as someone who has worked in a bank and has had bank capital placed on my ideas, I would very much hope that such a potential punishment would not hang over traders. Admittedly, I do realize that bankers are not particularly popular at the time of writing, owing to the financial crisis. In all seriousness, though, the example I have given concerning the Code of Hammurabi does illustrate how powerful incentives (or in this case disincentive is a better description) can focus and change behavior.

Today, the focus seems very much on creating more disincentives for traders in sell-side banks, following the Hammurabi model, to change their approach to risk-taking. I do of course acknowledge that the punishment is not as severe as in Ancient Babylon. In particular, this can be seen in terms of clawing back bonuses from traders should investments they undertake turn out to be loss-making in the future, even if they are profitable in the short term (and resulted in the initial bonus payments).

Some focus on the downside is justified as a way of changing the behavior of traders. The idea of exposing traders to some downside is at the crux of what Taleb writes when he discusses a trader having "skin in the game." In particular, I would say that this approach might be relevant particularly when looking at longer-term investments, where traders can often leave their employment before the maturity of these trades. In these instances these trades might appear very profitable when they are entered into, but this might not be the case over the longer term.

Certainly, it would be difficult to suggest anything else following the Lehman crisis and the fact that many banks have been bailed out using public money. If the public has been exposed to downside, it seems difficult to totally insulate traders from their losses at these institutions. It seems difficult to question the rationale of such claw-back schemes. The key is of course in how this is defined.

I would argue that changing the nature of upside incentives would be much more powerful, rather than purely emphasizing the downside potential for traders. The idiom of carrot and stick comes to mind, which suggests that the prospect of a reward with the possibility of punishment is a more effective way of changing behavior compared with just reward or punishment in isolation.

The idea would be to provide a different sort of upside incentive. The USD amount of profits would not be seen as a trader's overriding objective. Instead, individual traders' targets would be changed to include a mix of various risk metrics and reward. This type of approach would channel the behavior of traders toward generating a more responsible (and most importantly a less risky) form of profit. Perhaps on a year-to-year basis profits would be lower, but over the long term profits would be more stable and perhaps more sustainable.

If it is purely the downside which is emphasized, it might end up curtailing banks' risk-taking to such a degree that market liquidity is severely curtailed. The spreads between bid and ask prices would be increased. The indirect cost of this would be felt through the higher costs incurred by investors, such as through pensions. It might even be the case that sell-side banks would profit from more market illiquidity. It seems unlikely that this would be the intended by-product of discouraging risk-taking from sell-side banks. In a way, it is like our Babylonian builder refusing to build houses when the potential punishment is so great.

In buy-side firms, which manage investments for their clients, there is a slightly different approach to targets. On the buy side, the focus is very much on understanding risk-adjusted returns, rather than on the pure USD amount of profits produced by their portfolios. This is not to say that buy-side firms do not wish to make profits; indeed, this is how traders in hedge funds are ultimately compensated. It is merely that in buy-side funds they view investment performance in a way consistent with how (some of!) their clients would view it. After all, if funds produce very poor risk-adjusted returns, some of their investors will ultimately start to withdraw their capital, voting with their feet. As we have noted, though, some investors still place too much of a priority on annualized returns as opposed to risk-adjusted returns. Most funds do not benefit from a public bailout should they fail. This contrasts with very large banks, who are branded as too big to fail given their systemic importance to the financial system. The behavior of funds with regard to targeting risk and reward is obviously different from sell-side banks, where the links between risk and returns are much more opaque.

Looking at risk-adjusted returns as a single metric allows us to more easily summarize the performance of an investment, in a smarter way than simply looking at returns alone. Indeed, we have advocated how such a metric can be used as part of investors' targets for their portfolios. We shall write about such metrics in more detail next, including how to calculate them.

Using the Sharpe ratio as a target

We have looked at performance metrics in isolation, namely percentage returns, volatility, and drawdowns. However, we also noted that there are metrics which combine them in risk-adjusted returns. The Sharpe ratio (or information ratio; we shall use both terms interchangeably, although under certain definitions they are slightly different) is such a metric. It is named after William Sharpe, who later won a Nobel Prize in Economics for his work in 1990 (Sharpe, 1990), shared with Harry Markowitz (see Chapter 4) and Merton Miller.

This ratio is simply the risk-adjusted return, or more precisely excess returns divided by the volatility. Excess returns are the returns once funding costs have been taken into account. The cost of funding is the rate at which you can borrow money, and we assume this is a risk-free rate. Admittedly, the concept of a risk-free rate is a bit difficult to define when banks have the potential to go bankrupt, but for the time being we shall overlook this problem. Alternatively, we could use the excess returns over some benchmark (basically market beta), as opposed to risk-free returns, to isolate the performance from the alpha part of the strategy.

Let us illustrate the rationale behind looking at funding costs in the context of understanding the performance of an investment. We take the example of an equity which has annualized returns of 5%, but the cost of funding is 5%. This would imply a return over the funding rate of 0%. In other words you would do no better than if you held your money in a bank account. In practice, we might not need to put up cash for the whole amount of our investment; we might be able to put up a smaller amount of cash as margin at first, reducing our funding costs. Hence, we can view this funding cost as a worst case situation.

We have already described volatility in some detail, in Chapter 2. A clear understanding of the subject is necessary to comprehend the idea of Sharpe ratios. To illustrate how to interpret Sharpe ratios, we must first give a few numerical examples. Say our investment target was to have an information ratio of 1. This would imply that for each unit of risk we would gain precisely the same return. Hence, if returns were 5% and volatility was 5%, our information ratio would be 1. If returns were 10% and volatility was 5%, our information ratio would be 2; and so on. Clearly, the higher the Sharpe ratio the better, as we would be gaining more returns for a similar-sized risk. Later, though, we shall discuss that the Sharpe ratio does not fully capture all the dynamics of market returns.

Depending on the precise market, I would conjecture that most investors would be very happy if they managed to have a Sharpe ratio of 1. In practice, it is very difficult to achieve such an information ratio over a very long period in trading in the "wild." Generally the higher the Sharpe ratio, the more work needs to be done to achieve it, and the more "alpha-like" a strategy is likely to be. During shorter time periods, it might be possible to exceed this substantially. For those traders who are capable of delivering very high Sharpe ratios, there might also be other issues. Amongst strategies that are likely to generate very high Sharpe ratios are high-frequency strategies (it is possibly another question whether using a Sharpe ratio is the most appropriate method for measuring the performance of such strategies). However, as we noted in Chapter 2, these types of strategies generally exhibit a relatively low amount of capacity. Larger transaction costs render them unprofitable. If you are trying to capture a move of one basis point and it costs you over a basis point to enter and exit a trade, it is hardly the ideal trading strategy for large notional sizes. Hence, the amount of capital that can be deployed is relatively low in any particular trading idea. Obviously, the solution is to come up with many high-frequency strategies which can be run independently. However, this is time consuming and also difficult, as you might expect.

What does the Sharpe ratio fail to capture?

The Sharpe ratio tells us about returns when measured against risk in the form of volatility, so it improves upon the targeting of annualized percentage returns. Examining returns does not furnish an investor with knowledge about the risks involved. However, whilst the Sharpe ratio might capture some element of the risks involved (namely the volatility) in an investment, it does not fully capture information about drawdowns. In particular, it will not fully describe those drawdowns which make strategy returns non-normal. There is little use in having an absolutely fantastic Sharpe ratio if it somehow disguises potentially large drawdowns which you would have endured.

In Figure 5.3, we plot the returns from two investments with seemingly similar positive Sharpe ratios (close to 0.30). Whilst these Sharpe ratios are not huge, they are also not negative, yet they both appear to have quite significant drawdowns. Bailey & Prado (2012) discuss this issue. In particular, they suggest that Sharpe ratios can end up becoming inflated, in particular for hedge fund returns (and especially for high-frequency trading strategies). The difficulty is that there is always some temptation to use a statistic that overestimates how well your investments have performed, given that higher Sharpe ratios are likely to attract more interest. Indeed, comparing Sharpe ratios between various hedge funds can be a very quick (although perhaps an overly simplistic way) of choosing between them.

In their paper, Bailey and Prado suggest that one way to alleviate the problem of overinflated Sharpe ratios is to use a higher sampling frequency. If we simply monitor an investment on a quarterly basis and use that data to calculate volatility, we are essentially ignoring a lot of the price action. So potentially, if from quarter to quarter the value of the investment does not change that much,

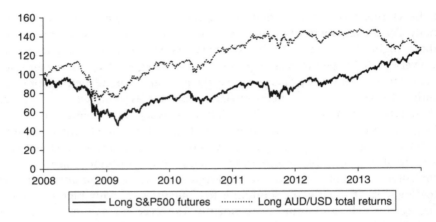

Figure 5.3   Long S&P500 futures and long AUD/USD have exhibited large drawdowns, whilst being on average profitable
Source: Thalesians, Bloomberg Finance L.P.

a calculation would show volatility to be low. Furthermore, our measurement of volatility would be low, even if day-to-day price action was volatile. These artificially lower levels of volatility, which ignore intra-quarter price action, would naturally translate into a higher Sharpe ratios. We also need to be aware of the length of the period used to calculate a Sharpe ratio. If a very short period is used, it will not be that informative. If we are "lucky" and we have a few good months of performance, we could achieve a very high Sharpe ratio.

If we take a strategy such as selling options this is fairly obvious. Typically, selling options can be a profitable strategy, as you are essentially collecting the volatility risk premium, which is the difference between implied and realized. However, it can be characterized by very large drawdowns. This is particularly true for very simplified versions of it. More involved implementations can reduce the drawdowns somewhat, but I would say it is extremely unlikely that they can be totally eliminated. For heavily leveraged option selling with any hedge, such as heavily out-of-the-money options, the risk of ruin is great. We discussed short volatility strategies in Chapter 2. We shall return to this topic in Chapter 6.

The presence of reasonably large drawdowns also makes risk-management of such strategies very difficult, in particular trying to gauge how much capital to allocate. If we simply measure the Sharpe ratio (or indeed any return statistic) over a period without any sort of market turbulence, it is likely we will come up with a very high Sharpe ratio for an option-selling strategy. This is misleading for the long-term behavior of such a strategy. It would be like visiting New York only in summer and concluding that it is sunny all year round.

Bailey and Prado have created a measure which they name the probabilistic Sharpe ratio (PSR). One of the applications of this measure is to answer the question about the length of the track record necessary to determine a statistically significant Sharpe ratio (in other words, one which is more a result of skill as opposed to a lucky stretch). I would argue that it is also necessary to understand the nature of a strategy on a more qualitative basis, to determine how sustainable its Sharpe ratio is. We have noted this with our option-selling strategy example.

Understanding drawdowns in investments

We have noted that the Sharpe ratio can mask large drawdowns. Hence, we cannot use the Sharpe ratio as our only measure of performance for an investment. In our discussion, we have suggested that understanding the nature of drawdowns in a strategy is important. It is very difficult for investors to ignore drawdowns. Severe drawdowns are the most likely factor that will force an investor to liquidate their exposure in an investment (or are the reason for a trader being fired). In such a situation, an investor will have taken the downside hit, without having realized the potentially higher returns from trading in the future. Just as with Sharpe ratios, we also need to be careful when we calculate drawdowns from historical data. Calculating historical drawdowns on a quarterly basis rather than on a daily basis can mask how large they are. Unfortunately, when we trade and we have a drawdown in the middle of a quarter, we cannot tell our counterparties to wait until the end of the quarter before coming up with further funds to cover our shortfall! Being able to calculate drawdowns on a higher-frequency basis, such as using daily data, does require however that we can price up our portfolio daily. This might be possible for heavily traded assets such as stocks, but it is unlikely to be possible for illiquid assets for which we do not have a liquid daily market, such as property.

Once we have a historical drawdown or an estimate for one, we then need to be able to interpret it. When judging drawdowns, just as with returns, it is difficult to judge them in isolation. For example, if we see that the largest drawdown of a strategy is 10%, in isolation this might seem like a high number. However, if annualized returns are historically 15%, such a drawdown might seem more reasonable, even if it would still not be entirely palatable. The potential drawdown is obviously still important, though, as it can help us with determining the initial size of our investment, by working backwards. The whole idea of a drawdown cannot be seen as a "target" in the same way that we might wish to target a Sharpe ratio. Experiencing a large drawdown is clearly a negative outcome, which we would prefer to avoid but we need to be prepared for.

We can give an example to show how to use a figure for potential drawdowns in practice. Let us say that our potential drawdown is 25%. We have gleaned this from the historical data of a similar trading strategy and some model-based estimates. Furthermore, we have added several percent as a safety cushion based

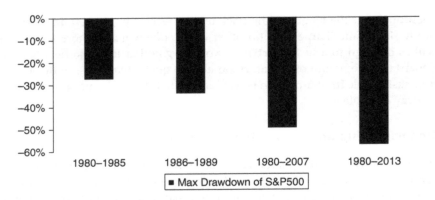

Figure 5.4   S&P500 drawdowns differ depending on time period we use
Source: Thalesians, Bloomberg Finance L.P.

on other estimates. This would imply that on an investment of $100mm we
could potentially lose $25mm, which seems quite large. The concept of "large"
in this instance is likely to vary between investors. For an investor whose total
notional available is $100mm, $25mm is likely to appear significantly larger
than an investor who has $500mm. We shall elaborate on this point in the next
section. If we think that $25mm is indeed a large loss, we could always opt to
underleverage our exposure until we get to a level of drawdown in USD terms
which we find acceptable. Once we have our notional investment amount set,
we can set about calculating what our returns potentially could be in absolute USD terms. We also obviously need to take into account that whatever
expectations we might have about drawdowns (or indeed Sharpe ratio or any
similar metric), these are only estimates as well. Hence, my inclination is to use
historic drawdowns as a conservative estimate and realize that potential losses
could eclipse them.

Let us illustrate our discussion by looking at S&P500. In Figure 5.4 we calculate various peak-to-trough drawdowns using different periods of history. It is
easiest to describe maximum peak-to-trough drawdowns using such a plot. This
drawdown is essentially the percentage difference between the highest and lowest points of an investment (see Figure 5.5). It is typically what most people
mean when they talk about drawdowns. Other common drawdowns could be
those specifically related to monthly, quarterly, and annual periods. This is a
somewhat more technical term for the most money which we can lose, which
we have discussed at length in the preceding chapters. This topic will come up
later too.

We see that, omitting the Lehman period, there are smaller peak-to-trough
drawdowns. We should note that if we had a much longer historical sample
for S&P500 going back to the Great Depression, we would have had a much

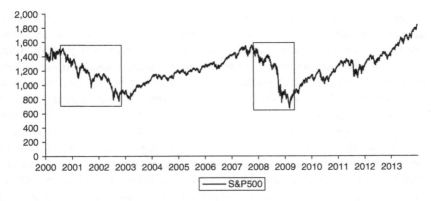

Figure 5.5 Identifying the largest peak-to-trough drawdowns in S&P500 between 2000 and 2013
Source: Thalesians, Bloomberg Finance L.P.

larger historical maximum drawdown, which would have eclipsed even the 2008 drawdown.

Once we have our drawdown estimate, whether it is calculated from historical data or by some other method, we can use another metric to help us, the Calmar ratio, to gain an idea of the relative size of the drawdown. This is returns divided by the maximum peak-to-trough drawdown (strictly speaking, the Calmar ratio is defined using the past three years of data). Evidently, a number greater than one is most favorable, implying that returns are greater than drawdowns.

As we have noted, we must be aware that it is possible to experience larger drawdowns in the future than we have had in the past. However, at the very least, historical data nevertheless gives us an indication of what a "large" drawdown is when we are trading on a live basis. If we have a drawdown which looks unusual against history, it will force us to assess whether there are deeper problems with our trading strategy. Furthermore, as a portfolio reaches such a limit, a trader would typically seek to cut leverage over a progressive period.

By targeting a multitude of metrics in a portfolio, such as Sharpe and Calmar ratios, it can help us to move away from overemphasizing returns. Instead, it helps investors to consider a more balanced approach, where they also take into account the potential risks as well as the rewards.

Is all volatility bad? Enter the Sortino ratio for targeting investment performance

From our discussion on risk in Chapter 2, it might seem to the reader that higher levels of volatility are always "bad" and always symptomatic of a more risky investment. Certainly, an investment with higher levels of volatility is indicative of potentially higher levels of risk. What we wish to discuss here is that the malevolence of high volatility is often dependent on the situation. If we think about the Sharpe ratio, in whatever scenario, a higher volatility reduces the final number. So if our investment has an annualized percentage return of 10% a year and the volatility of returns is 10%, the Sharpe ratio is 1. If volatility is 20%, our Sharpe ratio is instantly halved, and it seems as though this investment is worse. Hence, we see that the Sharpe ratio universally penalizes volatility. However, there can be instances where volatility is not as bad as at other times. Let us, for example, take a month where returns have jumped upwards. Jumps like this would be accompanied by increases in volatility. Under a Sharpe ratio basis, such price action would be penalized. This is in spite of the fact that as a trader you would probably welcome such an upward jump. Indeed, I do not ever recall getting upset when the P&L of any of my strategies heavily outperformed on a day, although such occurrences did heighten my suspicions that the strategy's P&L would see some reversal back to a lower point! Let us say that instead of a large jump upward, our portfolio returns suddenly see a big jump downward. This would also see volatility increase, but in this instance it would be very unwelcome, and we would like to penalize the strategy. Using slightly more statistical language, a strategy which has upside skew (big gains) in its returns distribution would be penalized just as much as those with negative skew (big losses). From an investing point of view, it seems counterintuitive to do this.

How can we alleviate this problem? The key is to penalize volatility when we have downside moves, rather than doing it for both downside and upside moves. Another type of returns metric, namely the Sortino ratio, can help to address this issue. With the Sharpe ratio, we divide returns by volatility to get a risk-adjusted return. For the Sortino ratio, we instead divide returns by what is termed as downside volatility. As a result we arrive at downside risk-adjusted returns.

The downside volatility calculates the risk only of those returns which are negative. Any positive returns in our time series are assumed to be zero in this downside volatility calculation. Through this approach, volatility which is the result of upside moves is not penalized. If we use a Sortino ratio in our targeting we shall end up preferring those strategies which have a positive skew, which are precisely the strategies which most investors would prefer.

We illustrate "good" and "bad" volatility in Figure 5.6 for long exposure to risky assets. S&P500 is plotted against rolling realized volatility since the financial crisis. We should note that when volatility spikes this tends to be "bad" volatility, and S&P500 tends to sell off. However, when volatility starts to come off from very high levels, we can see "good" volatility, which is accompanied by rises in S&P500. Hence, the level of volatility is not the only critical factor

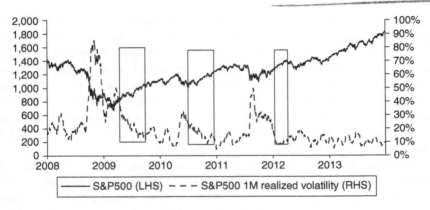

Figure 5.6 S&P500 1M realized volatility versus S&P500
Source: Thalesians, Bloomberg Finance L.P.

for determining if it is "good" or "bad" volatility. We should also be very aware that the direction of volatility has an impact.

Why should portfolio targets differ between investors?

In Chapter 2, we noted that groups of investors can be characterized by their differing appetite for risk. Speculators have more capacity to take risk. Pension funds, by their nature, are more conservative. So when it comes to creating targets for a portfolio, targets for some investors are unlikely to be suitable for all. The amount of leverage an investor is willing to take is also an important factor when creating targets. Heavily leveraged investors are unlikely to be able to sustain any large drawdowns. Hence, any strategies which they trade would need to adhere to this.

Say a heavily leveraged speculator is long gold purchased at $1,500 per ounce, using a margin of $100 per ounce. In other words, he or she is leveraged 15 times. If gold were to drop to $1,400, the speculator would need to come up with extra cash to pay for the loss. Such a speculator would be unable to ride out any large drawdowns in the price of gold.

Contrast this to property investors, who are buying up large amounts of London property with cash at the time of writing. If London house prices were to experience a slowdown, it seems unlikely that they would be as concerned as heavily leveraged investors, even though losing money is never a savory experience. If heavily leveraged investors were forced to sell their properties for a loss, they would have a shortfall to cover, between the size of their debt and the cash they actually received in the sale. This shortfall is known as negative equity. We can draw a similar parallel with our gold investor earlier.

Investors also have different priorities, which influence how they construct their targets. Say we take an investor who has accrued a large amount of wealth through other means. This wealth might have been gained through an inheritance or from founding some businesses. It seems likely that investment targets would be relatively conservative, given that he or she is already wealthy. The main priority would be preservation of wealth, rather than rapidly growing a cash pile, by taking large amounts of risk in financial markets. Hence, an investment which has very small drawdowns would be more attractive for such investors, even if potential returns could be lower.

We could also have investors who are unconcerned by a long period of drawdowns, given that their main goal is to protect against tail-risk events, so-called Black Swan events. Such investments by construction incur large drawdowns continually over time while waiting for a large risk event, in which case they can realize large profits. The P&L paths from such strategies end up looking like uneven heartbeats displayed on an electrocardiogram.

Hedging tail risks in this manner might sometimes be attractive, if we already have other investments. In Chapter 6, we elaborate on Black Swans in more detail. In particular, we note that purely trading Black Swan strategies can be somewhat more difficult these days, given that heavily out-of-the-money options are less likely to be underpriced than in the past. Such a strategy essentially relies on identifying such mispricing. In Chapter 9 we continue this theme, discussing how different trading strategies are suitable for different investors.

Is reaching an investment target fate?

In Chapter 2, we suggested that the reason the Ancient Greeks never delved into the subject of probability was the notion of fate. If they believed that the future was largely fate, then it would seem superfluous to gauge probabilities concerning outcomes. The importance of the idea of fate, or indeed destiny, was not unique to the Ancient Greeks. Lawson (1994) discusses the notion of "fate" in Ancient Mesopotamia and to some extent in Ancient Greece. He notes that at least in Ancient Greece, whilst it was said that the gods had knowledge of the fate which awaited man, they were not said to have control over humanity's fate, or *moira* as the Ancient Greeks called it. The origins of the English word fate seem to tally with this interpretation of what fate is. It comes to us from the Latin word *fatum*, which literally means spoken, in particular when referring to a god.

In Ancient Mesopotamia, fate was known as *simtu*. One of the most well-known stories in Mesopotamia, *Enuma Elish*, which takes the form of an epic poem, mentions the Tablet of Destinies. Whoever held this was said to be able to tell the future and rule the world. Just as with the Ancient Greeks and the Oracle of Delphi, which we discussed in Chapter 2, it seems that the idea of fate and seeing the future was something which concerned the Ancient Mesopotamians.

Maybe in the context of the ancients, given their strong belief in fate, the idea of rewarding a trader for reaching an investment target might seem unusual. If traders' decisions did not make any difference to some predetermined goal, why reward them for reaching a target? Of course, such an argument about fate in the context of trading might seem far-fetched, but it does bring up the very important point that external factors beyond traders' control can influence whether they hit a target.

As we noted in Chapter 1 Taleb (2007) does not quite frame his argument in such a way. He argues, though, that external forces, namely randomness and also broader market moves, can be very important factors which impact the performance of a trader. If a trader's strategy is basically following the market, in other words trading market beta (see Chapter 3), Taleb argues that we should not be surprised if this trader makes money when the market is in the midst of a multi-year market rally. His argument is that it is not so much the skill of the trader which has generated positive returns, but just luck from following the market. As he puts it, we should not be *fooled by randomness*. Over shorter periods, I would be inclined to agree with this notion, but over extended periods of time, I would find it more difficult to say that a profitable trader is consistently successful purely because of randomness, particularly if a rigorous investment process is being followed.

We can draw an analogy with rolling a die. Say we are playing a game where rolling a six elicits a prize. If we roll a six on our very first attempt, it could just be luck. After all, the chances are merely one in six. If we repeatedly throw a six, we can either conclude we are exceedingly lucky or that it is loaded in our favor. As a skeptic I would err toward the second conclusion!

Of course, you can argue that if there is a large enough pool of traders then at least one of them should be successful and manage to outperform the market, capturing that elusive alpha: throwing a six, to use our die analogy. If every trader uses a purely random trading strategy this might seem like a reasonable suggestion. Even if some traders might be trading totally randomly, it seemed difficult to believe that all traders who have been consistently successful are trading randomly.

The ability to trade profitably over many different market phases, during bullish and bearish runs, different interest rate regimes, and so on, is a relatively good barometer for understanding the ability of a trader. Success over many different regimes goes some way to allay fears that profits are purely related to following the market.

As we noted earlier in our discussion over the probabilistic Sharpe ratio (PSR), a longer track record can help us to more easily distinguish between skill and luck when it comes to trading. Furthermore, we also need to have an understanding of a trader's general approach to markets. Having an understanding of a trader's investment process aids us in identifying whether the deciding factor is skill or luck in his or her success.

In the end, our ability to identify whether a trader is truly skilled or simply lucky might be a moot point. In practice, when determining traders' compensation, it is inescapable that regardless of their individual performances, there is always going to be an external force impacting this decision, namely the performance of their own banks. If a bank is struggling, it becomes very difficult to justify compensating traders significantly, regardless of whether these traders have outperformed.

Deviating from our investment mandate can impact our targets

The main idea of the investment targets we have discussed has been to encourage investors to seek positive returns, whilst also being conscious of the risks involved. It seems obvious that taking outsized risks might deliver larger returns, but by definition it also increases the potential for large drawdowns. It is accompanied by greater levels of volatility, another measure of risk.

Let us say we are a fund manager with outside investors. When defining our various portfolio targets, we do so in parallel with our investment mandate, which has been discussed with our investors. The investment mandate stipulates our general investment style and is very much part of our pitch when attracting capital from outside investors. Simply saying that our fund "will make money" unfortunately does not tell an outside investor very much. It seems unlikely that any investment fund which is seeking to elicit funding will say that it wishes to lose money. Even if an investment mandate does not precisely stipulate our exact trading strategy, it will give various guidelines around which we trade. Outside investors would expect that we broadly follow these rules that we have set ourselves. We are selling a product to investors, and our original description of our product should align with what we deliver.

Our investment mandate will say whether we are trading more beta-like strategies or seeking alpha. It will define the types of assets that we intend to trade. There might also be strict numerical targets in terms of the volatility of our investment. Very often for hedge funds there will be a target for a specific level of volatility for their fund. We can see a parallel with sell-side traders having some sort of VaR limit as part of their trading mandate. Even if we do not have outside investors, I would suggest that it is important to understand what type of investment strategy we wish to follow, to give us some discipline in our trading.

Sometimes it can be tempting for investors to deviate from their original investment mandate. Their objective is often to seek higher returns elsewhere, away from the area where they are most comfortable. The problem is that other markets can be very different, as we noted in Chapter 3. If we are seeking to trade another type of contract heavily, and we do not understand it, this can pose problems. We might be facing all sorts of risks which we do not have the experience to manage properly. One such example is the case of relatively conservative investors who before 2008 were tempted to buy CDOs, because of the relatively high yields. These conservative investors included many municipalities, such as Narvik in Norway, which lost $64mm on US subprime securities (Landler, 2007). It seems difficult to think of a place more far removed from the housing bubble in US than a city in oil-rich Norway. However, many of these conservative investors were unaware of the full risks involved in these investments.

The idea of CDOs is to have several tranches. The safest bonds are in the senior tranche. In the lower tranches lie the riskier bonds. Before the financial crises, it was relatively common to wrap up mortgage-backed securities in such a structure. Investors were effectively loaning out cash to homeowners with poor credit histories, especially in the lower subprime tranches.

The problem was that in the credit crisis which started in 2007 many of these subprime bonds ended up defaulting at the same time. Consequently, there were little diversification benefits from having lots of subprime bonds. It also meant that the high credit ratings associated with their bundles of bonds were unfortunately not representative of the risk they contained. When one set of homeowners had trouble paying their subprime mortgage, so did many others. This goes back to the point that we have noted repeatedly that correlations are low until, to rephrase it crudely, feces comes into contact with the strong billow of air and a risk event occurs. Trying to capture higher-investment returns might have sounded good to investors before the credit crisis. However, it is likely that investing in an instrument like a CDO packed with subprime bonds deviated from their relatively conservative investment mandates. With quantitative easing in operation across the world for several years following the credit crisis and yields low worldwide, have investors made the same mistakes in their search for yield by overleveraging? Time may tell!

More generally, if we would like to deviate from our investment mandate we need to have a clear rationale for doing this. There is nothing intrinsically wrong in investing in an asset which yields more. However, we cannot use the excuse of targeting high returns without a consideration for the additional risks involved. Indeed, it goes back to our point that simply assessing percentage returns when understanding an investment is insufficient. Do we see strong investment opportunities? Furthermore, do these investment opportunities stand up to closer investigation? The difficulty is that very often investors might stray toward other markets, moving away from their initial investment mandate without thorough research because of tempting returns. If there is a substantial change in our investment strategy, we need to understand what impact it has on our investment targets. If we are managing money for outside investors, would they be comfortable with our new focus, or would they react by pulling money from our fund? If we are not willing to create the right environment to adhere to our investment target, then it seems unlikely we shall either hit our target or gain the benefits from it. Would we be happy placing our own money in this new investment strategy? This is always the crucial acid test of how comfortable you are investing in a specific idea! If you baulk at investing your own personal account into a specific strategy, it would suggest that you have reservations about the investment.

A view on targets and risk from an investor

Whilst writing this chapter, I felt it would be good to turn to Jan-Erik Skoglund whom I first met several years ago at a seminar of the Thalesians. As his name might suggest he hails from Sweden, and he also looks like a quintessential Swede, if there is indeed a stereotypical image of what a Swede looks like. His accent is not hugely strong these days, as he has spent over a decade in London. Although listen closely and it does become more noticeable with certain words (although their identity evades my memory at this point). However, I did not wish to quiz him about Sweden, a place which the reader must visit. (As an aside, if you do go to Stockholm, be sure to spend at least one night at the Grand Hotel and have dinner at Mathias Dahlgren: my expense budget did not quite extend to dining at the restaurant, although I did enjoy a meal at the brasserie.) Instead, I wanted to ask Jan-Erik about his thoughts on the investment process. For the past few years, he has been involved in creating investible model-driven index solutions for a company called QLAB Invest based in Zurich, of which he is the founder. Hence, a lot of what he does involves considering precisely the questions which I have posed in this chapter. They include the following: How much capital should I allocate to a strategy? What should I target in a strategy? How should we measure risk?

We had a chat in Starbucks discussing these questions amongst a whole plethora of others. This branch of Starbucks in the financial district of London was my usual habitat. I had already spent many hours there already, scribing much of this book in there. With the smell of coffee all around (which strangely I dislike, given I rarely drink it), his first observation was in the difference between systematic and discretionary trading, a subject which was touched upon in the earlier part of the chapter.

Jan-Erik made the very important point that it is actually relatively difficult to find a purely systematic trader. However, he did point out that the converse could be true: there are totally discretionary traders, who eschew systematic ways of trading. Very often there will be some element of discretion used when running a systematic model. Indeed, in the past when I have been involved running risk on a systematic basis, there were occasions when I changed the model whilst it was running with real capital. In particular, he noted a tendency for this to happen during periods of market stress, when a trader's judgment will be impacted by emotions such as fear, as well as behavioral biases. He added that it decreased the transparency of systematic trading. In such a pressured scenario, he said it is easier to make a rash judgment: anyone who has been anywhere near a trading floor during a market crisis would almost certainly witness the heightened tension. I would agree with much of this, but I would also say that having clearly defined rules of what to do when a model appears to break down would mitigate the problem. From my experience, I would also add that events can sometime force the hand of a systematic trader to make more discretionary decisions. It is difficult to trade in a perfectly modeled bubble when irrationality has its way of masquerading in the markets during crises, and indeed on many other occasions. Black Swan events will and do happen (see Chapter 6), catching investors by surprise.

In general, I would suggest, the key is not to modify a systematic model excessively, because it overrides the whole point of running a systematic strategy: the lack of discretion. Systematic traders might also tweak positions using some discretion, particularly around major scheduled events, cutting risk if they feel the market is too binary around those points.

Our discussion then shifted toward looking at returns and targets, the crux of this chapter. Jan-Erik said that returns should be seen from an unleveraged context to make them more comparable. Even when comparing strategies, we need to be aware of the relative liquidity of the underlying assets. Trying to compare a high-frequency FX trading strategy with a property investment is relatively difficult. Of course, in the real world investors have a massive universe of investments through which they need to navigate. It is just that the targets they will use when making investments in different asset classes are likely to differ considerably. He also suggested comparing returns against the amount of usable capital of an investor. This approach, he said, would provide a better estimate of how efficient an investor is when it comes to allocating risk. He said that this was a better approach than trying to calculate returns as a percentage of margin in a trading account.

When trying to understand precisely how much capital to deploy in a strategy, his approach was relatively similar to an idea I have discussed elsewhere in the book. The method, we agreed, was to stipulate the amount of a capital you are prepared to lose in your portfolio. With an estimate of the maximum drawdown, this allows us to scale leverage accordingly. Using this approach, if we are prepared to lose $1,000 and our maximum drawdown limit is 10%, it would suggest that our investment size is around $10,000. From this, he said, we could identify our potential return. This tallies with our earlier commentary.

However, there is little point having a maximum drawdown limit unless we are prepared to stick to it. An approach that makes it relatively straightforward to adhere to is crucial. Jan-Erik described a very simple systematic method for this. Let us say an investor has a current drawdown of –5%, where his or her maximum tolerance is –20%. If a forward-looking VaR measure is used (which could take into account non-normality, those pesky "tails") suggests a worse case of –10% over the chosen horizon, then the risk conditional exposure would be (20% – 5%)/10% = 150%). In other words, we would divide our exposure by 1.5.

Very often, I have seen traders adopting this approach of cutting leverage the closer they get to their ultimate maximum drawdown level, but generally in a more discretionary manner. Having a systematic method for managing drawdowns, even for discretionary traders, is often worth considering, as it instills some element of discipline. In a sense, it is like memorizing fire escape routes in a building. You hope you never have to use this knowledge, but it aids escape if a fire actually occurs. Whilst we might not be involved in a fire in our lifetime, for an investor to expect to avoid a drawdown during his or her entire career seems to be totally unrealistic. Hence, some sort of escape plan for a losing investment has to be considered.

One important point which Jan-Erik noted with respect to drawdowns is that we should use a worst-case scenario if we need to manage drawdowns: simply assume all the assets are fully correlated, and we will not benefit from any diversification in our portfolio to cushion us. As we noted in Chapter 2 on risk, during market crises correlations between assets increase massively. Hence, the benefits of diversification tend to be lost at these points.

Our discussion also strayed to understanding the relative riskiness of trading strategies, a topic we touched on in Chapter 2. Jan-Erik noted that volatility should not be the only criterion to use. He illustrated the problem by using the scenario of selling heavily out-of-the-money options. In a small sample, the returns would appear to be fantastic, exhibiting very little volatility, until the inevitable blow up which would destroy such a strategy. We discuss this in some detail in Chapter 6 on Black Swans and also earlier in this chapter. As opposed to purely using volatility, he also suggested looking at the serial correlation of returns as a measure of risk. Serial correlation means that returns from the previous period and the current period have a high correlation.

The rationale is that strategies which continually generate returns with very low volatility (and have higher risk of a structural break) would tend to exhibit high serial correlation in their returns. This could include those heavily short vol strategies, which we mentioned earlier, but also very high-frequency strategies, which rely on capturing very small returns on every trade. These opportunities can vanish if many other traders attempt to run very similar strategies. More broadly, we might wish to include strategies that harvest risk premium in this list. Selling heavily out-of-the-money options would be an extreme case of collecting risk premium.

On the subject of the Sharpe ratio, he noted some of the deficiencies related to it, notably, the way in which it fails to penalize those nasty tail losses which I flagged earlier in this chapter. We also strayed into discussing the information ratio. You will recall that this is similar to the Sharpe ratio, except that it compares a strategy to a benchmark.

For long only equities strategies such an approach might be reasonable, given that a benchmark (or beta) is readily available. Jan-Erik suggested we could simply use an equally weighted basket of stocks in the universe of our trading strategy and go long that portfolio. However, for scenarios where we both go long and short, it might prove more problematic (although not impossible) to create such a benchmark as a yardstick with which to compare the effectiveness of your particular strategy. If, for example, we are trying to assess the quality of a trend-following strategy, we might choose to find a relatively common generic trend-following strategy and use that as a benchmark. We can also use returns of funds which are likely to be using a similar trading strategy; although in that instance we have a lack of transparency around the precise strategies they use.

We also strayed into the area of selection bias and the criteria used by fund of funds for investing. As the name might suggest, a fund of funds allocates its capital to a portfolio of hedge funds. If fund of funds stipulate only investing in those hedge funds with a track record of many years, then there will be considerable selection bias. By implication, underperforming funds will never reach that stage of maturity. Furthermore, Jan-Erik suggested that with a big enough group we are likely to end up with at least one group of outperformers, which have arrived there as a result of luck rather than a superior investment process. It might be tempting in that scenario to find spurious reasons for the outperformance, rather than being more objective. This is known as confirmation bias, a topic which recurs several times in this book.

I think this point, which we have already touched upon, is crucial, namely that it is important to understand how returns were generated, whilst at the same time avoiding spurious explanations. Jan-Erik also agreed with an idea that I have mentioned before. If a fund has one big trade which goes well over several years, we might well attribute it to luck. However, if they are able to repeatedly enter into successful trades, it might be somewhat more difficult to say their performance was a matter of luck. On the whole, many of his thoughts on investment targets were articulated in a similar manner to me, but I was pleased that Jan-Erik brought up many points which I had not thought to articulate. That is the trick of the writer, to act as the mouthpiece of others whilst seemingly taking credit for the thoughts of others!

Summarizing our journey through investment targets

Throughout this chapter, we have gone through a multitude of different ways in which investors can target the performance of their portfolios. In particular, we have noted that targeting returns or an absolute USD amount alone could induce investors to take outsized risks. Indeed, this has been an issue in sell-side banks, where traders have often been given targets in absolute USD terms alongside a risk limit.

A more prudent approach would be to have investment targets in terms of risk-adjusted returns. The Sharpe ratio could be one possible metric. Although we noted that the Sharpe ratio does suffer from some deficiencies, it is still an improvement on targeting returns alone. Targeting using metrics other than purely returns would have the effect of engendering behavior which still encourages profitable investments but within the context of keeping risk in check. This contrasts to only emphasizing the downside risks for sell-side traders, which could end up reducing market liquidity and increase costs for everyone trading in the market. This includes pension funds, in which many of the general public have some exposure.

Sharpe ratios can sometimes mask large losses to some extent. Hence, we noted that other metrics, such as the Calmar ratios, are also important to give another perspective. Drawdowns are a crucial measure of risk (and possibly more important than volatility). We delved into the Sortino ratio, which extends the idea of the Sharpe ratio. Rather than penalizing high levels of volatility in all situations, including when we have positive returns, the Sortino ratio concentrates on penalizing volatility that is a result of downside moves. In any investment, having some upside limit for drawdowns as part of a target set seems prudent. We also noted that changing our investment style and deviating substantially from our investment mandate can impact our investment targets. In particular, trading other markets or contracts which we are unfamiliar with can open ourselves up to risks that we would not comprehend without a significant amount of research. Just as with Thales' olive trade, the target should be something other than returns. Essentially, by targeting another quantity we may end up realizing more returns in the end, by keeping our risk in check and avoiding outsized drawdowns. We also discussed the thoughts of Jan-Erik concerning investment strategies and in particular investment targets. Many of his points concurred with my thoughts on targets, although he also added a few ideas which I had not thought of before our conversation.

6

Predicting the Eclipse: Searching for a Black Swan and Windows of Doom

> As light will fade, begins to blacken through,
> A time will pause and life awaits that cue,
> Of the sun's shine, so bathed in gold, in heat,
> Eclipse will pass Mother Nature's one feat.

The solar eclipse foretold by Thales, and Black Swans

One of the most celebrated of Thales' achievements is his (claimed) prediction of a solar eclipse in 585 BC. The eclipse occurred during a battle at Halys between the Lydians and Medes in that year. Upon seeing the solar eclipse, the two parties at war decided it was a signal from the gods that they should pursue peace. The story is recounted by Herodotus as follows:

> After this, seeing that Alyattes would not give up the Scythians when Kyaxares demanded them, there had arisen war between the Lydians and the Medes lasting five years; in which years the Medes often discomfited the Lydians and the Lydians often discomfited the Medes (and among others they fought also a battle by night): and as they still carried on the war with equally balanced fortune, in the sixth year a battle took place in which it happened, when the fight had begun, that suddenly the day became night. And this change of the day Thales the Milesian had foretold to the Ionians laying down as a limit this very year in which the change took place. The Lydians however and the Medes, when they saw that it had become night instead of day, ceased from their fighting and were much more eager both of them that peace should be made between them.
>
> (Herodotus & Macaulay (trans), 1890)

Other ancient sources also mention Thales' prediction of the solar eclipse such as Laertius & Hicks (trans) (1925). Panchenko (1994) notes that whilst there are these various ancient accounts of Thales' prediction, there are no ancient descriptions which outline the method which Thales used to give his estimate. He also writes that some criticize the validity of the claim that he really predicted the eclipse, given we do not know the method he employed. These critics suggest it was unlikely that the prediction of solar eclipses would have been accurate until the time of Hipparchus, who lived 400 years after Thales. Critics might also ask why his prediction had a relatively broad window. After all, Thales was said to have predicted the year of the solar eclipse rather than the precise date. However, both Panchenko (1994) and O'Grady (2004) speculate that Thales could have known about the idea of solar eclipse cycles and had some knowledge of Babylonian astronomy, which would likely have aided his prediction. It is also noted that the Babylonians had some success at anticipating lunar eclipses. Both Panchenko and O'Grady seem to give credence to the idea that Thales really did make a prediction, and that it was not purely a coincidence.

Black and white swans, and proof by contradiction

So are solar eclipses Black Swan type events? We capitalize those instances of Black Swans which refer to events, as Taleb does, to help us distinguish between them and real swans that happen to be black. Before answering the question, let us first outline what a Black Swan event is. Taleb (2008) discusses the notion of Black Swan events, as the title of his book would suggest, and we use that book as a source for much of our discussion. (To be clear, Black Swan events have nothing to do with the film of the same name, featuring Natalie Portman, in spite of the fact that the film seems to saturate any Google search for the two words "black swan!".)

To illustrate the idea of what Black Swans are and to provide some background, let us first venture into the world of biology and the identification of "real" black swans. Historically, the existence of a black swan was deemed an impossibility by Europeans, and it was thought that all swans were white. Indeed, Puhvel (1994) notes that the origin of the word for swan in many Western languages is often related to terms for whiteness, an indication of how entrenched the idea was. The rationale was that since a black swan had never been observed, they did not exist, and hence all swans were white. However, Taleb argues that this type of thinking is flawed: the lack of a precedent does not imply that an event is impossible. In this specific instance, the discovery of Australia, which had black swans in abundance, totally disproved the idea that all swans were white. Mathematically speaking, this type of proof is known as a proof by contradiction (or *reductio ad absurdum* to use the Latin phrase), which is an idea that has been around since ancient times. Melis, Pollet, & Siekmann (2006) give several examples of these ancient mathematical proofs. Amongst the most famous of these is Euclid's theorem, which shows that there are an infinite number of prime numbers. Another well-known proof by contradiction is the one that shows that the number 2 is irrational (cannot be expressed as a fraction), which has been attributed to Hippasus who lived in Metapontum, a town which is situated in southern Italy. Hippasus was, like Thales, a philosopher. Hippasus followed in the Pythagorean tradition and lived in the fifth century BC, around a century after Pythagoras himself. Pythagoras is of course best known for his theorem relating to triangles, but he was also a founder of Pythagoreanism, a mystical blend of spiritual beliefs and mathematics.

Iamblichus, a Syrian philosopher who lived in the third and fourth century AD, wrote a biography of Pythagoras, entitled *Life of Pythagoras*. In what might be an apocryphal story, Iamblichus says that Hippasus was drowned by Pythagoreans for passing off the creation of a dodecahedron from a sphere as his own discovery. At the same time, he says a similar punishment was administered to the person who divulged the existence of irrational numbers. Indeed, it is possible that this also refers to Hippasus. In his book, Iamblichus tells the story of Hippasus' demise as follows (Iamblichus & Taylor (trans), 1818):

> With respect to Hippasus however especially, they assert that he was one of the Pythagoreans, but that in consequence of having divulged and described the method of forming a sphere from twelve pentagons, he perished in the sea, as an impious person, but obtained the renown of having made the discovery. (The same thing is said by the Pythagoreans to have befallen the person who first divulged the theory of incommensurable quantities.)
>
> (Iamblichus & Taylor (trans), 1818)

Whichever story is true (if any, I must stress), it does not appear that those using proof by contradiction in the Ancient Greek world were particularly popular amongst certain Pythagoreans! We should note that the definition of a Black Swan event does not require use of the proof by contradiction itself. We have merely discussed proof by contradiction, given that it can be used to prove that what were sometimes thought to be impossibilities are actually possible. We have used it in the case of our example of the discovery of the swans which were black in Australia or the existence of irrational numbers. Using proof by contradiction of course requires finding a contradicting example.

Defining a Black Swan with examples

We have circled around the subject of Black Swans, but now we shall try to more specifically define them. For the definition of Black Swan events, we defer to a very succinct version of Taleb's comments on the subject. He defines Black Swan events as those events which are unpredictable, yet which are significant, and which with hindsight appear to be totally predictable.

If we go back to our example of the solar eclipse at the battle of Halys, Thales would probably not have considered it a Black Swan event given that he was able to predict it. Certainly today, we would not think of solar eclipses as Black Swan events, even if at one time they might have been considered so.

What about market crises? Are they Black Swan events? Using Taleb's definition, it would seem so. After all, market crises are by their nature not predictable, unlike solar eclipses once we had a knowledge of solar cycles. There is no equivalent to a "solar cycle" which we can use to identify when market crises will occur. Even if an investor is able to seemingly foretell one market crisis, it seems doubtful that anyone is able to replicate such a magic act repeatedly, which would be an indication of some special ability as opposed to luck. Indeed, even if we might be able to make an accurate observation about the likely origins of the next market crisis, which is in itself difficult, the timing is unpredictable. For example, even without hindsight, it might have seemed to certain market observers that the dotcom frenzy of the late 1990s and the early 2000s was a bubble. In particular, Warren Buffett flagged it as a bubble and refused to buy these stocks (Schroeder, 2009).

However, being able to accurately predict when it would finally burst was something which escaped most market participants. Those who attempted to short dotcom shares too early, in an effort to profit from their potential decline, would have suffered losses at first, given that prices kept on climbing. One famous example was Julian Robertson and his Tiger fund, which lost money from shorting dotcom stocks (Strachman, 2004). Robertson was right to identify the bubble, but unfortunately his timing was too early to make it a profitable trade. Ironically, often being wrong with the right timing can sometimes be more profitable than being right with the wrong timing in financial markets. For Buffett, whilst he did not profit from the dotcom bubble, he also did not face losses when it popped.

In a sense, market crises share the same status as solar eclipses once did, before humans were able to predict solar eclipses. People would know that a solar eclipse would eventually occur at some point in the future, but would be unable (at least before Thales) to predict their timing. To some extent the same was true of hurricanes, until recently. Whilst hurricanes can be catastrophic events causing significant damage and might have been considered as Black Swan events before, in recent years meteorologists have been able to forecast them with some accuracy in the very short term. One such example was the warning concerning Hurricane Sandy in late 2012, which allowed many people to evacuate. Unfortunately, other natural phenomena remain unpredictable. In particular, earthquakes remain in the realm of the Black Swan. Whilst we understand the mechanics of where earthquakes are most likely to occur, we still cannot predict them even on a very short-term basis: we remain at their mercy just as those in the ancient world were. Hence, the only way to deal with earthquakes is to deal with the aftermath, by ensuring that buildings in earthquake zones are able to withstand the shaking of the ground. Recall our law regarding builders in Ancient Babylon in Chapter 4.

Just as with earthquakes, traders realize that market crises will happen in the future and are an inevitable facet of the financial markets. Furthermore, as we have already made allusion to, browsing financial data can very quickly show that market returns exhibit fat tails and are not normally distributed. In less statistical language, these fat tails can be characterized by relatively large if somewhat infrequent drawdowns. Market crises cannot be totally avoided by investors, but they can try to prepare for them.

Despite this observation that crises regularly impact the markets, the estimation of the precise timing of the next market crisis by market participants is unlikely to be accurate, whether it is the dotcom bubble or the Lehman crisis, two examples we have already mentioned. Furthermore, whilst the cause of financial crises is usually excessive leverage, the way in which this manifests itself is often different in each crisis. After all, consider that Ancient Rome succumbed to a credit crunch in AD 33, just as modern markets did over the Lehman crisis (see Chapter 3). Whilst there might be similarities, the precise epicenter was different in both cases. Hence, trying to predict the origins of a financial crisis based upon a previous template can be difficult. Taleb is critical of in particular of using historical data to try to estimate what might happen during Black Swans. Just because the market has never fallen by a certain amount before, it does not mean that greater downside moves are not possible (see Chapter 5 on investment targets).

Black Swans and probabilities

My opinion is that it is very difficult to predict market crises and tallies with Taleb's view. More likely, it might be more accurate to note that it is impossible to predict such events on a repeated basis. This hardly seems like a controversial view, and I suspect the vast majority of readers would agree with this. Even if we can make an educated guess about the likely nature of a Black Swan before it actually impacts markets, which is by itself challenging, we noted that it is extremely difficult to predict the precise timing. There are also instances when events can happen totally out of the blue without any major warning signs, such as 9/11. Although we face difficulties when analyzing Black Swan events, this does not mean we cannot make any observations about getting an incredibly rough estimate of their possible timing, a window. We give these estimated windows the apocalyptic name of "windows of doom." We can also attempt to assign probabilities regarding the likelihood of a Black Swan event during these windows of doom.

I will illustrate the point with a few simple examples. Let us create a window of (potential) doom, which encompasses the next 12 months from the current day. We wish to estimate whether a Black Swan event impacting markets could occur in this window of doom. Next, we create another window of doom, but this one covers the next 12 years. Without any reference to what is happening in the market or even making any complicated forecasts, it seems fairly obvious that the likelihood of a market crisis happening over the next 12 years is far higher than the probability of one occurring in the next 12 months. If we double our potential window of doom to 24 years, the probability of a market crisis happening is even higher. If we were to make our window of doom an entire human lifetime, the probability of a market crisis occurring would be very high. We can also observe the converse: that the larger we expand our window of doom, the likelihood of having no crisis becomes smaller and smaller.

Whilst history cannot tell us about the nature of the next Black Swan to impact markets, it does show us that what should be very unusual events, notably market crises, do occur repeatedly and with regularity. The notion of having no market crises over a lifetime would strike most people as highly unusual. Indeed, observing no market crises over a lifetime might actually seem like a Black Swan in itself. This would imply that a strategy which sold heavily out-of-the-money options would suffer no drawdowns during a lifetime: something which is extremely unlikely.

Are there varying shades of Black Swans? Can we decipher the relative Black Swan-ness of events?

So far we have lumped all Black Swan events together. This is despite the fact that some seem (just a tiny bit) more predictable than some others. We have noted that certain events adhere to the definition of being Black Swan events more easily than others. Notably, the terrorist attacks of 9/11 by any measure seem to have been Black Swan events. Even if there might have been some sort of warning, it was relatively vague (Lichtblau & Sanger, 2004) and would not have been seen by more than a small number of people. The financial crisis of 2008 was sparked by the collapse of Lehman Brothers in September 2008. I would conjecture that the timing of this collapse was a Black Swan event. However, were there absolutely no signs at all (without hindsight)? I think it would be difficult to say that there were no signs whatsoever. The crisis had been slow-burning, impacting markets for over a year, since summer 2007. Stocks had already begun to fall. A major investment bank, Bear Sterns, had been bailed out. The credit crunch had begun to impact markets. Hence, markets had already begun to move, even if the hammer blow had not yet been inflicted in terms of Lehman's collapse and the painful fallout into the broader economy. In a sense, it was more like a slow-motion car crash, which suddenly accelerated when Lehman filed for bankruptcy. At least in our small number of examples, there do seem to be differing levels of Black Swan-ness (to abuse the English language) in events.

In 2002, Donald Rumsfeld, the former United States Secretary of Defense, tried to describe the nature of Black Swan events, albeit in his own way. He was answering a question at a Department of Defense news conference. Indeed, so well known (no pun intended) for this statement was Rumsfeld that he chose to name his autobiography *Known and Unknown: A Memoir* (Rumsfeld, 2013). In the news conference, he said:

> Reports that say that something hasn't happened are always interesting to me, because as we know, there are known knowns; there are things we know we know. We also know there are known unknowns; that is to say we know there are some things we do not know. But there are also unknown unknowns – the ones we don't know we don't know. And if one looks throughout the history of our country and other free countries, it is the latter category that tend to be the difficult ones.
>
> (Rumsfeld & Myers, 2002)

In Rumsfeld's description, to somewhat rephrase his statement and fill in a few lines, true Black Swan events are those that we do not even know we have any idea about, which he labeled as *unknown unknowns*. This description might characterize the timing and the severe nature of the financial crisis following the collapse of Lehman Brothers. This came after the subprime market had shown some signs of fracture over the preceding year. We could argue that how the subprime market would turn out was a *known unknown*, which we could term as a Grey Swan. Whilst not quite as well known as the term Black Swan, scour the financial press and you will find the odd mention of a Grey Swan.

As an exercise, we can look at data from Bloomberg News stories which contained the word subprime in Figure 6.1. We see that there was significant media

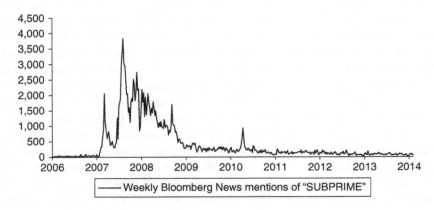

Figure 6.1 Number of mentions of "subprime" in Bloomberg News articles
Source: Thalesians, Bloomberg Finance L.P.

coverage of subprime, even before Lehman's fall. Hence, it was something which market participants were aware of, even though very few actually managed to predict the severity of what would ensue.

From that perspective, using these various examples for illustration, we might postulate that there might well be different shades of Black Swan, events which have a tiny hint of predictability. We have also suggested names for these, namely known unknowns or Grey Swans. Then there are events which have absolutely no predictability, which we might term as true Black Swans or unknown unknowns.

The extent of Black Swan-ness depends on proximity to historic events

Does the Black Swan-ness (again I realize that such a term really is an abuse of the English language) or the known-ness (if we wish to use Rumsfeld's termi-nology) of an event depend on the observer? We have already suggested that the historical time in which an observer lives impacts his or her notion of the improbable or novel. This was illustrated in our example of Westerners who believed that all swans were white before the discovery of Australia.

Let us say we are making prophecies. It is likely that events very far into the future will display more characteristics of a Black Swan. Take, for exam-ple, an Ancient Greek trying to predict the notion of powered human flight. That would seem outlandish, and in the realm of legends such as Daedalus and Icarus. To a Victorian, who had witnessed human flight through hot air bal-loons and mechanical contraptions such as cars, the idea of powered human flight, even if somewhat improbable, would seem closer to occurring than it would for an Ancient Greek. These ideas so far seem relatively straightforward.

I would suggest that the extent to which a future event can be considered a Black Swan might also be related to an observer's proximity to recent historical events. This is particularly true of those events which have directly been experi-enced by the observer. This is somewhat more useful for us in a trading context. After all, when trading, or indeed more broadly, we do not have knowledge of future events, whilst we do have information relating to past events!

We can identify examples of how the historical context of an observer impacts how he or she would estimate the probability of a Black Swan. In partic-ular, let us venture to Ancient Greece once again and think of the philosopher Plato, a pupil of Socrates. Like Thales, he was also a mathematician as well as a philosopher. Plato was born in the latter part of the fifth century BC and lived until the middle of the fourth century BC, in Athens. One of his most famous works is *The Republic* (Plato & Jowett (trans), 2000). Its form is that of a Socratic dialogue; in other words, a discussion between various characters, fea-turing Socrates as a main character. During my research into Plato, I randomly chanced upon a blog named the *Curse of Socrates* and an article entitled *Plato's Black Swan* (Fulton, 2013). Fulton makes the point that I have alluded to. He suggests that the ideas which might seem bold or original (Black Swan–style ideas) in the present may have been seen before in history. He notes that many of Plato's ideas might seem remarkably modern. One example is found in *The Republic*: the idea of giving women the same education as men. In the dialogue, Socrates, speaking as the narrator, expresses this in the following way:

> And if, I said, the male and female sex appear to differ in their fitness for any art or pursuit, we should say that such pursuit or art ought to be assigned to one or the other of them; but if the difference consists only in women bearing and men begetting children, this does not amount to a proof that a woman differs from a man in respect of the sort of education she should receive; and we shall therefore continue to maintain that our guardians and their wives ought to have the same pursuits.
>
> (Plato & Jowett (trans), 2000)

For an observer, for example in the Middle Ages, which was far removed from the time of Plato, it would have seemed like a Black Swan event to suggest that women would ever have equality with men, whether in education or any other sphere. It was only in modern times, for example that women were given the vote in the UK (in 1918), thousands of years after Plato wrote *The Republic*. Even today, it might be tempting (although wrong) to misattribute the ideas of equality purely to "modern" thinking, ignoring the fact that it was an idea discussed by Plato.

This argument about historical viewpoint is not purely relevant to the ideas of Plato and Socrates. It is also highly relevant to financial markets. Memories of recent historical crises can heavily impact how market participants view the likelihood of a Black Swan event in the present. One theme that we discuss later in the chapter relates to the relative cheapness or expensiveness of out-of-the-money options.

We can illustrate this with a small story involving two traders. Our first trader is called Ms. Volvo. Her hair is a bit greyer than it should be for her age. She never runs across the road. She always waits for the traffic light to change, just in case, she says. She still has her dependable Volvo car, which is nearly ten years old. She prefers to keep her savings locked up in a safe bank account (unfortunately she cannot easily find a bank which is rated AAA, which would indicate the highest creditworthiness). Why would she be so cautious? She worked on the trading desk at Lehman Brothers, where she witnessed the calamity of the bankruptcy unfolding. Whenever a client asks her for a tail-risk option, she takes a long pause and thinks about the Lehman crisis, which comes to mind very quickly. When she gives a price for the option, it is very expensive; she wants to make sure there is a very large risk premium. She realizes these are very difficult to price and would prefer to err on the side of caution. The client passes on the price and goes to another broker to ask for a quote. However, after ringing around many brokers, the client comes back to her. After all, most of the other traders have memories of the Lehman crisis, and they are not prepared to sell such an option without a chunky premium. This time Ms. Volvo says her price has expired, and gives the client an even higher price. However, the client is so keen to deal that he eventually accepts this price.

Our second trader is Mr. Ferrari. Ironically, although he is called Mr. Ferrari, he does not drive a Ferrari. Instead, he has a Porsche 911 painted in a shade of red not quite as bright as that found on a Ferrari. Markets have been relatively benign for a long period of time. In fact, Mr. Ferrari cannot remember a major crisis during the time he has worked in markets. There was this one time when a small country defaulted on its debt, but he was on holiday at the time and luckily did not suffer any losses from it. As a result, he is a bit more blasé about taking risks. He thinks it is basically free money to sell blow-up options, even at levels which clients seem to think are cheap.

The important point is that the historical contexts which Ms. Volvo and Mr. Ferrari use to frame their trading decisions are very different. For Mr. Ferrari, his estimates for the probabilities of Black Swans in the near future are likely to be skewed to the low side. This compares with those traders, such as Ms. Volvo, who have just been through a market which has been impacted by a Black Swan.

Indeed, it seems relatively intuitive that recent price action might overly impact the way that traders view the market. The pricing of heavily out-of-the-money options is one manifestation of this. We might conjecture that differing viewpoints around price action are likely to impact many other types of market behavior, which usually stem from taking too much risk.

Can we profitably trade Black Swans as a single strategy? Enter the window of doom

So what type of trading strategies could we employ in an effort to profit from a future Black Swan event in financial markets? Let us create a character called Mr. Pessimist. He is the man who sees the glass as always half-empty and sees problems everywhere. He smiles sparingly. He prefers salad to burgers, water to Coca-Cola, celery to cheesecake. His outlook on life permeates how he views financial markets. His pessimism dictates that he thinks stocks are due for a large correction lower, a good old-fashioned market crash, something he relishes as it will teach all the optimists a lesson. He is unsure, however, about the timing of such a market drop.

Let us say we share the views of Mr. Pessimism on markets, although most definitely not on food. Celery would never take precedence over cheesecake for me; furthermore, picking a salad over a burger would seem like an affront. We want to prepare for a massive market crash just like him. We also have no idea about the precise timing of this Black Swan event, which complicates matters. We cannot simply short beta persistently in the cash market, waiting for a market crisis during an extended window of doom. We illustrate this in Figure 6.2, where we show the year-on-year returns from being short S&P500. Yes, shorting beta in the cash market would have been profitable in some of the years, such as 2008; however, this would not be sufficient to make up for the years when long beta was profitable.

We can try other approaches, such as trading in the derivatives markets. This would allow us to use less capital to express our view. One common suggestion for a Black Swan-style strategy has been to purchase heavily out-of-the-money options, which is likely to be advocated by followers of Taleb (and Mr. Pessimist). Indeed, Taleb has also been involved with hedge funds, which aim to profit from Black Swan events. We might speculate that Black Swan-style funds use strategies which involve purchasing heavily out-of-the-money options. The idea of purchasing these is that they allow us to profit from very large downside moves, which are typically associated with market crises, whilst putting up less capital than we would use in the cash markets. Also, our losses are capped at the price of the options we are buying, unlike with shorting equities in the cash markets, where our losses could be unlimited (in particular if we eschewed the use of stop losses). In Chapter 2, we specifically noted that it is important to understand the downside associated with a particular strategy. Hence, it seems as though this strategy at least ticks that box.

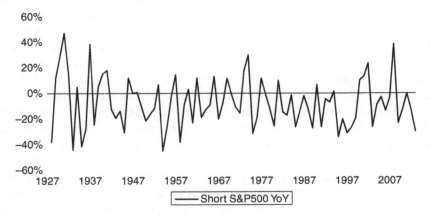

Figure 6.2 Short S&P500 has only made money in 32% of the years since the 1920s
Source: Thalesians, Bloomberg Finance L.P.

Typically during market crises, as we also noted in Chapter 2, risky assets tend to be sold aggressively. At the same time, safe haven assets appreciate. Investors effectively switch from seeking yield to safeguarding their capital. Thus to profit from such a scenario, these options could be a mixture of puts on risky assets and calls on safe haven assets, all heavily out-of-the-money. Hence, during a market crisis, the puts on risky assets would become very valuable, as would our calls on safe haven assets. Our earlier supposition was that even if we could not predict the exact timing of a market crisis, if we had a big enough window of doom the probability of a crisis occurring in our window would increase. Hence, if we keep buying these out-of-the-money options for a long enough period, they would (hopefully) eventually expire in-the-money. At least on a superficial level, this strategy seems quite reasonable. However, the problem is that it relies upon these options being heavily underpriced or mispriced. Before, this might have been the case (in particular in the time before Black Monday, the Wall Street Crash of 1987). Indeed, before, market makers might have over-relied on certain option-pricing models, which had deficiencies in terms of underpricing heavily out-of-the-money options, as we noted in Chapter 2, which essentially involved pricing them with the same implied volatility parameter, no matter what the strike was.

Even if strikes were priced differently later, there might also have been the tendency to underprice these options because the possibility that asset prices would move so much might have seemed "unlikely" (that most loaded of words in the financial lexicon). Of course, even if asset prices have moved massively in the past, traders' memories do tend to be relatively short. The relatively quick turnover in traders is probably one reason why market crises occur more often than we might expect.

In particular, following the most recent financial crisis of 2008, market makers are less likely to underprice such options, whatever a model might tell them. The sheer magnitude of the financial crisis makes it difficult to forget, and also the time elapsed has not (yet) been sufficiently large. Also, as we noted in Chapter 2, the final price that is output by models is ultimately a product of what inputs traders give. Whatever prices traders use to trade with their counterparties, they need to make sure that these prices pass their common sense test. We would conjecture that they would actually charge much more for these heavily out-of-the-money options than suggested by any of their option-pricing models, given the added risks from selling such blow-up options. Also, these options tend to be illiquid, making them more difficult to price. There might be instances where market makers would be unwilling to make markets in these options, given the potential risks from being on the other side of a tail-risk trade in the event that they cannot hedge out the risk. In more option-speak, a market maker does not wish to be selling tail risk outright and thus wants to have an elevated risk premium to compensate, if he or she is forced to hold it on his or her trading book.

If these heavily out-of-the-money options premiums are generally larger, an assumption which we think would be fair following the Lehman crisis, we need to consider several points. We would end up bleeding more capital whilst markets are benign. Hence, these options would expire out-of-the-money and worthless during these periods of calm. If we are "unlucky" and markets are benign for a very long period of time, we could potentially run out of capital before we hit a crisis. After all, the time value of the option is embedded in the premium. Hence, at expiry the intrinsic value needs to outweigh the initial option premium (which includes time value).

On the flip side, we might be "lucky" and a market crisis will occur very early, before we have paid out a large amount of option premium. Aside from relying on being "lucky," making money from such a strategy would require us to be able to predict the precise timing of market crises. However, we have already noted that predicting the precise timing of Black Swan events is impossible.

Even if we are running the strategy and we go through a market crisis, which triggers our options to expire in-the-money, the payout might not be sufficient to pay for our premium paid out during benign markets. So if continually buying heavily out-of-the-money options is not attractive as a stand-alone strategy because of option premium bleed (with some caveats), what about continually selling heavily out-of-the-money options?

Unfortunately, simply reversing the strategy would be very unattractive. We have alluded to this on multiple occasions. If we repeatedly sell heavily out-of-the-money options without any sort of hedge, we would pick up returns gradually over time, but we would suffer massive drawdowns during market crises. If we think about the maximum losses we could expect from such a strategy, they could potentially be unlimited, violating our rule in Chapter 2. We suggested that traders should have a reasonable idea what their potential downside could be. Even if these strategies might on occasion be profitable, the types of return characteristics from repeatedly selling heavily out-of-the money options are really not something to endear them to anyone wishing to run a strategy long term. Indeed, if we are "unlucky" and start running such strategies just before a market crisis, the drawdowns could bankrupt us. Taleb refers to such a strategy where we are selling tail risk as fragile (Taleb, 2013).

So, whilst it might seem like an attractive idea to search to profit from Black Swan events by continually purchasing heavily out-of-the-money options, practicalities make it difficult to trade profitably. Notably, we need to deal with the bleed from repeatedly buying these options when the market is not in flux. It might therefore seem more like death by a thousand cuts rather than a single sledgehammer blow. To make such strategies profitable would require a significant amount of work to identify specifically underpriced out-of-the-money options, and possibly to develop some sort of timing mechanism. We can no longer just simply assume that all heavily out-of-the-money options are "cheap" these days, related to unrealistic option-pricing model assumptions. This contrasts to a strategist who might be writing for years and years that a market crisis is coming. He or she will eventually be right: with a large enough window of doom a market crisis will eventually happen. Crucially, there will be little financial cost in repeating his or her prediction for years. Of course, there is an implicit reputational cost in repeatedly making a prediction which does not materialize, so we cannot say that a strategist has zero cost to their predictions: it is simply not a financial cost. Traders by contrast need to pay financially to express their views in the market. Talk is cheap, whilst option premiums are no longer always cheap for heavily out-of-the-money options.

Using Black Swan strategies as tail-risk hedges within a portfolio

We have seen that tail-risk-style strategies or Black Swan strategies which involve purchasing heavily out-of-the-money options might not be profitable on their own, unless the options we are purchasing are heavily underpriced. Indeed, this situation is less likely to be the case following the Lehman financial crisis. We would conjecture that finding such heavily underpriced tail-risk options would probably require a significant amount of work, and would also be contingent on the market environment. If the market has recently gone through a period of crisis, it is likely that these options would be significantly more expensive, and hence overpriced. This contrasts with periods of benign markets, when perhaps such options become underpriced as the market becomes less keen on buying insurance. However, strategies which profit from tail risks blowing up can still be an important part of an investor's portfolio.

Crucially, we need to think of a tail-risk-style trade as being one strategy within investors' portfolios, rather than as being a place where they deploy all their capital. First, let us think back to Chapter 5, where we discussed numerous ways in which an investor can create targets, which are an improvement on purely targeting percentage returns.

If we just think about percentage returns of a portfolio in isolation, adding a Black Swan-style strategy is unlikely to improve these returns. However, if we consider other factors such as volatility and drawdowns, as well as the Sharpe and Sortino ratios, we find a different situation. Typically, if an investor has capital invested in a beta-style strategy, such as long S&P500 or FX carry, whilst profitable, they can be subject to unsavory drawdowns during periods of market crisis. During calm markets, meanwhile, an investor would collect relatively stable returns. Even without any analysis, this type of observation is likely to be known to most market participants. It is a point which we have repeated on a number of occasions. Can we do anything about it?

One way to alleviate these drawdowns is to create a more active strategy, which exits these positions when we think there could be a market crisis. However, this is akin to predicting a Black Swan. This is something which is not possible, as previously noted. Hence, this does not seem like a feasible possibility. In practice, such strategies of actively managing exposure when risk sentiment sours can help to reduce drawdowns (at least around Grey Swans). However, I think it is difficult to totally avoid drawdowns, when your trading style is about collecting risk premium, no matter what supposedly fancy active trading technique you use.

A far more realistic objective is to employ a parallel strategy with statistical properties, which complements our beta strategy; in particular, one which would not suffer from timing risk – in other words, a strategy which is likely to be negatively correlated to our original beta strategy. Intuitively, a Black Swan-style strategy seems to fit, such as buying heavily out-of-the-money options which we have described earlier. After all, whilst tail-risk strategies are unprofitable during benign markets, our beta strategy should make money during these periods. Conversely, when there is a market crisis and our beta strategy experiences large drawdowns, a tail-risk strategy would be very profitable. As a result, by running both strategies in parallel we could mitigate our drawdowns, and it is likely that we could reduce volatility at the same time. As a result, we would probably see an improved Sharpe ratio. From a statistical point of view, we would hopefully be getting rid of some of the nasty tail of heavy negative returns within the distribution, which occur during Black Swan events. The cost of adding such a tail-risk hedge would likely be a reduction in returns (and the reason why we might not wish to run a tail-risk strategy in isolation), but we might judge that the beneficial statistical properties of our combined strategy justify this. In effect, we are using the tail-risk strategy as a hedge for the very large moves we could potentially see in markets during crises, something we discussed in Chapter 4.

In a sense, our tail-risk strategy would be akin to constructing a stronger building in an area known to be vulnerable to earthquakes or other calamities. Yes, it would be more costly than building an ordinary building, but it would better protect us during an earthquake. Whilst we cannot predict the timing of an earthquake, we can be prepared for it at any time.

Other ways to lessen the impact from Black Swans in the market: Leverage

We have established that Black Swan events are rather more frequent than we would otherwise think, if we consider financial markets. I admit this is hardly a revelation to anyone who has followed financial markets for a few years! One way of lessening the impact from a Black Swan event is to buy tail-risk hedges as part of a portfolio. If we take a step back, we have reasoned that one of the main causes of most market crises is excessive leverage or, more simply, borrowing too much capital which cannot be paid back.

Hence, it becomes relatively clear that one way to reduce the impact of Black Swan events on your portfolio is to simply employ less leverage in a portfolio. If we recall from Chapter 2, one key criterion whenever placing a trade is to have a reasonable idea of how much our downside could be as a USD amount, and from that extrapolate our leverage ratio. Let us say we leverage our position a lot, obviously the amount we are prepared to lose would not change. However, importantly, the level where we place our stop loss would have to be closer than on unleveraged position, perhaps nearer than we might otherwise want. So far, this sounds like obvious stuff.

The difficulty is that in the case of a Black Swan event we could be simultaneously hitting our stop losses in multiple trades because of widespread position liquidation. Hence, our problem about having excessively close stops would be compounded, causing even further losses. This resonates with our point in Chapter 5, about targeting return statistics other than annualized returns and instead considering other factors such as maximum potential drawdowns, volatility, and Sharpe and Sortino ratios. The difficulty we noted with purely targeting annualized returns is that it encourages overleveraging when investing. Once the Black Swan passes and the bout of forced position squaring has abated, we might find that the trades which we were prematurely forced out of have begun to recover. Unfortunately, we would have simply taken the losses in our portfolio on the way down. Furthermore, we would have not participated in any market recovery. Hence, our losses would be even larger than if we had simply remained passive over the whole episode. Obviously, this is just an example, but it does illustrate some of the issues with overleveraging: that it makes a portfolio very sensitive to losses and forces us to take short-term decisions which might be at odds with longer-term investment objectives.

So how can we avoid this vicious circle which can be unleashed by Black Swan events? The most obvious way is by not overleveraging a portfolio. Indeed, this is the approach that Warren Buffett has adopted, on average using leverage of 1.6x according to Frazzini, Kabiller, & Pedersen (2013). Whilst, for example, Berkshire Hathaway stock, the investment vehicle of Warren Buffett, declined during the Lehman crisis, it did so less than S&P500. This suggests that, whilst his investments were impacted by the largest Black Swan to hit markets in recent years, the relative lack of leverage helped to mitigate some losses compared with the market benchmark of S&P500.

We should not think we can totally eliminate drawdowns from Black Swan events. Indeed, we noted in Chapter 2 that filtering beta exposure was not a panacea. Our point, however, is that by keeping leverage relatively low, we can reduce some of the fallout from Black Swans, notably being forced out of trades we might prefer to otherwise hold on a longer-term basis.

Extended market positioning and Black Swans

The idea of market positioning has been broached on several occasions, notably in Chapter 3, where we discussed it in the context of foreign exchange markets. Understanding market positioning can help us to understand the possible impact from Black Swan events within the markets. At its most basic level, market positioning refers to the assets which traders are holding on their books. As we noted earlier, there are many different market participants, and this can impact how they view risk. Hence, we need to be careful about how we interpret market positioning. If possible we should understand how various types of investors are positioned. In Chapter 3, we discussed how retail investors as a group can often have positioning on the wrong side of the market.

This contrasts with speculators whose positioning tends to be correlated with market moves and is relatively short term in nature. In Figure 6.3, we illustrate this point by plotting EUR/USD spot versus speculative net long EUR/USD futures positioning on the Chicago Mercantile Exchange (CME). This data is published weekly by the US Commodities Futures Trading Commission (CFTC).

Pension funds have a much longer-term outlook. As a result their market positioning tends to be a lot slower to change. As a group they do not tend to flip their positioning very quickly. For one, the size of the assets they have under management (or AUM in asset management lingo) means that they would have a large impact on markets if they repeatedly changed their exposure significantly. In a sense, we can think of the way they turn over their portfolios

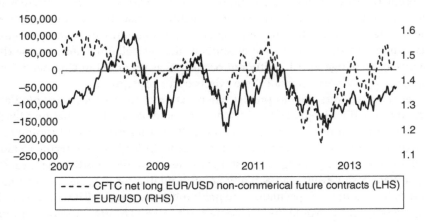

Figure 6.3 Net long EUR/USD speculator positioning on CME versus EUR/USD spot
Source: Thalesians, Bloomberg Finance L.P.

as being like a supertanker turning. The sheer size of their holdings necessitates a relatively low turnover in their portfolio, as does their conservative nature.

If we think about extremes in market positioning, these are typically the times when market crises have most potential to strike, or at least those occasions when their impact can be the most devastating. At these times sentiment might have swung to an extremely positive outlook. Hence, speculators and longer-term investors might be heavily invested in risky assets. However, owing to the saturation in exposure to risky assets, it implies that there are fewer investors to come into the market and sustain further moves higher in risky assets.

A market crisis might occur for a multitude of reasons and can emanate from many different markets. The expression of a crisis within markets is a rapid liquidation in market positioning. We can think of extreme market positioning as the fuel necessary for market crises to explode. Speculators are often the first to react to a market crisis, and attempt to get out of their exposure quickly. When a market crisis becomes particularly potent, longer-term accounts such as pension funds might also join in the position unwind, adding further fuel to a market crisis. Essentially, too many investors are trying to offload their exposure in a massive fire sale, but there are few buyers willing to take it off their hands at high prices.

The important point is that an unwind in positioning does not necessary mean the market is actively putting on positions to profit from falls through short positions. At first, it is simply a damage limitation exercise to get rid of risk whilst the focus for investors shifts from seeking profits to safeguarding capital. As we have repeatedly said, Black Swan events in markets are impossible to predict. However, there are conditions in the market, notably extremes in market positioning, which increase the likelihood that they can occur (or at the very least indicate that the subsequent market fallout will be more severe). Also, more broadly, factors such as shifts in market volatility can increase the chance of a change in risk sentiment occurring, as we noted in Chapter 2. The difficulty is that very often all these events occur concurrently.

Hence, if we were able to predict when extremes in market positioning are starting to be liquidated in every instance, it would be akin to predicting a Black Swan event on a repeated basis! The difficulty is that market positioning can remain extreme in one direction for a long time. Indeed, merely trying to fade (a trader's way of saying "go against") extremes in market positioning, expecting a Black Swan event, can actually be unprofitable for long periods of time. Hence, for example, if speculators are predominantly long S&P500 futures, fading the positioning would involve going short S&P500 futures, hoping to profit from a fall. Or alternatively another way to "fade" the move could be to buy heavily out-of-the-money puts on S&P500.

This is similar to the idea we mentioned earlier about repeatedly buying out-of-the-money puts on risky assets, which would profit from large falls in the underlying assets. Of course, at some point extreme positioning will eventually be unwound, but by the time it actually does, an investor repeatedly fading the market might have lost a lot of money already. So are there any hints which we can use to give us an estimate of when extreme positioning could get unwound? One trick we can try is to estimate the profits and losses of speculators. Publicly available positioning data is published by the CFTC for a multitude of different futures for speculators (and also other market participants), which we have seen earlier. Indeed, we have already used this data in various plots. We can crudely estimate speculator profits and losses by simply multiplying their market positioning by price changes. If speculators are losing money on their positions, it increases the chances of a position unwind and also increases the potential for a market crisis, if this is done rapidly and simultaneously by a large segment of the market. The "pain trade" occurs when price action is forcing a large number of market participants to experience losses on the assets they are holding. It is also possible to do historical studies to gauge the average length in time for extreme positioning, although in my experience this has been very tricky (at least in the currency markets).

In summary, extreme market positioning might give us some small indication about Black Swan events, which are related to pressures building up within the markets, the known unknowns or Grey Swans. Timing when these positions will be unwound is still problematic. However, it obviously cannot help us to predict many true Black Swan events, such as 9/11, where both the nature of the event and the timing are totally unpredictable, or unknown unknowns as Rumsfeld would term them or true Black Swan events. Positioning in these instances would not give us a warning sign. Even if it cannot help us predict a Black Swan, positioning data might be helpful in identifying the possible market impact from such an event. The larger the positioning the more potential there is for liquidation, and the larger the market impact could be. If positioning is extremely light, the fallout from position squaring is likely to be less.

A final word on Black Swan events

We have discussed Thales and the solar eclipse at the battle of Halys. Whilst there are some skeptics, on balance it seems reasonable to conclude that he probably did predict the solar eclipse. We discussed Taleb's definition of Black Swan events. These events have several properties: firstly they are unpredictable, they have a large impact, and with hindsight they seem predictable. Whilst, solar eclipses might be rare events, we cannot say that they are Black Swan events anymore, given that they can be forecasted in advance. The same is true of hurricanes, which we have had some success in forecasting at least in the very short term in recent years. This contrasts to market crises, which are by definition unpredictable, in particular when it comes to forecasting their precise timing. This does not mean we cannot say anything about roughly when they will occur, and assigning a probability to this. If we keep extending our window of doom, as we called it, we increase the probability that a market crisis will occur during that period.

We also noted that there might be differing shades of Black Swan events. There might be those which happen totally out of the blue, such as the 9/11 attacks, unknown unknowns to use Rumsfeld's terminology. This contrasts to certain market crises, which can have a slow-burning quality to them and a tiny amount of forewarning about them. This could be said about the financial crisis of 2008. Whilst the hammer blow to the markets might not have been predictable, the subprime crisis had simmered for over a year until that point, causing equities to sell off and suggesting that something was afoot.

The ability to estimate relatively rough probabilities of crises during very large windows of doom might seem to suggest that we can employ strategies to protect against and possibly profit from Black Swan events (or tail risks). In particular, we discussed the idea of purchasing heavily out-of-the-money options over long periods of time. Unfortunately, we noted that these are unlikely to be profitable, unless these options are heavily underpriced. Finding such options is trickier today. Whilst this might have been the case before (such as before the 1987 Wall Street Crash), market makers are far less likely to price such options cheaply on a persistent basis. This is particularly the case following the financial crisis triggered by the bankruptcy of Lehman Brothers. Perhaps it will require a whole new generation of traders to come along, without any strong memories of the Lehman crisis, to once again appreciably underprice such tail-risk options.

Whilst these tail-risk strategies might not be profitable on their own, we discussed how they can be used in conjunction with beta-style strategies in a portfolio. They can help to reduce the drawdowns associated with some beta strategies such as long S&P500. The cost is likely to be a reduction in returns for this improvement in the statistical properties of the beta strategies, in particular in terms of reducing drawdowns and keeping volatility in check. However, it is likely that many investors will think that such an improvement is worth the cost of slightly lower returns.

We also discussed the idea of market positioning in the context of Black Swan events. We noted that whilst we cannot predict Black Swan events, extreme market positioning can provide the fuel for crises to manifest themselves truly in the market. We suggested that market positioning which is heavily extended is in itself not a reason for a large unwind in positioning to occur at a particular time. Importantly, extended positioning can increase the chance of a rapid squaring of exposures. We also commented on various techniques which we can use to estimate whether the probability of an unwind in these positions has increased. In particular, we mentioned how estimating the profits or losses speculators, as one way to do this. Our writing on market positioning followed from earlier discussions in Chapter 2, where we talked about how shifts in certain factors such as market volatility tend to be associated with changes in market risk sentiment. These factors can help to increase the chances that a Black Swan might indeed be ahead, even if they might not be good enough to predict its timing with any accuracy. Admittedly, our single chapter was a relatively brief introduction to the area of Black Swans. For readers wishing to learn more about Black Swan events, I would recommend Taleb's series of books about the subject, most notably Taleb (2008), which have a far more thorough discussion on the topic.

7

In the Stars: Lateral Thinking to Understand Markets

Amongst the stars there lies the light,
Of Rome, of Mars at war, Neptune at sea,
Venus in love, emotions now still here,
For man remains the same today as then.

Thales: A polymath of the ancient world

As civilizations have progressed, specialization has prospered. At first we were hunter-gatherers. Then we began to farm the land as agriculture took hold. Later other industries grew, and with this further specialization was undertaken. The idea was that a specialist could be more efficient than a jack of all trades. Indeed, this is the idea behind the efficiency of a production line, something we mentioned in Chapter 3 in the context of decathletes and athletes specializing in specific events. Adam Smith (1776) gives an example related to the manufacture of pins. A quotation from this is on the back of the £20 note:

> The division of labor in pin manufacturing and the great increase in the quantity of work that results

In modern times, knowledge has evolved to such an extent that it has accelerated the process of specialization. In the ancient world, the relative simplicity of life meant that it was possible to be accomplished at many disciplines, perhaps in a way that might be difficult today, as specialization had not yet evolved to such a lofty degree.

If we think back to Ancient Greece, Thales was a philosopher, yet he was also a mathematician. Indeed, Thales' theorem is one of his contributions to geometry. Then again, we cannot purely label him as a mathematician, given he was an astronomer who was sufficiently skilled to predict an eclipse (see Chapter 6). Yet, he was also a trader able to profit from one of the first explicit derivative trades. Thales' expertise in many fields can be summed up by a story mentioned in Plato's *Theaetetus* from the *Dialogues of Plato* (Plato & Jowlett (trans), 1892):

> the inner man, as Pindar says, is going on a voyage of discovery, measuring as with line and rule the things which are under and in the earth, interrogating the whole of nature, only not condescending to notice what is near them ... I will illustrate my meaning by the jest of the witty maid-servant, who saw Thales tumbling into a well, and said of him, that he was so eager to know what was going on in heaven, that he could not see what was before his feet.

It seems difficult to create a precise label for describing Thales, given his multitude of talents. If anything, he could be described as a Renaissance man, millennia before the term reached its apex with people such as Leonardo da Vinci, who could straddle diverse areas in both the arts and science.

The idea of a Renaissance man (or woman) seems less common in finance: namely, someone who can be an expert in the many different areas of the subject. Within financial markets the idea of specialization has evolved to a significant degree, in particular in recent years, where the complexity of markets has catalyzed the process. Yes, there are "top down" traders who digest small snippets of knowledge from many different markets to make their decision-making, so called macro-traders. However, there is a growing army of specialists amongst them, looking at the market from the bottom up. Sector-specific stock pickers are not the only market specialists.

Furthermore, this complexity can also been seen in highly exotic derivative contracts, an area which is perhaps less exciting after the Lehman crisis than before it. We remarked earlier that even what might appear to be very simple asset classes (such as currencies and equities) can have large differences, explaining why market professionals have become so specialized. Indeed, we have noted that it is because of the differences that investors really need to do a significant amount of research to trade in markets which are new to them. Before we address this issue of specialization within finance, we shall briefly digress to the field of lateral thinking.

What is lateral thinking, and how does it differ from vertical thinking?

The term lateral thinking was coined in 1967 by Edward de Bono (Bono, 2009). The approach involves solving problems in a creative manner, rather than always undertaking the most obvious entry point or trying to use a linear-based step-by-step approach. It is primarily used as a way to come up with new ideas.

De Bono contrasts the idea of lateral thinking with logic and mathematics, which tend to be more associated with vertical thinking.

He suggests that the two approaches of lateral and vertical thinking can work together. We can use a simple metaphor to illustrate this point. Lateral thinking can be seen as a way of quickly scanning an area to find points of interest. However, it is through more vertical-based thinking that those points can be explored in more detail. It is like a tourist picking out interesting towns by placing pins on a map, and then spending an extended period visiting those destinations. The limiting factor is that there is not enough time to visit every place on a map, necessitating the creation of a shortlist of destinations.

We can think of technological innovations, where a modicum of lateral thinking was involved to kick-start a project and then vertical thinking was used to create the finished product. Let us take the Walkman as an example, the precursor to Apple's iPod. On the thirtieth anniversary of the Walkman's introduction in 2009, *Time* magazine told the story of how it was invented (Haire, 2009). The cassette tape had been invented in the 1960s. It was, of course, small enough to be carried easily, which was clearly not the case with vinyl records, which were also comparatively fragile. Sony's co-founder, Masaru Ibuka, had a problem. He found Sony's large cassette player too heavy to carry whilst travelling, so he called on his engineers to find a solution, something that could be used with headphones. The result was a cassette player small enough to be hand held. Hence the Walkman was born. Before Sony introduced the Walkman, the idea that people would be walking around listening to music via headphones would have seemed remarkable. Lateral thinking provided the idea: the pin on the map, using our earlier terminology. It was then up to vertical thinking to provide a workable solution.

The risks from blinkered trading, the opposite of lateral trading!

We can relate these ideas of lateral and vertical thinking to trading markets. The difficulty is that with today's silo-based market, where specialization is so heavily prized, it is often easy to ignore the fact that markets are indeed so heavily interrelated. A modicum of lateral thinking can help identify opportunities in such a situation. In effect, it is like trading with blinkers, precisely the opposite to the approach which would be espoused by lateral thinking. This is not to say that investors should always trade every asset under the sun. Indeed, a deeper understanding is required for that, and would require a multitude of traders! It is just that having a broad comprehension of financial markets can help investors to understand the specific market they are trading. For example, even for a trader who is simply trading stocks in individual companies in a single equity sector, it would seem reasonable to understand what is happening in the broader market. It would explain the market-wide risks underpinning his or her stockholdings, even if it would require his or her specialist knowledge to grapple with the idiosyncratic risks.

This is one problem that I encountered when attempting to decipher markets from a systematic perspective in the past. At the beginning of my career, when I was much less experienced in the field, I was much keener on finding trading ideas which simply worked, a relatively narrow objective. Indeed, this is something which can afflict those with a mathematical slant: numbers are the grail, whilst words and explanations might appear to be purely window-dressing. Luckily, I was guided by senior colleagues, in particular Jim McCormick and Alexei Jiltsov whom I mention in the acknowledgments, toward using a more considered and diligent approach for analyzing markets. When it comes to analyzing markets, data should be your servant and not vice versa!

In retrospect, such an approach of simply generating a bundle of trading rules would not have yielded the most robust strategies. Not understanding why a strategy should work raises questions about its likely effectiveness in the future. In Chapter 9, we discuss the use of historical data when testing trading strategies. We also refer to the possible pitfalls if it is done incorrectly.

Indeed, just because my specialism is systematic trading, it does not mean that I should avoid having a view on the market or having an understanding of markets in a more qualitative way. In recent years, I have come to appreciate that having a deep and rounded understanding of markets has aided me significantly when it comes to finding systematic trading ideas. This does not mean every systematic trader must also trade discretionary ideas. It is simply that having knowledge of something other than your specialty can add another dimension to how you view the market. From this, it becomes easier to have the confidence to place real money on ideas, rather than simply talking about it (as we noted before, whilst talk is cheap, losses are not!).

To some extent, currency markets force investors to have a rounded understanding of financial markets, given that foreign exchange transactions are often a by-product of so many other markets. Admittedly, I have had endless discussions with traders about whether it is currency markets or indeed other markets which lead price action, which somewhat clouds my point. What I would say is that whilst it is difficult to prove if one leads the other definitely, understanding what happens to rates markets certainly informs how currency traders view (as an example) the FX market. As another illustration, understanding how currency flows move with other portfolio flows is crucial. We see this type of behavior repeated across markets too.

There is a counterargument to my point about the benefits of having a broader knowledge of markets. Namely, some market participants have said to me that having a deep understanding of markets can be detrimental when analyzing the markets from a systematic perspective. The main reason, they suggest, is because previous knowledge might bias the types of trading ideas you have. Hence, it might reduce the chance of seeing something new. Indeed, certain systematic trading funds often employ analysts who have had no experience in finance, but specifically have knowledge of areas in science and engineering which are relevant to systematic trading. Again, the notion is to be able to think laterally, specifically to bring novel ideas from science to trading. I can see the merits of such an approach, but I still believe that there is some value in having an intuitive grasp of the market, even if that means using ideas learned from others.

Of course, I do not doubt that there are traders who are hugely specialized in a very small sector of the market and who can generate large profits. I would argue, however, that such an approach opens up traders to a lot of risk when that very small slice of the market no longer yields such bountiful opportunities. Also, more simply, they need to understand the very small sector of the market in sufficient detail.

I would term this type of silo-based problem as knowledge diversification risk. We have seen this in recent years for those who were involved in the CDO market. Before the Lehman crisis, this market was very buoyant. However, following the credit crisis, the CDO market froze over, as investors avoided trading such products. Hence, some traders whose expertise was purely in CDOs would have needed to move to other areas to secure employment. To some extent, it can be difficult to escape this risk, even when trading the broadest and most liquid of markets. After all, no specific market will offer fantastic trading opportunities all the time, but the more specialized the market the larger this risk will be.

Lateral thinking can also become more crucial in other trading situations. In particular, it comes into play when attempting to answer the question of why a certain trade or strategy is likely to work. The question "why?" is one which we continually advocate answering, when it comes to investing. We shall discuss this in some detail in Chapter 9 when we look at analyzing historical returns. This is regardless of whether our strategy is something heavily quantitative or qualitative; the principle is the same. As mentioned earlier, if we cannot ascertain why an idea should work, then we increase the chance that we are essentially trying to kid ourselves with numbers from a spreadsheet or because of a lucky run trading. In addition, having no idea why a trade should work seems to sound more like gambling then investing. If we wish to roll a die, roll a die, but do not trick yourself that it is anything more than a purely random outcome! In the case of gambling, there is only one long-term certainty: the house wins, you lose – as we noted in Chapter 2.

Lateral thinking can also work at other levels when investing. For example, having ideas totally outside financial markets can cross-pollinate knowledge to help investors to identify trading opportunities. Information is the blood which forces the movement of markets. After all, assets are generally the paper representations of a real world asset, whether it is a stock, a bond, or an equity. It is just that sometimes this obvious point can become blurred, as markets have become increasingly electronic and thus more "invisible." For a farmer, trading corn has an intuitive relationship with the land. For a trader sitting in Chicago, who does not have such knowledge, he or she must try doubly hard to understand the factors that impact corn.

We can also use the example of an investor trading stocks on luxury goods. Having an understanding of which luxury goods are in fashion can inform the investor. I have specifically given an example of a trade in a market in which I have no huge insights, to illustrate my point! The markets are essentially a chain which begins in the real world, well before assets are traded on exchanges back and forth between market participants. Somewhere along the chain there could be something of importance for future price action, which we might identify if we were to undertake further investigation. Getting to the start of the chain can help us understand where price action might end up. Admittedly high-frequency traders are unlikely to be impacted by such notions, given that fundamentals do not change rapidly, but for the rest of the world which is investing on a longer-term horizon rather than purely intraday trading, this point is worth considering.

Lateral thinking to the path of an investment idea

We can take this idea further by asking the most abstract question: why do people put on a trade? We shall ignore the answer "to make money!" More seriously, there can be many reasons for entering into a trade. Obviously, the objective is to reach some sort of financial target, which is dictated by their circumstances. We discussed this idea in Chapter 5 in some detail. In particular, we noted that targeting returns by themselves can be counterproductive if we ignore all other factors. Instead, we suggested targeting some sort of risk-adjusted metric, and trying to keep drawdowns in check can be very important. This is particularly true for more leveraged traders. Large amounts of volatility and drawdowns can be the factors that can quickly force heavily leveraged traders to exit their exposures rapidly. More broadly, the circumstances of an investor can impact how they use targets. For retail investors managing their pensions, their objective is to have a reasonable income when they retire. They would expect their investment to grow slowly, thus providing a future income comparable to their current wage. However, for very rich investors, their main objective might be wealth preservation rather than targeting a large increase in their investment. More simply, they have more to lose than to gain, and hence act accordingly.

Before we even have considerations concerning investment targets or returns and so on, it seems obvious that every trade starts with an idea. From this idea, the trader can see some sort of opportunity which he or she thinks is likely to yield results. More justifications are built on top of this, before eventually a trader decides to pull the trigger to execute the trade. Even though the direction of the trade might have been decided, just as important is the money management behind it. The size of any trade should match the conviction, and the downside to any trade needs to be capped, drawing upon our ideas on diversification from Chapter 4 and risk from Chapter 2. Hence, any trading decision involves of course the direction, but just as importantly the ability to manage risks around it. There is little point having the right calls and allocating too little capital toward them. Equally frustrating is sloppy money management, where a couple of bad decisions can overshadow a generally profitable portfolio.

Noise and signal and time: The battle in making decisions

During the course of writing this book, I read Nate Silver's book entitled *The Signal and the Noise*. As the name suggests, it is all about trying to strip away the noise from a deluge of information to identify something of utility, namely the signal (Silver, 2012). Silver's fame stems from his predictions of US presidential elections, most notably through his FiveThirtyEight blog, which was previously part of the *New York Times* and is now a website in its own right at www.fivethirtyeight.com. The question of trying to sort the wheat from the chafe (another reference from the ancient world, from the Bible), finding the signal in amongst the noise, is nothing new. Indeed, in Chapter 2 on risk, we discussed Croesus' attempts to filter out the noise from the various oracles spread throughout the Ancient Greek world. His aim was to find the most accurate one. In his test, he deemed the Oracle of Delphi to be a provider of a signal, whilst the others provided the noise. Clearly, it was the signal which interested him, even if he famously misinterpreted this signal in the end.

As a whole, in the ancient world the amount of information available was obviously a lot less compared with what we have today. There were also considerable barriers to the flow of information. I know this point is fairly obvious, given it was millennia even before the printing press! There was also a considerable amount of noise, despite the fact that there was a dearth of information compared with today. We only have to think about some of the stories Herodotus told, about the nature of cinnamon that we shall quote in Chapter 8 to observe noise. Herodotus suggested that cinnamon was obtained from the beaks of the birds, who picked it from plants growing at the sides of mountains.

This story might have come about through miscommunication. However, as we shall note later, it seems more likely that this very unusual story came about through deception by the real traders of spices. The obvious motivation would be that traders wanted to keep the secret of spices to themselves, hence elevating their value. We might therefore conjecture that this was an intentional example of noise. Indeed, as we note in Chapter 8, we can draw a parallel with traders today who might be overly secretive about their strategy to protect the origin of their idea. I suspect this excessive secrecy also adds an element of mystique to what they are doing. Exclusivity is costly, whereas commoditization is cheap. If you are selling something, you can charge more for exclusivity.

Today, we have a far larger flow of information feeding into the markets than at any time in history, and this is likely to increase with time. The amount of noise has also exponentially increased at the same time. More information does not imply more of a usable signal. The difficulty is that if we indulge in too much lateral thinking, we might cast our net for capturing information too widely. The result will be an exponential increase in the problem of too much noise. The key to the approach of lateral thinking within the context of the market is to avoid the digestion of every facet of information we can find. The optimal approach is instead to try to take small snippets of assorted information from a diverse array of different sources.

Hopefully, we shall not be overrun with data if we adhere to this approach, whilst at the same time we should benefit from lateral data sources. Of course the idea of Big Data, which is a particular buzzword in the Internet age, is that we can take vast quantities of data and somehow distill something useful from it. I accept that it can provide investors with a new tool to trade, but I would suggest that even this needs a directed approach. I have written some research for the Thalesians discussing the use of data gleaned from Google searches and Bloomberg News articles. The general gist of my research was that they can add value when a careful approach is used. The crucial point in such an exercise is how you direct the searches through the deluge of Big Data. Perhaps unsurprisingly, I found that Google search data around terms relating to unemployment are of particular importance for generating profitable trading strategies for risk-premium trades. It is just data mining (and subjective) if we use words which refer to specific crises to try to detect market turns; this is not an issue when using generic terms such as unemployment. On a more unusual level, Big Data can be used for more eclectic purposes. One of the most innovative uses was to identify Hurricane Sandy's path via the GPS location tags of uploaded photos to the social media website Flickr (Preis, Moat, Bishop, Treleaven, & Stanley, 2013). Approaching a problem like that from such an innovative angle surely requires a great deal of lateral thinking.

The analysis of Big Data, especially in its rawest form, requires time. If we consider the costs of trading, we observe that capital is not the only cost. The other cost is time, which is somewhat overlooked on a day-to-day basis. Just like capital, time needs to be allocated effectively to provide a return on investment. So what techniques can we use more broadly to find interesting data or ideas when we allocate this precise resource of time? We discuss this in more detail in the next section.

Lateral thinking to a different data angle

What is a trader's edge? Some profitable traders will probably tell you it is their intrinsic genius which explains their success, or a so-called "secret sauce" that we discuss in Chapter 8. However, that will not help the rest of us. As you will read later, I am somewhat skeptical of this type of reasoning to explain the "secret sauce" of trading success.

If we think more seriously, we can come up with explanations of what can provide an edge for traders. Often their edge might be their experience, and how they can learn from it: experience has little value if you cannot interpret it. At other times it might be a specific idea that they have dreamt up. This goes back to the "genius" point! I would suggest that there are many smart people in the markets, so this is not a unique attribute. Furthermore, being smart alone is not a guarantee that you will have positive returns; it is all about being market savvy. In Chapter 9, we also discuss the point that certain strategies by their nature will suit certain traders more. A winning strategy in the hands of one trader will not necessary be such a winner in the hands of another trader.

It can also be the case that profitable traders examine different sorts of data which are not commonly used by other market participants, and this provides an edge. We have already given an example of an innovative way to use data outside the trading sphere, in the case of using Flickr data to map Hurricane Sandy. The ability to use unusual data for an advantage is of course not a new phenomenon. Sun Tzu's *Art of War* (Tzu & Giles (trans), 1910), written in the fifth century BC, discusses a more deceptive way to obtain this information, namely spying (which we do not advocate):

> The enemy's spies who have come to spy on us must be sought out, tempted with bribes, led away and comfortably housed. Thus they will become converted spies and available for our service.
>
> (Tzu & Giles (trans), 1910)

At the very least, the above example illustrates the value of information. The idea of doing something unusual or generally overlooked when trading goes back to our thoughts in Chapter 3 concerning alpha and beta strategies. Recall that beta strategies tend to be related to typical strategies employed by investors, whilst alpha strategies are (supposed to be) the more unusual approaches to trading, which are (supposed to) bear low correlation to market beta. By their nature, alpha strategies require more work.

As we noted, one advantage can come from unusual data, which has the potential to make a strategy "alpha" or to "alphafy" it, if there can be such a word. We can define several different types of private information. Within banks, market makers will be privy to information about client flows, which can provide valuable information and is obviously not available on a fully public basis to other investors.

In more illiquid asset classes, market makers generally have to take more risk because they cannot immediately hedge out positions offloaded on them by clients. If they see a large amount of flow in a specific direction for an asset, this might impact how long they wish to hold that inventory and will impact the skew of their quotes in that asset. Typically, if banks do publish such market flow or positioning data, they tend to reduce the frequency of its publication and tend often to release it on a lagged basis, by which time it is likely its usefulness has diminished somewhat. Obviously, in any data published by banks, they cannot (and should not) identify specific client trades, given rules concerning client confidentiality. Wherever I have worked at the past, it has been a disciplinary matter to reveal such information publicly. If a client wishes to affirm he or she did a specific trade that is obviously a different matter.

There might also be non-public information which has not been gleaned through the course of business and is by any definition obtained illegally (recall our spying example): in other words, this is insider information. Insider information is unfortunately still a problem, as evidenced by recent SEC investigations (Anon, 2013).

So what of public data? There is a vast quantity of public data that can be used by market participants but is not. In many cases it is totally free to obtain or sometimes it might require the cost of a modest subscription fee. Why is so much freely available public data seemingly ignored by market participants?

It goes back to our point about time being a valuable resource. Just because information is available, it does not imply that it will be used or processed by investors. That is the problem about the efficient market hypothesis which stipulates that public information is already in the price of an asset. It might well be the case, but only if all investors actually look at all data (how many of these perfect investors exist?). Furthermore, even with all the data, they might misinterpret it! There are often snippets of news that are ignored by the market, only to be seized upon later by market participants to move prices. This would not happen if every piece of information was already in the price. In the next section, we shall outline the various groups of public information available, splitting them into foreground and background information.

Foreground versus background versus processed background public information

First, there is what I would term foreground public information. These include events known to all market participants (or at least those trading actively). In particular, this can include events such as rates decisions by central banks and the outcome of important economic data releases such as the change in non-farm payrolls in the US. Those who follow a newswire service will have such information blasted onto their screens. Admittedly, high-frequency traders willing to pay for expensive data feeds will obtain such information quicker and execute trades quicker than a human trader would be able to react. However, setting that aside, if we are considering anyone who trades over longer-term time periods, they effectively receive this type of data at around the same time. The further complication is that whilst some immediate market reactions are "obvious," sometimes the market itself can be confused about how to interpret newswire data. If we think of statements from the FOMC concerning US monetary policy, sometimes intraday price action can be very volatile around the release in both directions, as market participants digest the news and try to convert qualitative ideas mentioned in the statement to actual trades. Often when monetary policy has not been changed, even the general tone of the document and particular phrases can move the market. The market can simply change its mind about the interpretation of events such as FOMC or ECB: maybe it is all that lateral thinking by the market! There might also be keywords in rate statements, which are well known to flag intentions. When former ECB president Jean-Claude Trichet mentioned "vigilance" or "strong vigilance" on inflation, for example, the market often interpreted his statement as indicative of higher interest rates in the future.

Second, I would create a category which covers what I would term as background public information. Let us consider the US employment report, which contains a multitude of labor data and is released once a month. The headline figure is the change in non-farm payrolls, which market participants focus on. The report also includes the unemployment rate, which garners less focus from short-term market traders, but is key for the longer-term health of the economy. Furthermore, keeping the unemployment rate low is part of the mandate of the Federal Reserve. In addition, they have also sometimes given numerical thresholds for unemployment, which need to be satisfied for future interest rate moves.

However, the US employment report contains a myriad of other statistics such as "average hours worked" and data revisions. How many market participants delve into this data? I suspect very few traders do. Indeed, I think it is only economists covering the US economy who are likely to get excited by it. I have never heard a trader jumping up and down after the US employment report was released, commenting on a "shocking" average hours worked number. The market can often be very myopic when it comes to data, looking at one component and then trading on that, and then possibly scouring another component at a later stage. However, it is rare that it will drill down into much more detail.

Do the other components of the US employment report have no use from a trading perspective? I really cannot say over the longer term, even if from a short-term perspective this seems unlikely. However, I do think that the reams and reams of additional data in the US employment report do have some potential to be analyzed further. The main reason I have not done this personally, and the likely reason many market participants do not, is of course a lack of time.

Time spent undertaking such analysis means a reduction of work done elsewhere to examine another facet of the market. It is only through experience and a considerable amount of work, that investors gain an insight into which ideas should have time allocated to them (and are likely to yield results). By the same rationale, experience will also help to guide them toward the ones that are more likely to be a waste of effort. The better and more experienced traders are, the fewer wild goose chases they will have to endure, investigating what turn out to be valueless trading ideas. I have endured many hours investigating some supposedly interesting market trading approach only to find that it has little applicability.

Lastly, I would define a last group, which I call processed foreground information. It would be wrong to assume that every successful strategy has at its core only very esoteric data. Instead we can use foreground public information for the basis of further analysis, which might squeeze some interesting observations from it. Here the difficulty is not so much thinking about which dataset to focus upon (as with background public information); it is more in the small "twists" and details we use in our analysis to provide a novel angle on what is very common data. Often it can be the case that combining relatively mundane bits of data together can add value. In Chapter 8, we discuss our thoughts for the basis of a successful trading strategy. In particular, we note that the profitability of a strategy is often likely to be related to the details of an implementation, rather than some totally different factor, the so-called "secret sauce" of trading. Historically, it might have been easier to argue that investors could discover totally different approaches to trading. However, today this seems a lot more difficult. To use a cliché that I absolutely hate, the low-hanging fruit has already been picked. However, what might appear to be very commonplace strategies now were historically in the same league as complex trading ideas today.

A spurious warning

With all this chatter about lateral thinking, it might seem to be the panacea for creating robust trading ideas. Provided you can navigate through the noise and avoid becoming too sidetracked, more data should (theoretically) aid trading decisions? Unfortunately, this is a best-case scenario. Any sort of interpretation of data needs not just an ability to process data but also the ability to rationalize the outputs. The difficulty is that lateral thinking can be misused in this scenario. In particular, it can involve trying to think of anything to explain the outperformance of a strategy when an obvious explanation cannot be found. This urge to over-explain is known as a confirmation bias and is one of the subjects discussed in Kahneman's brilliant book *Thinking, Fast and Slow* (Kahneman, 2012). The alternative would be to flag that this superior outperformance could be a result of being *fooled by randomness*.

Indeed, this is something we have raised throughout this book, mainly because it is such a crucial point. This concern was mentioned by Jan-Erik in Chapter 5 in a specific example. He noted that fund of funds might be tempted purely to pick the best-performing funds in their portfolio and then try (too hard) to come up with reasons why the investment process of these funds is superior, to justify their decisions.

Lateral thinking should be seen as a way of finding trading ideas. It should not be used to force a trader to use an outperforming strategy, which on the surface seems both illogical and irrelevant. This issue is not purely confined to the (misplaced) justification of certain outperforming trading strategies; it can also be found when trying to explain the relationship between financial time series. Indeed, there are many spurious correlations we might be able to find in finance. Given the number of financial time series available to us, it is surprisingly easy to do this.

One of my favorite examples of a spurious relationship can be seen when cattle futures prices are plotted against various exchange rates. In certain cases there appears to be a link. However, there is very little rationale to explain the link (unless I am missing something!). You might be able to argue that, broadly, some countries are commodities importers or exporters. This would imply a broader relationship between currency moves and commodities, rather than something related specifically to cattle futures.

I was chatting with Fred Goodwin (no, not Sir Fred Goodwin, formerly of RBS, but a friend and former colleague of mine at both Lehman Brothers and Nomura). Fred's nicknames at various times have included Mr. Prop, Mr. Macro, and most recently Mr. Risk, in his guise as a macro-strategist, writing insightful articles that are doused in his trademark humorous style. Although he has spent many years in Britain, his accent remains distinctly American. In the past he has also been a trader, spending a number of years in Chicago, a city where even the snow is frightened of the winter cold. Luckily the city is released to bask in sun during the summer. Whereas New York might be the city most associated with finance in the United States, it is Chicago that is most closely associated with the futures and options markets.

When I told Fred that I was writing a section of my book about spurious relationships in finance, he gave me possibly the most ridiculous example anyone could muster. It is a plot which has been a favorite amongst Twitter users,

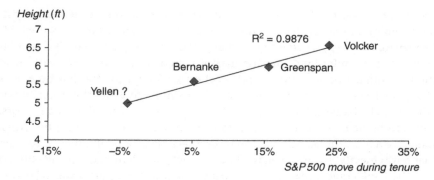

Figure 7.1   Fed chair heights against S&P500 returns during their tenure
Source: Thalesians, Bloomberg Finance L.P., Wikipedia.

although I have never been able to find out precisely who discovered it. Fred's plot shows the heights of Fed chairs against the moves in S&P500 during their tenures (see Figure 7.1). It appears to show a positive correlation. Hence, the tenure of taller Fed chairs have historically been accompanied by more gains in S&P500. We could no doubt compute an R^2 which was very high (99% in fact), which "shows" that the variables had a strong relationship. We can engineer such a statistic, despite the fact that there is little rational explanation for it.

In general, it can be very easy to create fictitious arguments to explain the cattle correlation (although it would be a challenge to explain the outlandish Fed chair height example) and indeed many other sorts of market behavior which would not stand up to further study. Just because we might be able to come up with some sort of explanation, we sometimes need to accept that one of the reasons for certain market behavior or outperformance of a trading strategy could simply be randomness.

There is unfortunately no simple rule to identify when market behavior is either spurious or has a valid explanation. I can, however, offer one heuristic: the longer you spend seeking an explanation for certain market behavior, the more likely it is to be spurious, and your eventual rationale is likely to be an example of confirmation bias. In Chapter 9, we shall specifically discuss the issue of data-mining, which can undermine the historical backtesting of trading strategies.

It's all so obvious (with hindsight)

After any major market event, in particular a huge market crisis, it is easier to find how the crisis evolved and to locate its root with the benefit of hindsight. This was part of Taleb's definition of a Black Swan event, which we talked about in Chapter 6. After the event, with that magical thing called hindsight, the lateral thinking involved seems far more straightforward to explain why it happened. However, when we are actually trading during an event, it can often be difficult to understand that the market is in a slow-motion car crash until the final impact occurs and the price action goes haywire. By that time, it is obviously too late to profit from an event or simply to avoid the losses in our portfolio. The bankruptcy of Lehman Brothers, where I worked for many years, seems to be such an obvious event now, many years removed from the crisis. Indeed, even on the day after Lehman Brothers filed for bankruptcy, it seemed that it was inevitable. However, weeks earlier, whilst I identified some likelihood that the bank could collapse, the probability I attributed to this was relatively (and mistakenly) low. To some extent, my wrong assumption was clouded by a recent experience. The market had seen Bear Sterns, a smaller investment bank, being bailed out and sold to J.P. Morgan several months earlier. Hence, much of the market, including myself, mistakenly made the assumption that Lehman Brothers would benefit from a bailout if it was needed. It is an entirely different question whether saving Lehman Brothers would have averted a crisis or simply delayed it. Our point about Bear Sterns links back to our earlier point in Chapter 6, that expectations are heavily impacted by the observer's viewpoint.

Part of the difficulty with market crises is that they are by their nature unpredictable and often emanate from different places, even if the final price action is woefully familiar: a pummeling of risky assets. The cause is also frightfully common, namely too much leverage. There are many (novel) ways in which an excessive amount of leverage can manifest itself. As a result, the path from the cause to the ultimate result of a market crisis can be difficult to predict, and sometimes requires some lateral thinking. The problem is, of course, that even if we might be able to identify many possible scenarios it is relatively easy to assign misguided probabilities to them.

Lateral thinking to a conclusion

Throughout this chapter, our focus has been on espousing the benefits of lateral thinking for investors wishing to make decisions. In part, owing to the increasing specialization in markets, it can be tempting for investors to view the market purely through the prism of their home market and ignore everything else. This is the precise opposite of a lateral approach to trading.

In particular, we held up the example of Thales, who was successfully active in many areas, including philosophy, mathematics, astronomy, and trading. Indeed, his polymath approach heavily contrasts to that of specialists who are trading the markets today. In general, even outside the world of finance, professional roles are becoming ever more specialized.

Admittedly today, given the progress of knowledge and the time we have, it would be difficult for anyone to become an expert in many fields, as Thales was. Indeed, whilst the tasks we do in our day might differ today, compared with Thales' era the time you have remains a limiting factor.

However, this should not imply that we cannot use small insights gained from a multitude of different areas to inform our view on markets. In particular, we should always remember that markets are interrelated. Hence, even if we are trading just one market, we should be conscious of what is happening in other markets. It might even help identify a new trading opportunity, which would never have occurred to us. The key is to make a judgment call when allocating time to various potential trading ideas. With experience and a considerable amount of work, investors can slowly get a feeling for which types of investigation are likely to yield positive results and which are less likely to be successful. If you think laterally too much when it comes to trading, eventually the noise will overwhelm you. Lateral thinking should also not be used as an excuse to justify trading ideas which appear to have no plausible explanation but seem to have reasonable historical performance. However, no lateral thinking at all would be like trading with blinkers on, and would involve ignoring risks. It is all about balance: listen enough, but not too much that it proves distracting.

8
The Silk Road and Its Secrets: Is There Really a "Secret Sauce" in Trading?

> So soft to touch its threads so deftly weaved,
> By hands Asian to flow to Rome so eased,
> Carried across deserts and paths and more,
> Destined for those Romans never called poor.

Images from the Silk Road

Think of the Silk Road for a moment. When I do this, several images seem to project themselves inside my mind. I see rich Romans clothed in Chinese silk, the colors bright and slightly intoxicating. I visualize large caravans of traders and their camels traversing central Asia, laden with luxurious goods destined for the West. However, other than these intensely clichéd images, before writing this book there was little else I could tell you about the Silk Road. I suspect that you, the reader, will probably be endowed with more knowledge.

To try to alleviate my ignorance of the subject, I sought an introduction to the route by reading Colin Thubron's *Shadow of the Silk Road* (Thubron, 2012). Rather than seeking to buffet the reader with fact after fact, Thubron instead undertakes his own modern journey along the Silk Road, interweaving his experiences with its history. I also used as a reference Valerie Hansen's *The Silk Road: A New History* (Hansen, 2012). She takes a very different approach to telling the story of the Silk Road, using as the basis of her investigation contemporary documents detailing specific trades along the route amongst other things, as well as some more unusual sources, such as the graffiti painted by travelers and other archeological evidence.

However, having read Thubron's observant account and delved into various sections of Hansen's book, it seems that to some extent the whole notion of a Silk Road is a misnomer. Silk was of course carried from the East to the West. Spices were another high-value commodity which travelled along the route. But it was not purely goods which travelled along the Silk Road; just as important as the actual goods were the ideas that were able to travel this route. For example, the technique of papermaking made its way from China to Europe along the road. Somewhat fortuitously, Hansen points out that the high value of paper at the time meant that many documents relating to the Silk Road were preserved (which is somewhat ironic: it seems equivalent to preserving a painting for the value of its frame). The actual volume of trade along the routes was relatively small, Hansen suggests. However, the relatively exotic nature of the flow and also the nature of the cultural exchanges made possible has elevated the Silk Road's importance in history. For example, it aided the exchange of languages between travelers at a time when it was more difficult to hear or learn foreign languages. Most notably, the cultural exchange from the Silk Road came from the movement of people along the route. Refugees brought their cultures and beliefs to places where they settled.

The term the Silk Road is actually a concoction from the nineteenth century, invented by Friedrich von Richthofen. Whereas the phrase seems to suggest that it was a single road, it was actually a collection of paths which intersected at major oasis towns. Hansen contrasts the lack of a clearly marked path with major Roman roads such as the Appian Way. Indeed, she notes that guides were often hired to aid travelers find their way along the Silk Road, given it was relatively ill defined. Whilst goods might have travelled the entire way between China and Ancient Rome, contrary to popular belief, the same merchants did not accompany these goods for the whole distance. Instead, the goods passed through multiple traders along the way, progressively becoming more expensive. Today, the same phenomenon occurs with global trade. Goods which at their source are cheap are progressively marked up by intermediaries before they reach the hands of consumers, often in the West.

Blurring the origins

Aside from escalating costs because of a large number of middlemen, goods being passed from source to origin in this way had another effect. Unsurprisingly, there was often a relative lack of knowledge about the true origins of some of the goods, in both the East and the West. More simply, their origins were blurred. In the case of silk, Thubron notes, some Romans thought it grew on trees, perhaps because of their familiarity with the production of cotton. Some had theories which were much closer to reality. Pliny the Elder, writing in the first century AD, had a somewhat different idea:

> The larva then becomes a caterpillar, after which it assumes the state in which it is known as bombylis, then that called necy-dalus, and after that, in six months, it becomes a silk-worm. These insects weave webs similar to

those of the spider, the material of which is used for making the more costly and luxurious garments of females, known as "bombycina".

(Elder, Bostock (trans), & Riley (trans), 1855)

Indeed, Pliny the Elder's description seems much closer to the real way in which silk is produced. It is obtained from the cocoons of mulberry silkworm larvae, feeding on a diet of mulberry leaves. At the same time, the Chinese, who were familiar with silk, thought that there was an animal whose young created cotton. If we consider how silk is created, then maybe this was a reasonable guess, even if wrong. Sometimes investors familiar with one area of finance make similar mistakes, thinking that whatever approach they use for their home market can automatically work elsewhere. This is a theme we have discussed already.

Thubron tells the legend of how silk was discovered. The Yellow Emperor reigned from 2697 to 2597 BC. It is said that his wife, Empress Lei-zu, witnessed the flight of a moth from its cocoon, after seeing a silkworm eating mulberry leaves. She unwrapped the cocoon after accidentally dipping it in tea, to reveal silk. It is said that she eventually became a teacher in the art of creating silk and farming the silkworm. There is some archeological evidence which suggests that silk production was actually undertaken earlier, however (Tsang, 1995).

As we have noted, what were considered to be exotic spices were also carried westwards. As with silk, there was a lack of understanding about the precise source of these exotic spices. Herodotus, writing in the fifth century BC, somewhat earlier than the establishment of the Silk Road but at a time when the Persian Royal Road was in existence, mentions a "probable account" of how cinnamon was obtained:

Cinnamon they collect in a yet more marvelous manner than this: for where it grows and what land produces it they are not able to tell, except only that some say (and it is a probable account) that it grows in those regions where Dionysus was brought up; and they say that large birds carry those dried sticks which we have learnt from the Phoenicians to call cinnamon, carry them, I say, to nests which are made of clay and stuck on to precipitous sides of mountains, which man can find no means of scaling. With regard to this then the Arabians practice the following contrivance:- they divide up the limbs of the oxen and asses that die and of their other beasts of burden, into pieces as large as convenient, and convey them to these places, and when they have laid them down not far from the nests, they withdraw to a distance from them: and the birds fly down and carry the limbs of the beasts of burden off to their nests; and these are not able to bear them, but break down and fall to the earth; and the men come up to them and collect the cinnamon. Thus cinnamon is collected and comes from this nation to the other countries of the world.

(Herodotus & Macaulay (trans), 1890)

In the case of silk, we have tried to explain some of the misunderstanding around its origins by using the historical viewpoint of ancient Romans, in the context of their understanding of cotton production. We have already used this idea of differing viewpoints when discussing how the different viewpoints of traders can impact how they judge the likelihood of Black Swan events in markets (see Chapter 6). In particular, we focused on differing viewpoints with respect to proximity to historical events.

For Herodotus' "probable account" of how cinnamon was obtained, it seems very difficult to give an explanation like this, related to a misunderstanding based on the context. I somewhat doubt that in Ancient Greece it was common for agricultural produce to be delivered in the beaks of birds from the sides of mountains! A more plausible explanation is that some entrepreneurial spice traders took it upon themselves to spread this wildly imaginative story: it would add to the exoticism of the product they were selling and also help to justify its expense. It would also no doubt discourage others from entering the cinnamon business and thereby increasing competition. In a sense, this is no different from financial markets, where there is often said to be a "secret sauce" encompassing magically complicated ideas, which supposedly underpin very successful trading strategies.

Later in the chapter, we discuss the idea of a "secret sauce" in financial markets in more detail. In particular, I give my opinion about whether or not I think such a "secret sauce" exists for trading strategies. We also ask whether, like the cinnamon-carrying birds, it is mystique rather than anything else. However, first let us discuss the secret of silk!

The secret of silk

Whilst there was some confusion over precisely how silk was created, what was certain was that it was a very desirable and expensive commodity for ancient Romans. We have noted that whilst there might have been some confusion about how it was made, some ancient Romans had a vague idea about how it was created. However, it was not until the sixth century AD that the precise knowhow spread to the West. This smuggling exercise is summarized by Hunt (2011), based on an ancient account in the eighth book of Procopius' epic *History of the Wars* (Procopius & Dewing (trans), 1989). The series of books largely tells the story of Justinian's various wars in the sixth century AD, as well as telling how silk was finally smuggled to the west. It is said that monks were sent to China, and on their return they secretly brought back silkworms in hollow bamboo walking canes. They were also able to bring back mulberry plants, another crucial part of the silk-making process. As a result, a Byzantine silk industry began to grow, becoming an important part of Byzantium's trade. Hence, the monopoly which China had on the silk industry and Persia's control of the flow of silk to the West were weakened.

In the case of silk, the "secret" of how it was made was not so much the problem. Knowledge of this slowly seeped out to the West, as we have indicated. In the end, the main issue was access to the raw materials for silk manufacture. In trading, the equipment in most cases, unless we are talking about very high-frequency trading, is generally not the limiting factor. Most banks already heavily invest in their technology infrastructure. I have yet to hear traders complaining that they lost money because their computers were too slow. Clearly, capital is also a factor. Without any capital, it is not possible to trade. Could it be that what separates traders the most are their ideas (and, broadly speaking, human capital, the "software" which runs capital)? The question of whether these ideas constitute a "secret sauce" for markets is a pertinent question. It is this that we shall explore during the rest of the chapter, following a brief interlude.

Different route, same destination, and the "secret sauce"

We take a brief digression from the Silk Road for a moment, although keeping with the idea of a "secret sauce." Some of the tales of *The Thousand and One Nights* or more simply *Arabian Nights* (Burton, 2004) are very well known in the Western world, such as Aladdin and Ali Baba (Britannica, 2013); the first Western translation was made by Antoine Gallard in 1704 (Galland, 2004). Less well known, perhaps, is the central story which acts as a frame for all these various tales. King Shahryar discovers his wife has been unfaithful. He proceeds to vent his anger upon all the women of his kingdom, marrying a new wife each day and then executing her. Eventually, only the two daughters of his vizier remain, one of whom is named Scheherazade. Rather than accepting her fate, she starts to tell the king stories to save herself and her sister. So enamored is he with the stories that he wishes to hear more, so each night he spares her for another day.

However, there is someone who could put even Scheherazade to shame with the number of interesting stories he knows, gathered from living in a varied array of places in Europe and also Down Under. That person is Kurt Magnus, one of my former colleagues who has been working in the foreign exchange market since the 1990s, both as an options trader and as a salesman. Perhaps my favorite Kurt story is the occasion when he was on his regular Stockholm flight (he commutes between London and Stockholm every week). To his left, he struck up a conversation with a Swede, who I imagine make up a large contingent of the passengers on a Friday Stockholm-bound flight. As you would, he asked his neighbor his name and what he did. Acting was the reply. After a hearty conversation for the rest of the flight, it was only when Kurt returned home that he realized this man was rather more famous than he had let on. To prove that the episode had taken place, Kurt had a photograph, which he showed a group of us at drinks.

I recently had lunch with him in the City of London whilst I was trying to gather ideas for my book. He assured me that the pub we were in had the finest fish and chips in London, and I must confess it did. For whatever reason, whilst London has foods from every possible place on earth, it is rare to find an exceptional plate of fish and chips. With his tie emblazoned with kangaroos and cufflinks shaped like a map of Australia, Kurt then proceeded to make suggestions about my book in his trademark Australian twang (he is Australian, in case you haven't already guessed). He noted how money provided liquidity in a way which bartering, a feature of some ancient societies, could not do. Very often with bartering, the problem he noted is that the two parties might find it difficult to exchange services or goods which both parties actually want.

Whilst much of what I mentioned to Kurt about the book was about Ancient Greece and Rome, alongside a dose of finance, he noted that I had not discussed the Incas at all. I had to confess that I knew very little about them. However, the day after our meeting I immediately proceeded to research the subject.

The Incan civilization was somewhat later than the Ancient Greeks or Romans. Like other civilizations of the Americas it grew up totally independently from the rest of the world, notably Europe, Africa, and Asia. Indeed, given this independence, it is not surprising there were notable differences. In particular, the economy did not use money extensively; instead, bartering was the most common medium of exchange. Necessities including food were organized by the state, which helped reduce the need for anything resembling money (McEwan, 2006). The economy was heavily centrally managed in contrast to a market economy.

Despite having a very different economy, the Incas were still able to create a sophisticated and relatively wealthy civilization. Their skill, for example, in building can be seen today in the ruins of Machu Picchu in Peru. They did not learn how to build such magnificent structures from the Romans. If we think back to the Silk Road, we see something similar. We noted that it was a collection of various paths, which allowed goods to travel between east and west. Which path was traveled was immaterial, however, provided the goods reached their intended destination.

Within the market, we can see very similar parallels, of traders taking different paths but reaching the same endpoint. Whilst different traders work totally independently of one another, there seem to be commonalities in how they trade and the various strategies they employ. If they are trading the same market, using the same data and the same approach, then perhaps this outcome is expected. Admittedly, the fact that traders move around various financial institutions does cloud this point (contrasting with the lack of any information flow from the Romans to the Incas). Very often hedge funds will be highly protective of their intellectual property in terms of how they implement specific trading strategies, in particular when it comes to systematic trading. Whilst they will often describe the general approach they use, for example saying that it is trend-following or statistical arbitrage, to give a couple of examples, they are unlikely to go into particular details. This is not surprising given the likely investment which needs to be undertaken when implementing such strategies, both in terms of time but also technology, as well as the issues around crowding.

As we have noted, trading strategies will often have been developed independently of their equivalents at other firms. I have never heard of two competing hedge funds sitting down with one another to compare notes about their precise trading strategies. I remember an occasion, whilst I was working at Lehman Brothers, when I was helping to host a models dinner. Unfortunately, it was quantitative trading models we were talking about, not stunning women off the Parisian catwalk, who could also do with a burger and chips every so often. It took place in the client meeting rooms at the top of our skyscraper in the Canary Wharf district of London, which afforded panoramic views over much of the city. Some of our client attendees were relatively animated at the dinner, describing their approach to trading. However, when it came to some funds who were direct competitors, they were very careful not to say anything which could potentially be heard by one of their rivals. Yet, in spite of this anecdote illustrating the relative lack of communication between funds, there is often some element of correlation between fund returns and direct competitors. As an example, the returns of various funds which predominantly use trend-following have a reasonable amount of correlation with each other.

This observation should not be a surprise. Even if they are working independently of one another, if their general objective is to use trend-following strategies, then there should be some element of correlation. If there were no correlation, then it would imply that they were implementing a totally different type of strategy, which could not be classified as trend-following. Even more broadly, it is likely that many funds within a specific asset class will exhibit some level of correlation, given that they will probably employ similar strategies. At least on a generalized level, at least in FX, we noted in Chapter 3 that most fund returns can be approximated by a mixture of relatively generic strategies (trend and carry). Hence, at least within FX, this point suggests that generally the majority of funds are employing relatively similar strategies. We might expect that these findings are likely to apply to other asset classes too, not purely to FX funds.

So what could be the "secret sauce?" The details, rather than the grand idea

So, if many strategies are similar, what precisely could constitute a "secret sauce?" We may conjecture that the differences between various funds are more in terms of the details of implementation, rather than the general strategies they employ; we suggest these are likely to be similar and account for the high level of correlations between funds. When all these subtle differences are added up, they can considerably improve the performance of the strategy. This also includes the skills required to run and implement a trading strategy. It could also simply be a case of having sufficient knowledge gleaned over years about a particular market to be able to squeeze out the last few cents from a trading idea. These barriers to entry could also constitute part of the "secret sauce." At the very simplest level, a trader needs access to capital, another barrier to entry. Stating the blatantly obvious, without capital a trader is not going to be able to generate returns. Indeed, the same was true of silk. Even if at some level some of the Ancient Romans seemed to have a general idea of how to create silk, it would be futile without silkworms.

Hence, the idea of some amazing "secret sauce" based upon a single secret in trading seems unlikely, and indeed this is the message from Narang (2009). Just because a strategy is complicated it does not necessary mean that it is better. Whilst there might be some appeal in a super-complicated black box trading strategy which has amazing returns, I for one would have difficulty running such a trading strategy with my own money! If a trader has no idea why a trading system is undertaking a trade, it becomes very difficult to remain invested in a strategy when it starts to perform poorly. The inclination is simply to throw away such a model when performance starts to deteriorate. By contrast, when a trading strategy is simpler and a trader can understand why it is making or losing money, it is easier to allocate capital to it and to have some confidence in it. Keep trading ideas simple: the detail is in the precise implementation.

The mystique of a "secret sauce"

So what is the value of perpetuating the idea of some "secret sauce" that is based upon some very novel trading idea, rather than saying it is related to the precise details of an implementation? If anything, from a marketing perspective there is value in framing a strategy as more complicated than it really is. If a fund is trying to attract investors, it probably does not want to say it is just running the same strategy as all its competitors with a few interesting tweaks (my definition of "secret sauce"). This is probably more difficult to sell as an idea, even if the strategy performs far better than competitors. Hence, sometimes excessive secrecy in a trading strategy has the added by-product of creating mystique. When something is unobtainable or has some element of mystique around it, it suddenly becomes that bit more appealing. I would call this excessive secrecy and mystique which accompanies trading strategies the "cinnamon complex," harking back to Herodotus' outlandish explanation for the origin of cinnamon. This "cinnamon complex" can work both ways, however. For example, if a fund's strategy is totally opaque, investors might not be so willing to hand over capital to invest, regardless of the performance. They might also be less willing to accept periods of underperformance, which are inevitable for any trader.

From a trading perspective, the benefits of being secretive are largely dependent upon the capacity of a trading strategy within the market. This is a factor we have discussed before, in Chapter 2 for example. If we are running a trading strategy which trades on a lower frequency, we might be able to be more open about the general idea, given that it is less likely the strategy could be crowded out quickly. This might not be true of very high-frequency strategies, where any leakage about the precise details of a strategy or even the general idea behind it could blunt its effectiveness through crowding out. In this instance, perhaps the "cinnamon complex" is more justified than in other parts of the market.

There is another point against the idea of a "secret sauce" relating to a very novel trading idea, which we mentioned before in Chapter 2. Trading strategies do not work forever without some element of adaptation through time, especially when they are more specialized and have more characteristics associated with alpha. This is true in particular when the market capacity is less, such as in high-frequency strategies, when too many investors are chasing the same strategy. Indeed, my personal experience of having real money invested in strategies that I have developed and my discussions with traders seems to add credence to this point. I remember running a profitable intraday FX strategy for just over 12 months with real cash at Lehman Brothers several years ago. Ironically, in theoretical simulation it did extremely well in the weeks following the Lehman bankruptcy, although for obvious reasons Lehman Brothers was never able to run the strategy with real cash during that period, given it was a bankrupt institution! However, the last time I looked at the very same strategy, several years later, it had become unprofitable. There could be several reasons for this. We might suspect that the strategy had been crowded out. However, I suspect the more important reason was simply a change in the way the market traded with the advent of quantitative easing. Later strategies I developed, whilst having some similar characteristics, were profitable. Hence, the ability to continually come up with new ideas, especially if we are seeking alpha, is necessary if one is to be an effective trader, and can also be part of the idea of a "secret sauce."

It is a misconception that some within the market think they can run someone else's trading strategy without having knowledge of all the various intricacies. If you have not spent the time developing an idea and are not familiar with the details, it is very often difficult to begin trading it. Yes, you might be able to place some risk on it and even profit from it, but what would happen if the strategy starts to develop problems? It amounts to not having a clear understanding of the risks involved. This brings us back to our point about black box trading systems, where we have no idea why they are generating specific trades:

when they go wrong, the only solution is to turn off the system, even though it could mean missing out on future outperformance. In Chapter 9, we describe how certain trading strategies will suit different traders. Very often different investors will also have varying ideas on how to construct their investment targets (see Chapter 5).

In summary, my opinion is that the "secret sauce" is more a case of a trading strategy known to market participants which has been implemented very well, rather than a single overriding near-mythical idea. It is likely that it is the subtle details that make the difference between profitability and mediocrity. These details constitute the strategy's "secret sauce." There is certainly a case for protecting these details, to give a competitive advantage. It can also be the case that the continual improvement of a strategy over time can end up constituting a "secret sauce."

I think it is more the case that marketing (or excessive secrecy, which we named the "cinnamon complex") is the likely reason why some investors seem to think there is a "secret sauce," based on very unusual trading approaches. In some cases, this type of secrecy might be justified if a strategy has very low capacity and the spread of the idea might render it unprofitable. However, in cases where capacity is high, perhaps this is more of a marketing exercise.

The lack of a "secret sauce" based upon very unusual trading strategies explains why strategies between competing funds can be correlated (as you would expect). At the same time, the differences in the details of implementation go some way toward explaining the relatively large discrepancies in the performance of what appear to be similar funds.

Adaptation and diversification is another element of the "secret sauce"

We have suggested that there is not really a "secret sauce" in trading (in particular in systematic trading) as some market participants would think of it. Indeed, very often, having a super-complicated algorithm which is difficult to understand can be counterproductive. This is particularly the case when it is impossible to understand why it is losing money. Instead, we think that the "secret sauce" can be a combination of factors, with hard work at the source of it. One important element which we have noted is being able to implement the details of a particular trading strategy effectively.

Aside from how a specific strategy works, we think that there are actually many other elements which should be adhered to which constitute other elements of the "secret sauce." Amongst these elements is the ability to continually work on new strategies, hone existing ones, and adapt to new market environments. It is also the case that through experience we might be able to identify new strategies. If I think of the types of strategies that I have developed in later years, I am quite sure that these would not have been things I would have even considered earlier on in my career.

Just as key to the "secret sauce" is money management. Understanding how to allocate capital to various strategies and diversification, as we discussed in Chapter 4, is one of the most important parts of the investment process. No matter how good your individual trade or strategy might be, the amount of money you make is proportional to the amount of capital allocated to a particular strategy or trade. If too little capital is deployed in a strategy, even if risk returns are favorable, the actual USD amount of returns might be minimal. Furthermore, allocating too much capital to a strategy increases the risks: in particular, what would happen if we had a drawdown which consumed a large amount of our capital.

Also, the ability to decipher the performance of a trading strategy is a key element of the "secret sauce." At the very simplest level, this involves assessing what the returns are. However, on a deeper level it requires an understanding of how the returns of a trade or a particular strategy are related to the markets. Notably, we need to ask the question why, something which has cropped up in various guises in this book.

When is a strategy simply underperforming? Or is the underperformance severe enough to indicate a structural break in the idea? If this is the case, we should reduce exposure to that strategy quickly. It is also just as important to ask these questions when a strategy is outperforming. If we are unable to understand why this is occurring, we might suddenly get all bulled up and allocate a lot of extra capital to it. This is fine if it manages to outperform in the future, but would result in outsized losses if that performance does not persist.

In Chapter 9, we shall go into more detail about understanding historical trading performance, and in particular the question of why rather than simply how much it returns. Very often, it is "how much?" which takes precedence in investors' minds, rather than "why?".

Further thoughts on the "secret sauce"

Whilst I have my own view on the "secret sauce" of trading, I was also keen to ask others working within the industry what they thought, given it is something that is very difficult to evaluate objectively. There is little chance of proving the idea, as the only way in which this could be done would be to have all the various trading strategies of the most successful funds and assess their complexity. That seems to be a very unlikely scenario.

Hence, our only alternative is to answer the question with a more subjective approach: by canvasing opinions on it. In particular, I thought I would ask one of my friends who is a financial markets researcher. He has worked on the buy side for many years (more than me, I might add), and he possesses a strong background in quantitative trading models within foreign exchange markets.

Also, more recently he has worked on a more cross-asset basis. As a result, he possesses more cross-market knowledge than I have gathered.

Many of his comments on a "secret sauce" echoed my thoughts, but at the same time he added some interesting points that had escaped my consideration. At a philosophical level, his first point was that the idea of a "secret sauce" belonged to the realm of concepts such as "talent" or "discretionary management." Indeed, how can you define if someone is "talented" in a broad sense? Furthermore, is success in any enterprise simply a result of "talent" or a product of hard work and a methodological application of a learnable process? I certainly do not wish to attempt to answer these questions, as I am not a philosopher, unlike Thales of Miletus. By implication, if we cannot define a concept easily, it makes it difficult to replicate. Indeed, I suppose this is the idea behind labeling someone as "talented" or a trading approach as a "secret sauce." If anyone or any strategy earns such labels, it becomes more valuable because it cannot be easily replicated. It goes back to my earlier point about the notion of a "secret sauce" within trading being partially motivated by marketing considerations and the creation of a mystique.

My friend made the point that at least when it comes definable strategies, particularly in systematic trading, most specialists know all the different types of strategy in their particular asset class. I would have to concur with him on this from my currency-centric viewpoint. There are notable exceptions, such as very high-frequency strategies (so-called algo trading) or what he would term "rocket scientist" concepts. To some extent these concepts are not as well known because it is a newer field, and also because the mathematical complexity can create a barrier to entry. Significant time is required to overcome these.

In general, though, my friend said that making strategies as simple as possible is important, to paraphrase Occam's razor. William of Ockham lived in the Middle Ages from 1287 to 1347. He was born in the village of Ockham in Surrey, today a short drive south of London. As well as being a philosopher he was a Franciscan friar. The term Occam's razor was coined by Sir William Hamilton in the 1850s. The sentiment has been explained in many ways over the centuries by many philosophers, as evidenced by the countless quotations available on Wikipedia (Wikipedia, 2014) on the topic, right back to Aristotle. One of the most popular ways of expressing the idea was written by John Punch in the seventeenth century:

entities must not be multiplied beyond necessity.

(Bauer, 2007)

Whilst the idea has its origins in the ancient world, it is just as relevant today when it comes to trading. Unnecessary complexity simply burdens a trading strategy with more parameters and gives more opportunity to data-mine too much, resulting in a model which is highly unstable. The same is true when you make discretionary decisions. If you look at too many factors, it can complicate the decision-making process. If you fly between two cities you can take a connecting flight. However, it would be far quicker and more efficient to fly directly. Simple is usually best. It is a topic we shall return to later in the book, and have touched upon already.

Another point my friend made is that he is relatively open with the general idea of the strategies he has employed, even if he is not willing to describe the details, which is totally understandable. Indeed, I have found this to be the case with many clients whom I have talked to over the years. Whilst some have been very secretive, a large number have been relatively open with the types of ideas they use, especially those who trade at lower frequencies. The main rationale is of course that these strategies are not really secrets anymore. This goes back to my earlier point that the value is in the details of a strategy rather than the general principles, which tend to be relatively similar across various hedge funds in a particular sector. This can be seen when we calculate correlations between funds in a sector. Often we find large positive correlations between many of them. For example, a point my friend made is that from his experience it is likely some CTAs base their strategies around relatively similar trend-following rules, even if this is not outwardly what they say.

Whilst money management is important, as I have alluded to before, my friend notes that it can sometimes be used in inappropriate ways: for example, using stops and take profits to make an unprofitable strategy suddenly profitable. Intuitively, if a simple version of a strategy is not profitable, it would point to the fact that the initial idea might need some work. Furthermore, money management should not mask the original ideas behind the strategies being employed. If a strategy which uses trend-following ideas makes money during ranging periods in price action, but not during trending periods after some funky jiggery-pokery has been employed, it suggests that money management has interfered with the original rationale of the strategy. It returns to our earlier point: how are you supposed to risk-manage strategies which are incomprehensible to you?

If anything, my friend suggests, he would much rather have a suite of relatively simple strategies. He thinks the real value of money management is in terms of allocation of risk toward these strategies, and that is where considerable energy should be spent. Finally, he jokingly adds that perhaps the "secret sauce" is related to a bit of humility and common sense. I have in the past witnessed an absence of both of these. Success suddenly causes humility to vanish and in its place an idea that risks are asymmetric, where the downside is minimal and the upside is without bounds. Unfortunately, such behavior ends in tears (or in bonuses, on occasion).

So, in summary, my friend doubts the existence of "secret sauce" in the way that some investors might define it. Indeed, if there is any sort of "secret sauce" he can point to, it is the use of sound and well-established methodology, which can result in profitable trading strategies. The only way to prove that a "secret sauce" exists would be to learn about it. By then, it would hardly be a secret anymore; it would just be a sauce.

Concluding our discussion about the Silk Road

We began this chapter by discussing the Silk Road. We noted how it became a route to exchange between east and west not only goods but also ideas. As goods were passed through multiple hands, their origins became blurred. In the void, stories were conjectured up about their origins. In particular we noted the example of cinnamon. There are significant parallels with trading today and the Silk Road. For one, we noted that many Silk Road traders took different routes to get to similar end points. This seems to have a parallel in trading strategies, which can be independently created yet amount to something relatively similar. At the same time, there is often said to be the notion of a "secret sauce" to trading, which encompasses some grand ideas. Like the tales told about cinnamon, we think that they are largely exaggerated and are what we term the "cinnamon complex." The ability to come up with new ideas and the ability to continually hone them is key. Resting on your laurels is not the way to become a successful trader! Incidentally, the idiom "resting on your laurels" has its origins in Ancient Greece. Laurel wreaths were associated with victory and were presented to winners at the Pythian Games, part of the Panhellenic Games.

Aside from honing a strategy, money management is also crucial: understanding when to cut off losing trading strategies and when to allocate more capital to them. There needs to be a decision about whether under- or overperformance is purely a temporary phenomenon or something more permanent. Perhaps the best way we can encapsulate it is in the following. Whilst it is somewhat less sexy than the notion that there are grand ideas which can generate hugely profitable trading ideas, we think that it is the details that make the difference. These differences in the details explain how relatively similar funds can have such different performance.

9
The Father of History: This Time Is Sometimes Different in Markets

> The words of men they tell us the stories,
> Of times gone past written in The Histories,
> Of wars of Greece, ancient, fought with Persia,
> So told to us for our memories' nurture.

Herodotus, the "father of history"

We have peppered a large amount of the book with quotations from Herodotus' mammoth text *The Histories of Herodotus* (Herodotus & Macaulay (trans), 1890), also known more succinctly as *The Histories*. It remains a very well-known work millennia after it was written, as evidenced by the plethora of translations available. These include a recent one by Tom Holland, which was published whilst I was writing my book (Herodotus & Holland (trans), 2013). I found Holland's translation very readable, and the book also contains an enlightening introduction by Paul Cartledge. Alongside this, I have used quotations from an older text (Herodotus & Macaulay (trans), 1890), which I would also recommend. A somewhat lighter introduction can be found in *Travels with Herodotus* (Kapuscinski, 2008), which mixes the thoughts of Polish journalist Ryszard Kapuscinski during his own travels with passages from Herodotus. If you enjoy Kapuscinski's take on Herodotus, I would also recommend his book *The Shadow of the Sun* (Kapuscinski, 2002) about his experiences in Africa.

Herodotus was born in Halicarnassus (earning him the name Herodotus of Halicarnassus), which today is the town of Bodrum in Turkey. His birthplace lies nearly an hour and a half's drive from the ancient site of Miletus, Thales' home. Much of what we know about Herodotus is based on his own writing. He lived in the fifth century BC, around a century after Thales. Cartledge also notes that he is likely to have spent a large amount of time in Athens, given it was the hub of intellectual activity, and that his last days were probably spent in southern Italy.

Herodotus' book largely concerns the wars between the Greeks and the Persians, the Greco-Persian Wars in the fifth century BC, as he recounts in the first line:

> This is the Showing forth of the Inquiry of Herodotus of Halicarnassus, to the end that neither the deeds of men may be forgotten by lapse of time, nor the works great and marvelous, which have been produced some by Hellenes and some by Barbarians, may lose their renown; and especially that the causes may be remembered for which these waged war with one another.
>
> (Herodotus & Macaulay (trans), 1890)

Herodotus is well known as the "father of history," a title given to him by the Roman politician and philosopher (amongst many other roles he had) Cicero. Cartledge writes that many of the techniques that Herodotus uses would be familiar to modern historians, for example the way he distinguishes between various sources, such as those of eyewitnesses and secondary sources. In some instances, he comments on the validity of his sources, at times affirming his skepticism of them. Furthermore, Cartledge suggests that he is keen not only to recount events, but also to understand the reasoning behind them. Notably, he tries to address the causes of the war between the Greeks and Persians, which we see in the opening quotation. It is often the question "why?" rather than purely "what?" which makes history so engaging.

However, others have been less flattering in their descriptions of Herodotus; he has been called the "father of lies." One criticism is that Herodotus too often attributes the outcome of events to the will of various Greek gods.

Indeed, some of his stories seem slightly outlandish to a modern reader (or even perhaps to an ancient reader). At times, they appear to be more fictional than a purely objective view of historical events, even if Herodotus does sometimes note his own skepticism. Indeed, Herodotus has been named a "storyteller" by some, including Aristotle. This seems at odds with the concept of him as a chronicler of events. Whatever view you might have concerning Herodotus, though, it seems difficult to deny that he was a pioneer in the field of history. He raises the notion that looking at history was important and, as he notes in his first line, the events he writes of should not be forgotten.

That is at the crux of the study of history, of course: that the lessons and events of the past should not be forgotten. As we discussed in Chapter 6, the way we think about Black Swan events is related to our historical context. If we have not lived or worked through a Black Swan event which has afflicted markets, we are less inclined to think about the likelihood of similar events. As a result, our decision-making process is likely to be different from that of market participants who have been through such upheaval. Furthermore, even if we have lived through such events, memories are short. In particular, our viewpoint could be skewed by events which have occurred more recently. Hence, we are tempted to avoid taking a more rounded view of both the history of markets and our own experiences in markets. Having no knowledge of history sets us up to make precisely the same mistakes.

Markets change, even if people don't

We generally observe that markets change over time following general economic cycles. Mirroring this, investors often change their behavior within an economic cycle from pessimism in a crash to euphoria as the market rallies. We might conjecture that this pattern ends up being repeated. Certainly, the repeated cycles of boom and bust over the ages seem to confirm this idea. Folly has been the friend of any ruler who thinks he or she can banish the economic cycle. I shall refrain from bringing up various quotations from politicians who have claimed to banish the notion of boom and bust, but I am sure a few examples spring to mind!

Hence, the general behavior of investors can be seen to persist over a long period of time around the various machinations of the economic cycle. A theme we have repeatedly discussed throughout this book is that the cause of market crises is often too much leverage. This occurs when greed has overridden an investor's other emotions. Conversely, during crises it is fear which overrides all else and causes the rapid capitulation of investors. Indeed, the fact that we regularly have market crises seems to add credence to the point that there is some persistence in how investors behave in different eras. What else would explain why market crises impacted the ancient world just as they do today? Whilst technology has obviously become more advanced, humans are still governed by the same emotions when it comes to trading. They just use different trading instruments to inflict pain in times of market crisis.

Hence, looking at historical data and also our experience should be able to provide some insight into how we trade in the future (even if it is not a perfect prediction), provided we do it in a diligent way. In particular, we need to make sure that we do not simply frame trading decisions by viewing the very recent past only. Our time frame should not simply be the past few weeks, but at least the past few years and perhaps even longer. This is particularly the case when we are attempting to analyze market crises. We discuss these themes in more detail in the remainder of the chapter.

Why backtest a trading strategy?

We have discussed the relevance of looking at history, in particular examining the approach of Herodotus, the "father of history." Our emphasis has been particularly on viewing historical data and trading experience as a whole, rather

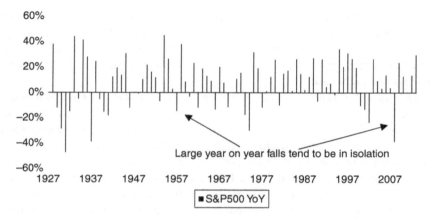

Figure 9.1   Large falls in S&P500 tend to be isolated in specific years
Source: Thalesians, Bloomberg Finance L.P.

than falling into the trap of only focusing on the immediate past. There are several questions we wish to answer.

First, what is the point of looking at the historical performance of a trading strategy (or more simply backtesting a trading strategy)? After all, as anyone can tell you, strong historical returns cannot guarantee that future performance will be quite as rosy. In particular, performance in the very short-term future need not be rosy. In Figure 9.1, we plot the year-on-year returns from S&P500, which illustrates both these points. We note that historically stocks have risen, as the reader is no doubt aware. However, there are obviously years when there have been deep falls, which have occurred in isolation. These would be very difficult to predict simply by using the very simple metric of examining the previous year's performance. Major exceptions can for example be seen around the Great Depression and the dotcom crash, where weakness persisted for several years.

Despite this, I would say that looking at historical performance is still important. To some extent it helps to validate (or invalidate) the general thought processes behind an idea.

As an example, let us say you have an idea about using a specific type of trading strategy. Let us assume that after testing the trading idea historically, you find that it is heavily loss-making. What we can gather from this is that for our strategy to be profitable in the future, there has to be a significant change in the way that markets behave; either that, or our strategy is doomed to failure and we should reconsider whether we would like to deploy real cash in running it live. The key point, which we have rattled on about on many occasions, is to have an intuitive understanding of why a trading idea has performed in a specific way historically. If we are able to understand the reasons behind historical performance, it helps us to understand the conditions required for the future profitability of the strategy. Indeed, this is the approach of historians and something introduced by Herodotus. The question "why?" is just as important as recounting events in the past or, in our case, knowing what the historical returns of a strategy are. This is even more important when the strategy is being run live with real cash.

If we have the converse situation, where a trading strategy has performed well in our historical sample, we still need to be diligent when analyzing the result. We need to be asking precisely the same questions. If we are convinced about the idea, we also need to decide whether it might persist into the future. Just as Herodotus was prepared to use some skepticism, so should investors when it comes to testing a trading idea. Furthermore, what do others think of the same idea? I am not saying that other traders have to approve of every idea you have before you run it live (on the contrary, sometimes being against the crowd can be very profitable). However, the exercise of discussing a trading strategy or even a specific trading idea can help to pick holes in your arguments. It can often be tempting to look only at positive historical returns and to use them as the sole motivation for a trade. At the same time, we might overlook any possible difficulties which might ensue from the trade.

Furthermore, backtesting a strategy need not always be a mathematical exercise which involves examining the historical returns of a trading model. Trading experience can also be seen as a backtest of sorts (possibly the best sort of backtesting). Indeed, when traders make decisions about trading, they are often implicitly leaning on their experiences and using them as a proxy for backtesting. Backtesting a strategy aims to replicate this "experience", but in, ideally, as objective a way as possible.

The key point with both backtesting and using trading experience is that we need to use a reasonable sample to make any judgment. Simply looking at price action over the very recent past as opposed to a longer period will fail to give an accurate representation of how a strategy or a trader has performed. Viewing the market through the prism of his or her recent trading performance will skew a trader's perception. We mentioned this idea in Chapter 6, on Black Swans. We noted how it is likely that a trader's proximity to historical events would impact the probability he or she would attribute to a Black Swan event in the near future. Obviously, there are cases where risk-management takes over and worst-case scenarios force the closure of trades. I admit, though, that advice such as this is easier to write than to trade in practice. The difficulty is that from a psychological perspective it is far easier to overemphasize recent trades and the profits and losses from these.

Backtesting versus real track record

We have debated the difference between the historical backtesting of a strategy and the live trading of an investor with real cash. Whether a trader is using some sort of systematic trading strategy or making discretionary trading decisions, the experience gained from trading with real cash can be very different to purely theoretical analysis.

Here we delve into this in more detail. The most obvious difference is that investing with real cash adds a strong psychological element compared with doing a historical backtest. It is not possible to backtest the pain of losing money. Your perceived pain thresholds when backtesting historically could well be far higher than when you invest in real cash. A dip on a graph showing historical theoretical losses is difficult to make more tangible in your mind.

Even once a backtest has gone well and we are happy with our general approach, there are several steps we need to take. We need to consider paper trading, basically executing trades with virtual cash. This can be seen as an out-of-sample test (we shall address this in more detail later). Even when we are happy with it, we should consider running with a small amount of real cash. We can then slowly increase our risk as we become more comfortable with our strategy and create a positive cushion of returns.

Perhaps unsurprisingly, you feel pain far more when you experience losses from real cash. Would such losses cause you to prematurely reduce risk on a strategy? When running a strategy for real, we also need to continually risk-manage the strategy and assess the P&L continually (that question "why?" again!). In particular, if a trading strategy has recently lost money, is this the result of a temporary blip or noise? Alternatively, is there some sort of structural break in the strategy related to big changes in the market? Repeatedly changing a systematic trading strategy, as we noted in Chapter 5, will render it a fully discretionary strategy. This defeats the point of a systematic trading strategy.

Furthermore, when running a trading strategy with real cash, an investor experiences all the pitfalls associated with real trading, such as the cost of execution, slippage in execution, market impact, and so on. In a theoretical backtest, a strategist needs to be very careful to simulate these real world issues. In practice, when making allowances for real world transaction costs, I try to err on the side of caution. It is better to assume slightly larger costs than you might incur in reality than smaller. At the same time, assuming massive transaction costs in backtesting can make what should be profitable strategies unprofitable in testing. This has the effect of excessively reducing your universe of possible trading strategies.

Despite the advantages of a real track record, the major disadvantage is that it takes years to accumulate. Furthermore, a real track record will be most relevant for the strategies you have selected in the past and for validating your general trading approach. It will not necessarily tell you whether totally new strategies will also be profitable. Whilst it might be the only real test of how good a trader is, producing an extended track record is often non-trivial. This is particularly so if you wish to use it to seek capital from others to trade. In that case, any track record would have to be verifiable by a third party. When the veracity of a track record is simply down to your word, investors will obviously have more difficulty accepting it, for obvious reasons.

Another advantage of a backtest is that it can be extended over a longer period of time. It can also be produced for strategies which you are not running with real cash in your portfolio. As a result it can be applicable for new strategies. We can also use backtesting for scenario analysis of trading strategies. For example, what would have happened if we had tweaked this parameter? What if we had tried a specific level of stop loss? What would have happened in the strategy over major periods of risk aversion? The list of variations and investigations is of course endless. Admittedly, the main issue with backtesting is data-mining, a topic we shall delve into in the next section. We shall also show ways of testing the robustness of strategies in later parts of this chapter.

When the data-mining gets too much

Backtesting is supposed to give some level of confidence that a trading idea has worked historically. However, there can be a significant side effect from a poorly run backtest. Notably, backtesting can fall foul to the scourge of excessive data-mining. This occurs when a strategy is overfitted on historical data. As a result, all the various model parameters have specifically been picked so they improve the various return statistics for the historical data being tested. Unfortunately, we cannot trade with real money on a historical sample. Hindsight is unavailable for the future.

The result of excessive fitting is that a trading strategy can be susceptible to breaking down in the future when there are small changes in market behavior. So you have a lovely line going upwards of returns when using historical data, which has been superfitted, and then a line which moves down when it is run live! I have observed this many times with systematic strategies, which look great historically, but out-of-sample, when money is applied to the strategy, performance starts to turn. Whilst the culprit can be a very sudden change in market behavior, my suspicion in such scenarios also points toward excessive data-mining.

The art of creating a robust trading strategy is knowing the amount of data-mining which squeezes reasonable performance from a strategy without overdoing it. Doing absolutely no data-mining (or indeed directed research) might result in missing what are otherwise good trading strategies. Also, if a strategy has absolutely appalling returns, it can be a good sanity check on the initial idea.

One way to check the stability of returns is to rerun the backtest with a variety of different parameters. This can be a good way to test whether a backtest is showing good returns because of data-mining. If it works with many different parameters, then we might consider that such a strategy is more robust. It also increases the chance that data-mining was not the overriding reason for strong performance. We also need to be aware that data-mining is not always purely a matter of parameter selection; it can also be a result of testing many different types of related trading rules.

There is also the question of whether a trading strategy works with different types of assets, which can be another test of robustness. If we are trying to use a very broad strategy such as trend or carry, extracting risk premia, then if our approach totally fails with another asset class, it would arouse suspicions that our trading approach has some flaws. One of these flaws could be related to data-mining. As ever, there are always exceptions. There can be instances where the specific microstructure of a market makes a strategy very difficult to replicate in another asset class. For example, differing levels of liquidity might make it problematic to move certain strategies between asset classes.

Considering out-of-sample backtesting is also a useful check for any trading strategy. Let us say you develop a trading strategy on data trading S&P500 between 1995 and 2005. We can then check that it works on a later sample. This helps us ascertain whether we have data-mined it too much. If it fails on the out-of-sample part, it could be the result of indulging in excessive data-mining. The alternative hypothesis is that the market has changed considerably in our out-of-sample area. The risk is obviously that when you find a strategy does not work that well out-of-sample, you go back and "optimize" it again. Then you check if this revised strategy works out-of-sample again. If this is done repeatedly, it does in effect negate the benefits of out-of-sample backtesting. If we think about it, we are fitting parameters on the part of the time series which we have defined as out-of-sample. This is precisely what we wished to avoid. One approach which traders sometimes use is to fit parameters on a recent window and then to update the parameters as new information comes in.

Historical robustness of a strategy in different market regimes

There seem to be lots of differences between backtesting and real trading. What about the similarities between backtesting and real trading, we might ask? In both cases, something we have already noted is that there is a tendency to place too much emphasis on recent performance in both instances. We should try to take a reasonable sample when analyzing performance.

In both cases, if we are using a very short time period, whether it is a backtest or a real track record, a trader might have the problem of being *fooled by randomness*, which we noted in Chapter 1. For example, if his or her strategy was to be long risky assets when markets were saturated with liquidity during their track record, low borrowing costs would be conducive to an overall market rally in risky assets. Hence, the investor was simply riding the prevailing "beta" (investment) wave which dominated the sample period, rather than extracting alpha as he or she might claim. It becomes more difficult to make this point if a real track record is for an extended period and covering a whole multitude of market regimes. With a backtest we often have larger amounts of data for our analysis. When extending our backtest history, we also need to use a bit of common sense. In the next section we shall expand upon this point.

Once we have sorted these various issues which can impact longer term backtesting samples, we have an extended canvas to work upon to try to avoid being *fooled by randomness* as much as possible. At the very least, we need to test how robust the various parameters are, to reduce the impact of data-mining, as alluded to earlier.

We also need to ask many questions to check a strategy's robustness to market regimes, ranging from short-term fluxes in the market to the longer-term macroeconomic environment. Importantly, we need to check whether its behavior over those regimes is consistent with what we expect.

For example, is the strategy sensitive to short-term shifts risk sentiment? How did it perform over a bear market in stocks, if the strategy is supposed to deliver alpha rather than beta? If a strategy is supposed to be an alpha strategy, yet only makes money when stocks are rallying, it suggests the strategy has not worked as intended. This would raise some issues with the implementation of the idea. Did it outperform during different parts of the monetary policy cycle? Did it perform better during periods of rate hikes or cuts? If a strategy that is largely designed to be long bonds profits mainly during rate hiking cycles, when yields tend to rise (and bond prices tend to fall), we might question whether our methodology is flawed. Aside from factoring in transaction costs, we also need to be very careful to properly calculate returns when we backtest. For example, carry costs can be considerable, and without them backtesting results might not be reflective of real trading results you might obtain. A backtest which fails to accurately reflect what your returns would have been over the period is unlikely to be that useful.

All these questions are not purely academic. They can help us overweight or underweight a strategy, depending on our view about the general macro-environment in the future. Sometimes this weighting can be done on a more discretionary basis. Alternatively, this approach can give us an idea for identifying systematic ways of allocating risk to various strategies, depending upon the underlying environment. We touched upon this topic in Chapter 3, when we discussed allocating capital to different market betas.

How far back should we look to test a trading idea?

It can be somewhat difficult to write a book by yourself. I have found that by far the easiest way to write a book or indeed to undertake any sort of research is to allow others to write it for you. This is possibly a facetious way of putting it. Perhaps a better way to express this sentiment is by noting that research need not always consist of having your head stuck inside a book. Very often the best research can be done by talking to other people. Journalists know this, but perhaps I was not as aware of it before as I should have been. After all, people talk back to you, people debate with you, and a book does not, even if it may inform. One of my aims when I visited Budapest whilst writing this book was to ask for ideas to fill these previously blank pages. The other (more important) reason was to spread the Thalesians from our base in London into Eastern Europe. At our very first Budapest meeting, I presented some of my work on FX volatility to an audience of quant finance professionals.

The whole idea of starting up a branch of the Thalesians in Budapest began quite randomly. I chatted with Mark Horvath after he attended our Thalesians meetings in London, and he recalled how in earlier days he had taken part in similar events in Budapest. We thought therefore that it would be a great idea to resurrect these events under the Thalesians banner. Help from Mark's friend Attila Agod proved invaluable. Attila went through the grueling logistics work of finding a venue and, more importantly, attracting an audience.

Following my presentation, discussion turned toward the idea of this book: the link between the ancient world and trading today. Many members of the audience were keen to hear more about this. Some also offered their own anecdotes concerning trading in the ancient world. One example I recall was given by Imre Koncz, one of both Mark's and Attila's friends. He noted that in the Bible Joseph suggested to the pharaoh that he should hedge the risk of seven bad years of harvest. The idea of hedging is therefore far from a modern practice. The story is explained in a somewhat tongue-in-cheek way by Kaminska (2013). Indeed, in another example from the ancient world, in Chapter 4 we noted how insurance, another way for individuals to reducing risks, was present in Ancient Babylon.

On a broader basis, I was asked whether it was relevant to make these parallels at all. After all, trading today is so different to the ancient world. Was it actually counterproductive to draw these parallels? There are instances where I would say it is totally irrelevant to make detailed comparisons. For example, we can find data on commodity prices from Ancient Babylon – but would anyone think these are of any trading relevance today? Most likely, the answer would be no, even if we might well conjecture that seasonality could be observable in these prices.

When it comes to details, I would agree that it is difficult to compare totally different eras. However, I would suggest that the general principles of how markets trade actually make certain comparisons relevant. The one caveat is that we make these comparisons in the broadest scene. We expand upon this in the next section, where we approach the question from a more philosophical point of view.

If we stick to detailed analysis of markets, the question of precisely how far we look back is very important. It is a matter which we touched on in the previous section. We have market data going back many decades; in addition, we have news feed data. Hence, if we wanted to do so, it would often be possible to backtest trading strategies going back 30 or 40 years (more for certain strategies) on daily data. Is it really necessary to go back so far? In most cases, I would argue that this is likely to be of interest as an academic exercise, but from a pure trading perspective the dynamics of how markets have traded have changed over time, as we noted in the previous section. Yes, relatively straightforward strategies (beta) may have delivered profitable returns over this long period of time, so such an exercise might be useful. However, when it comes to strategies that are less correlated to beta, essentially more specialized trading strategies (alpha), it could be that in many cases we are attempting to exploit behavior which is by its nature less sticky. Often this might be a product of more specific market microstructure, which can change over time. Furthermore, market liquidity is likely to be vastly different during a long sample, complicating any sort of backtesting. Hence, we would have to make many different assumptions about the cost of trading in different times. This is a point very often overlooked by very long-term backtests I have seen in the past. Furthermore, in certain cases some strategies might have been impossible to execute in practice, so the whole exercise of backtesting would be totally futile. We also need to ask for more exotic derivative instruments whether any price we generate for a backtest would be representative of what a trader would have quoted at the time.

This is not just an issue for exotic derivatives. For example, attempting to do a backtest of strategies which trade most emerging market currencies during the 1980s, a time when many were very difficult to trade (if not impossible), would yield results which would be purely theoretical. We would need to restrict ourselves to backtesting strategies which trade those contracts which were tradable at the time, such as futures on S&P500 and US Treasuries. If we have to generate prices for specific contracts, we need to be sure that they are realistic.

There is also a question of polluting our results by using redundant information in a backtest. This predicament can face an analyst who uses very long historical samples for backtesting. We can illustrate it through a simple comparison. Let us say that we wish to build a rollercoaster ride, and use the heights of people in Victorian times up to the present day for building the seats. Of course, it is likely that such rides would have terrified Victorians if they had been around then, just as people are terrified today: the basic human psyche is still the same, and we still feel fear. However, by using data for heights going back to Victorian times, we would have ignored the fact that people have grown taller over time (Dougherty, 1998). Thus our estimate for heights would be skewed to the downside because of the older data, and our ride would be incorrectly proportioned for people today. This case is perhaps an extreme example, but it does illustrate that using very old data can be counterproductive, even if that is clearly not the intention. More data is not always better: it can sometimes increase the noise (see Chapter 7).

Also, the insistence that strategies need to have been profitable in testing for a very large sample will force traders to ignore many strategies that would be more appropriate for recent years. These might need forms of data or technology to trade which could have been unavailable in the past. It would mean ignoring higher-frequency data, for example. Unsurprisingly, the further back we go in the search for data, there are generally a smaller number of types of data too. Furthermore, the data quality can become more questionable. If this is awful, can we really place much credence on the results of a backtest? It is one thing creating a pretty plot of a strategy's returns and quite another thing to have confidence in the results being realistic.

Once we have answered the conundrum of the length of our data history, we need to interpret our results. When evaluating our historical performance, it can be very easy to exhibit biases. We have already stressed how traders can have excessive focus on their most recent performance. The difficulty with focusing only on very short-term returns is that we could end up making the wrong future decisions, purely because of short-term noise (and fear). This is indeed the issue that Jan-Erik mentioned when I interviewed him (see Chapter 5). There is a very fine line between a strategy which has "broken" and one that has temporary underperformance. Both scenarios face even the most profitable of investors.

There are issues aside from the bias of overweighting recent performance when evaluating a trading strategy. Even when looking at historical price action, certain periods will stick out in the memory more; in particular those periods of very volatile price action. From personal experience, this chiefly includes those periods of very large losses. For example, I can tell you from memory the worst trading days for models I developed: there is absolutely no need for me to retrieve the data, as the memory of pain is always fresh. As we noted earlier, backtesting a trade idea can give you statistics about the returns of a trading strategy historically, but it cannot replicate the pain of incurring drawdowns.

If you ask me about the best P&L days for these same trading strategies, however, I might have more trouble recalling them. My memory is not quite as rich in these instances. Yes, I can recall periods of outperformance, but specific days are more difficult to recall.

So, whilst trading experience is an important pool to draw upon, we need to be conscious of bias we might have when using it. We can "enhance" our experience if we examine the time series of our real trading P&L and analyze it in a similar manner to how we would for a theoretical backtest. Such an exercise can help fill in missing parts of our memory when it comes to recalling our trading experience. It can help to remove some of the biases when we use our trading experience. Another method is to write a trading diary each day, picking out the winning and losing trades every day. I did something like this in the past, when I helped to create and run a trading model in tandem with the bank's trading desk. I know some analysts who do something similar for price action, using diaries to note important price changes and technical levels. More simply, just looking at a plot of P&L can be an important exercise for recalling the reasons for gains and losses. Indeed, it is not purely when analyzing P&L that this exercise can be done. I find the same happens when I view the plot of a very liquid currency pair, such as EUR/USD. Following the jagged time series quickly brings to mind the events which caused those gyrations.

So to sum up this section, testing ideas on very long price histories can often be interesting from an academic standpoint. From a pure trading perspective it is perhaps not as crucial as we might think. In some situations, it might be totally irrelevant to backtest a strategy going back a long way, because in practice it might have been impossible to execute. Alternatively, there might have been insufficient high-quality data available. At the same time, we would add that only taking a very small sample when testing a trading strategy is also not ideal. In such a situation you might simply be testing over a period which was "lucky" for your particular idea. The key as ever is balance, not too little and not too much.

The trading style depends on the trader, not on the style

Let us make the assumption that we have spent a lot of time developing a trading strategy. It has been rigorously backtested by a team of quant analysts. They like working with numbers a lot and wear glasses (as a disclaimer, both of these are true in my case). Alternatively, we might have thought of a particular discretionary trading style that we wish to employ. There is significant rationale for why the strategy or our trading style should work. For example, it could be based on some macroeconomic or perhaps a more behavioral rationale. Hence, we have answered the crucial question of why this trading strategy should work. The returns have been strong historically. Admittedly, for more discretionary approaches this might be more difficult to check without a real track record. However, it is something we can check for rules-based trading strategies.

In our strategy, we see that drawdowns have historically dragged on for relatively long periods of time. This is hardly a plus point, but it is something we need be aware of. Generally, most trades in our strategy are losing trades. However, those trades which end up being positive have historically had very high returns. Hence, most of the time we have small losses and occasional big wins; thus on an aggregate basis it is profitable. The volatility of the strategy is relatively low in our historical sample. The resulting Sharpe ratio is also reasonable. After all our analysis, we have also conducted paper trading. During this period it has also performed well. After all these various steps, one key question remains, which is perhaps the most important: should I run this trading strategy with real money?

It would be fantastic if I could reel off a stream of relatively straightforward bullet points which could be applied to answer this question. Unfortunately, trading does not lend itself to such simple generalizations, especially when it comes to such crucial decisions. The true answer is a rather convoluted one.

This subject came up in conversation with Mark Cudmore and Cameron Millar. Both Mark and Cameron are veterans of Lehman Brothers, trading there in various guises before it closed in 2008. At the time of writing, Mark has been in markets for nearly a decade, mostly trading in emerging markets currencies and also in currency sales covering hedge funds. Cameron meanwhile has been trading for 25 years, primarily in the currency spot and options markets. They have therefore both had a considerable amount of experience in the markets. I have often exchanged views with them and have found this a great learning experience. I invited both Cameron and Mark, alongside Barney Singer, the head of emerging markets trading at Nomura, to speak on a Thalesians panel that was discussing market views whilst I was writing this book. I had been planning to moderate the panel myself, but luckily Katie Martin from the *Wall Street Journal* accepted an invitation to do so instead. The panel spurred a lot of debate, with both a considerable amount of agreement and disagreement, and a modicum of audience participation, on what at the time were some large moves in emerging markets. More broadly, if there is one thing I would advise to any traders reading this book, it would be to talk to others in the market. Reiterating an earlier point, it allows you to test whether your ideas are able to stand the scrutiny of others. It might not always be the case that you will agree, but that is what a debate is all about. Is there any point debating with someone who agrees with every point you make? In trading in particular, I would suggest that always being in the consensus need not always mean a trade will be profitable. If anything, it might be an indication that market positioning is skewed heavily in one direction, increasing the chances of an unwind (see Chapter 6).

After the panel, we discussed markets from a more abstract level, and Mark gave an answer to the question I posed earlier in this section. He suggested that particular trading styles suited different traders. What might appear to be a profitable (and logical) trading strategy might not be appropriate for every trader, when it comes to deciding where to allocate capital. This is independent of whether a strategy is perceived as "good."

If we think about this carefully, there is a reasonable explanation for Mark's answer. We have noted that trading objectives and risk appetite differ significantly between the various groups of investors and traders in the market (see Chapter 2). Pension funds do not trade markets in the same way as short-term speculators. There is also a matter of how this impacts their investment mandates and how they create their investment targets (see Chapter 5).

Hence, the decision whether to run a certain strategy or to invest in a particular fund is cloaked in all these considerations. It is not simply a case of placing capital in what appear to be good ideas. Abusing Descartes' famous statement "cogito ergo sum" (I think, therefore I am), the notion of "it works, therefore I trade" is generally an inappropriate criterion if used in isolation when picking trading strategies. We need to understand how a particular trading approach can fit in with your risk appetite, even ignoring that pesky "why?" question, which has come up so often in this book. Would you be prepared to invest in a trading strategy which generated no income for long periods of time, with short sporadic profitable periods (Black Swan-style strategies as discussed in Chapter 6)? Alternatively, would you prefer strategies which deliver relatively consistent returns but face large infrequent drawdowns, such as being long S&P500? It goes back to our discussion of investment targets and mandates in Chapter 5.

If a trader runs a strategy or tries to adopt a trading style which does not fit with his or her psychological preferences or specific investment goals, then there is little point running it. After all, in all likelihood, he or she will end up exiting the trading strategy as soon as there are short-term drawdowns. The key is to find the style or particular systematic trading strategy which suits you, the trader. It is for this reason that the idea that traders can simply "take" models from others and expect to run them profitably is a fallacy. Simply copying other traders who are successful does not automatically mean that returns will follow into your trading account. An idea will only be profitable with the right trader who can allocate the appropriate amount of risk to it. Furthermore, the trader needs to be aware of both the advantages and potential drawbacks of a particular strategy. A good trader shows his or her worth, not purely in the decisions made when winning, but moreover in the way he or she adapts in more difficult times.

Why should history matter for trading?

We have looked at the reasons why examining historical data is useful when looking at trading strategies. The main caveat is that we do not attempt to data-mine too much in such an exercise. We also need to have an understanding of the historical time series that is relevant. Here, we look at the more philosophical question of the benefits of looking at history with respect to trading. We draw a parallel with how historical work is viewed in the humanities and in science.

While writing this book, I have read many others on a wide range of topics. There have been books with an ancient focus, for example on olives (Foxhall, 2007) and on Thales (O'Grady, 2002). Other books I have read exhibit more of an obvious relationship with modern finance, about Warren Buffett for example (Schroeder, 2009). Totally unrelated to my writing here, I also started reading *Cultural Amnesia* by Clive James (James, 2007). I had been exchanging Twitter messages with Nassim Nicholas Taleb on a topic totally unrelated to finance when he mentioned James' book. (this might seem like a case of name dropping. I have to admit I have never met Taleb in person, so I can hardly be accused of this!) Seeking some solace from the relentless (but still fun) reading for this book, I decided to distract myself by reading *Cultural Amnesia*. Clive James' book discusses an eclectic array of public figures largely drawn from modern times, neatly arranged in alphabetical order: some are quite fascinating and others definitely evil. It proved to be a thoroughly entertaining book, whilst making me feel slightly ignorant for not previously knowing the names of a large number of people he describes.

Perhaps unexpectedly, I found certain points made by James to be very relevant to trading. In one particularly pertinent section he notes a crucial difference between science and the humanities. He suggests that this can be seen in how they absorb previous work (to paraphrase him in my prose, which is unfortunately not as lucid as his). In the humanities, it would be difficult to study philosophy without understanding the work of ancient philosophers and to read their work. Indeed, we have quoted Thales on numerous occasions in this book. Many of his more philosophical ideas, many thousands of years later, still have relevance. In science, the rapid rate of change means that examining a computer built in the 1950s is unlikely to tell you much about a computer today, if we are looking from a purely superficial level. There have been so many iterations of development since the 1950s that today's computers appear unrecognizable. This is despite the fact that at their roots the principal idea behind both computers is the same. Of course, this is just one example, and we could come up with many counterexamples from other areas of science, notably in mathematics, where there is a more obvious link between ideas from the past and the present. Ancient mathematical proofs, such as those related to proving the irrationality of certain numbers, are just as true now as they were in ancient time.

However, by and large the explanations that science gives us today are very different from those given during ancient times. If we think back to Chapter 2, we discussed Thales' idea that the principle of everything was water. Whilst the idea of an underlying unit, which provided the building block for the world, was correct (namely atoms and subatomic particles), he was clearly wrong to think that water was this special unit.

In the humanities, the differences seem smaller over the ages, or at least the similarities are easier to spot when compared with science, if we are willing to make a very broad and crude generalization. After all, humans are still the same, despite all the technology which we seem to enjoy today. Indeed, this is a point we made earlier in the text. Namely, we noted that the persistence of human behavior over the ages has given rise to what appear to be relatively similar market crises throughout time.

Humans have not changed to such a degree as to overcome emotions such as greed and fear. Indeed, we might argue that humans have not really changed at all. This is a point we made in the most recent section and at many other points in the text. Greed and fear are the emotions which are central to how investors trade markets. Their effect is clearly greatest when many investors share the same emotions of fear or greed. When there is a balance in the market between investors who are fearful and greedy, then we might expect market volatility to be lower.

If it was not for fear during a crisis, why would an investor sell stocks in a crisis incurring a loss, when in the longer term he or she might be bullish? Clearly, the fear of further falls in the short term and the potential further pain from that can inhibit the expression of a longer-term view at all times. A successful trading strategy might sometimes be clothed in statistics and executed on a computer, but both developing such a strategy and in particular running real cash on it is still very much an art rather than a science. If it were not, then there would be a fairly straightforward approach for trading markets successfully, maybe an easily implementable "secret sauce" and a way to inhibit the second thoughts which are inevitable when you go through a poor trading period. Part of the reason why trading is more an art than a science is that you are trading against other investors, rather than nature, whose objectives change depending on their circumstances. Hence, simply assuming some sort of continuing rationality (or at least a rationale to you) in every market move would be a mistake. After all, if the market were totally "rational" then going with the consensus view would always be profitable. If anything, it might be more profitable to buck consensus sometimes. I have opted to use speech marks around the word "rational" simply because traders often perceive a market to be more rational when they have positions profiting from the market and irrational otherwise. It is the same argument that blames losses on luck and gains on skill: a sort of skewed view of being *fooled by randomness*.

As we have noted before, scientists have been able to model certain natural phenomena such as hurricanes. The irrationality of human behavior is hopelessly difficult to model. In particular, the issue of how investors' priorities change in different market conditions, which has cropped up on several occasions in this book, is perhaps what makes investing so challenging and can be why the market sometimes appears to move in an "irrational" way. We could also refer to "animal spirits," to quote John Maynard Keynes, as one of the drivers for the markets.

Given the relative persistence of how investors behave over the ages ("animal spirits" remain prevalent), historical analysis can provide insights into future price action. Even taking this into account, we need to be aware that events never observed in a historical sample can occur in the future, as we noted with Black Swans (Chapter 6). Just because historically markets have never fallen by a certain amount, it is does not mean that we should assume such moves are impossible.

If investors were persistently in wealth-seeking mode, risky assets would go up indefinitely without the specter of drawdowns. In practice, these periods of the market seeking wealth are broken up by periods where the market pivots toward wealth preservation (see Chapter 2). Yes, past performance is not indicative of future performance, but it would seem difficult to simply ignore what has happened in the past and expect markets to behave totally differently from how they did historically.

Now we elaborate on our earlier question. If trading is better described as a part of the humanities than a science, would it be more literature or art? Paraphrasing Clive James again, a phrase he used had resonance for me when I was considering this question: "art takes the words away, writing gives those words back." With that in mind, I would suggest that running a trading book is perhaps more like art, whilst the planning and preparation is more like writing. I shall leave you with one thought: it is difficult to be both an artist and a writer.

And then it was history!

If there is one theme from this chapter which we have repeatedly returned to, it is the importance of understanding why historical events have occurred. When we began, we told the story of Herodotus, the "father of history," documenting the wars between the Greeks and the Persians. As opposed to simply telling the reader what happened, he was also keen to understand why events occurred, and furthermore to pass a judgment on the veracity of the observations he was making. Admittedly his judgment was not always right, notably when he seemed to believe the story of how cinnamon was found.

When it comes to trading, we can use the same ideas in terms of deciphering the rationale for a trading idea. In particular, when examining either backtested historical performance or when evaluating the live performance of a trading strategy, crucially we need to understand why the strategy is making money or indeed losing money.

Of course, we cannot seek to rationalize every single gyration of market price action and what it might mean for our trading strategy. Indeed, a lot of very short-term price action is likely to be very noisy. Trying to understand the "cause" of every move in the price can end up being a wild goose chase, particularly on an intraday basis. Whereas we might be able to rationalize moves following economic events and in the midst of news flow on other occasions, price action might gap for entirely different reasons, such as stop losses going through the market, which are difficult to pick out. Rather than trying to understand each one of these moves, we can try to examine the general performance of a strategy more broadly.

The advantage of a live trading history is that it is real and hence cannot be the result of excessive data-mining. This is an issue that can impact backtested strategies. The disadvantage of a real track record is that it is often very short. In particular, over very short periods it can be the case that the success of a trader's strategy might be the result of luck rather than anything smarter. If a trader maintains profitability over an extended period over different market regimes, then it becomes more difficult to say that success was purely down to luck. We also noted that a rigorous investment process needs to be observed to reduce the luck factor, whether we are looking at a backtested sample or a real track record. With a backtested sample, we usually have access to a longer data history, compared with a real track record. Hence, we can test the robustness of backtested strategy over many different market regimes. We also grappled with the idea that making parallels between different eras is justified, provided we do not use it as a basis for detailed analysis (grain futures might have been referred to in the Bible, but they were not exactly trading on the Chicago Mercantile Exchange!). There is the caveat that events can occur which never happened in our historical sample. As we noted, just because a market has never moved by a certain amount before, it does not imply larger moves are an impossibility. However, there are numerous other examples we might give.

We have also suggested that the reason why examining historical returns is so crucial is that trading is more an art than a science. Whilst technology has clearly changed some facets of trading markets, in particular high-frequency trading which can become a technological arms race, it is the basic human emotions of greed and fear which still pervade markets. Hence, examining what has happened before can provide insight into the future, even if it does not guarantee that history will repeat itself in quite the same way. I found a quotation in Ronald Wright's book *A Short History of Progress* (Wright, 2006), which seems like an appropriate way to end this chapter on history. The original source is unknown, although it sounds very much like a warning to a trader who refuses to examine the past. The quotation notes that "Each time history repeats itself, so it's said, the price goes up." Learn from your trading mistakes and hopefully you will not pay for them again. That is the intention at least!

10
A Last Word to Conclude

In conclusions very last words are said,
Of what has passed little will be recalled,
Towards the end, the words will shine instead,
Valued in mind yet dull when only scrawled.

We started our book by discussing why we started the Thalesians. In particular, we recounted the story of Thales of Miletus and his profitable olive press option trade. The creation of the Thalesians gave me the idea that there was something today's traders could learn from the ancient world, starting me along the path which culminated in this book.

Our first major discussion concerned how investors could measure risk, citing the importance of understanding the maximum possible losses associated with a trading strategy. We noted how even in ancient times such a concept could still be articulated. Later, we delved into the differences between alpha and beta trades, illustrating them with the example of the olive industry in Ancient Greece. We later moved on to the idea of insurance, and ways in which investors can mitigate risk in a portfolio.

The idea of what an investor should target constituted the next chapter. We noted that returns are not the best metric to target. In particular, trying to maximize returns in the short term can perversely impede longer-term returns, because it encourages overleveraging. Instead, investors should think about other measures such as information ratios and maximum drawdowns. It is drawdowns which can ultimately cause the abandonment of a trading strategy. We discussed a multitude of these various metrics.

We explored the field of Black Swans, a topic that has been ably covered by Nassim Nicholas Taleb. We agreed with many of his notions. However, we also noted that trades which try to take advantage of Black Swans, such as continually investing in heavily out-of-the-money options, can face issues.

Notably, these options are no longer always as undervalued, as they were historically, such as before the Wall Street Crash of 1987. To make such an approach profitable requires identifying specific parts of the vol surface which are undervalued, which is trickier to do these days. Furthermore, we need to consider the bleed from these trades when markets are more benign.

The area of lateral thinking was then up for discussion. We noted how it can be used to find new trading ideas. The key to lateral thinking is to brainstorm a wide variety of potential ideas, before focusing on specific areas for more detailed analytical study. The risks are in trying to explore too many areas. The key, as we noted, is to listen, but not to listen so much as to confuse.

We reverted to the ancient world, and in particular the Silk Road and the idea of a "secret sauce" for trading success. We disagreed with the idea of a grand idea constituting some sort of "secret sauce" that allows someone to become a successful trader. Instead, we conjectured that it is the details of a trading strategy and the precise implementation that can constitute this "secret sauce."

Lastly, we discussed the writings of Herodotus. We noted how it is important that historians do not simply reel off events which have happened, but that they have an understanding of why those events have happened. We suggested that a similar approach is important for traders when analyzing their historical performance. Whilst being profitable is clearly the aim, just as crucial is understanding why historically a strategy has exhibited strong returns. If we are unable to answer this question, then it might suggest that a similar approach is not likely to yield good results in the future.

Whilst you, the reader, may not have agreed with everything you have read, given that a lot of these pages are filled with opinions which are difficult to prove, I do hope you have found the book enlightening. My aim is to provoke debate, and I hope I have succeeded; but of course only you, the reader, can judge that, not me. Do you have a profound understanding of markets? That is a question for other Thalesians to answer!

I leave you with a few words that I hope will inspire you as you travel your path through investing and perhaps even through life. Although I am certainly not qualified to advise anyone how to live, I shall endeavor to write words that give that illusion, although a friend has told me the Danish philosopher Kierkegaard expressed a similar sentiment nearly 200 years ago. *Life is lived forward, experience is experienced backward. Yet it is at the intersection of these paths where life is richest of all: the present.*

A yard to end

> Beneath the whisper are words to rise and strive,
> That seek to break apart the sentiments,
> Which say no and never and don't and won't,

To trounce the dreams, to pounce upon what seems,
Go wipe away the false and grasp the truth,
So seek the path and endeavor and rise,
Go forth traverse the lows and climb the highs,
Ignore the pain, the fails and the near just,
A yard to end, that goal it'll be your pole,
And turn to back and smile in that last mile,
Year next will rise in mind as you'll sure find,
If simple were life, boredom would be rife!

Acknowledgments

I save my greatest thanks for my family, Baba and Mama, Furrat and Dunia, Samar, Mia, Amer, grandparents, aunts, uncles, and cousins. After all, we are the sum of our experiences, both past and future, but only so much as we reconcile them with where we came from.

I would also like to thank my fellow co-founders of the Thalesians, Paul Bilokon and Matthew Dixon. I strongly suspect that without Paul's idea of creating the Thalesians, I would have never written this book (or if I had never met my friend called Thales, who told both of us the story of the philosopher!). I would also like to thank all those at Palgrave Macmillan who worked so hard to enable this book to be published, including Aimee Dibbens, Gemma d'Arcy Hughes, Grace Jackson and Pete Baker. Throughout the course of writing the book, I discussed it on many occasions with Iain Clark, who is already a successful author of finance books. Iain deserves a lot of thanks for being a sounding board throughout this project.

In terms of colleagues, the list whom I would like to thank is relatively long. I would especially like to thank Jim McCormick, who gave me my first permanent job after leaving university, at Lehman Brothers. Together with Alexei Jiltsov, they both provided me with an excellent grounding in financial markets and in particular in currencies. I would also like to thank Brent Donnelly and James Pearson, trading desk heads who placed their faith in me to put real cash behind my systematic trading model ideas. You learn far more about the market when real cash is placed on your ideas and from working with excellent traders such as Brent and James. I want to thank Will Johns from Nomura for teaching me about the various intricacies of how FX options are traded, a topic which is very difficult to understand purely from literature. There is a large disconnect between how options are priced and how traders actually trade options. Understanding an option-pricing model does not always imply an understanding of the latter; but the latter is of course necessary to be able to trade options profitably. I'd also like to thank many more of my former colleagues, including Shruti Sood, Anne Sanciaume, and Pallavi Borse, part of my team at Lehman Brothers. I extend my thanks to the many students who worked with me on industrial placement at both Nomura and Lehman Brothers, including Thales Panza de Paula, Tim Davis, and Jordan Rochester. Tim has always been a good friend and has been a great source of advice over the years.

I'd also like to thank are those who managed me at Nomura, including Des Supple, Stephen Hull, Geoff Kendrick, and Jens Nordvig. I would like to extend my thanks to all the team at Nomura, which I had the pleasure of working with, including Kurt Magnus and Mark Cudmore, who both championed my research work. Mark has always offered excellent advice to me throughout my career! I hope one day to be on hand to offer him equally great advice (with respect to a subject other than my favorite burger joints). Kurt is both a great salesman and a great storyteller, with a sense of humor which seems akin to mine. I shall defer judgment on whether this is a positive.

Geoff Kendrick invited me to cowrite a chapter with him in the *Handbook in Exchange Rates*, which encouraged me to write this book, and most importantly having a published chapter was helpful when it came to finding a publisher. I would like to thank Jessica James, who co-edited that book and gave us a lot of feedback while our chapter was being written. Matthew Slade deserves a mention for putting up with my jokes at work for many years and the good advice he offered me whilst I wrote this book. I'd also like to thank

Ylva Cederholm, for somehow managing to work in the same team as me for nearly five years in my time at Lehman and Nomura, the longest of any colleague!

A great thanks goes to everyone whom I have not already mentioned who gave their comments on the book whilst I was writing it. They include Jacob Bartram, Zeiad Idriss, and Chiara Albanese.

I would also like to thank my many clients who read my research work over the years, and provided me with feedback on it. They include Bhupindra Bahra, Frederick Bourgoin, Alessio de Longis, Martin Richter, and Francois-Xavier Adam. I would also like to thank Nazli, Toro, and the rest of the team at my local Starbucks, who grew accustomed to seeing me write this book over many months, keeping my mind alert with a plethora of hot drinks.

With due acknowledgment of the help and advice from everyone listed above, I accept full responsibility for any errors and omissions in this book. I intend to list these on the Thalesians web page (www.thalesians.com) in due course.

Lastly, a great thank you is reserved for you, the reader, for offering me hours of your time to read this book. I have one piece of advice: keep reading. Read for leisure, read for pleasure, and read for everything else in between.

Please follow me on Twitter @thalesians for finance-related commentary (but not investment ideas).

Further Reading

I used numerous references throughout the writing of this book, which are detailed in the bibliography. However, I would like to flag up several books which I found particularly useful. Before beginning work on the book, my knowledge of Thales and ancient philosophers was relatively sketchy. I knew the story of Thales and the olives, but precious little of his other accomplishments.

To help fortify my knowledge of all things Thales, I read *Thales of Miletus* by Patricia O'Grady (O'Grady, 2002), and a large part of what I have learnt about Thales has been taken from that book and also from the shorter article O'Grady wrote summarizing Thales' life for the Internet Encyclopedia of Philosophy (O'Grady, 2004). It serves as a very comprehensive account of Thales. Given that no written work by Thales survives, understanding Thales' life is quite difficult. However, O'Grady manages to cut through a lot of the conjecture, to ascertain which stories are likely myths about his life and work, and which are most likely real events. A somewhat more concise introduction to Thales' life and work can be found on Wikipedia, and I would thoroughly recommend reading that. I would also recommend reading the section about Thales in *The Lives and Opinions of Eminent Philosophers* by Diogenes Laertius, as well as reading Aristotle's references to Thales. To better understand the importance of olives in Ancient Greece I read Lin Foxhall's tremendously detailed book *Olive Cultivation in Ancient Greece: Seeking the Ancient Economy* (Foxhall, 2007). Before reading this, I had never really contemplated precisely how important olives were in that part of the world during ancient times. Other books also furnished me with knowledge about the ancient world, most notably Marc Van De Mieroop's book *King Hammurabi of Babylon: A Biography* (Mieroop, 2004).

Before undertaking this project, I knew little detail about the life of Herodotus. I have extensively used several texts on Herodotus, including *Travels with Herodotus* (Kapuscinski, 2008), and the two translations of his book *The Histories* (Herodotus & Holland (trans), 2013) and (Herodotus & Macaulay (trans), 1890).

The bulk of this book, however, is about finance and specifically ways of better understanding markets. Before I began this book, and also through the course of my writing, my best references for market knowledge were those colleagues whom I have been lucky enough to work with over the past decade at Nomura and Lehman Brothers, as well as fellow finance professionals who have attended the talks of the Thalesians.

In addition to these many discussions over the years, reading books about finance have also shaped my ideas, both in this work and in the numerous papers I have written on currency markets over the years. It is unlikely I would have written this book without reading Nassim Nicholas Talib's *Fooled by Randomness* (Taleb, 2007), *Black Swan* (Taleb, 2008), and *Antifragile* (Taleb, 2013), in which he cites the story of Thales and the olive press. I would heartily recommend all these books to any reader (especially *Fooled by Randomness*), and I agree with large parts of them (although admittedly not all). I suppose that is the point of reading: to spur your thought processes, not necessarily to agree with every sentiment expressed. To that end I would wholeheartedly recommend that anyone working in finance read his work. I also read a large number of books on the field of technical analysis, including many by Murphy. Whilst such a discipline is lauded as mumbo-jumbo by some of those in academia, after seeing numerous colleagues employ technical analysis profitably I would have to disagree.

Bibliography

Adkins, L. & Adkins, R. A. (1998). *Handbook to Life in Ancient Rome*. Oxford University Press.

Amen, S. (2013, August 30). *Beta'm up – What Is Market Beta in FX?* Retrieved from *The Thalesians*: http://www.thalesians.com.

Anon. (2013, June 1). *Ship of Knaves*. Retrieved from *The Economist*: http://www.economist.com/news/books-and-arts/21578633-rajat-gupta-had-everything-why-did-he-blow-it-ship-knaves.

Aristotle & Ellis, W. (trans). (1912). *Politics 1259a*. J. M. Dent & Sons.

Aristotle & Tredennick, H. (trans). (1933). *Metaphysics 963b*. Loeb Classical Library.

Bailey, D. H. & Prado, M. L. (2012, July 1). The Sharpe Ratio Efficient Frontier. *Journal of Risk*, 15(2), Winter 2012/13. Retrieved from SSRN.

Barr, A. (2010, January 13). *Soros Among Firms that Made Money in 2008, 2009*. Retrieved from MarketWatch *Wall Street Journal*: http://www.marketwatch.com/story/soros-among-firms-that-made-money-in-08-and-09-2010-01-13.

Bauer, L. (2007). *The Linguistics Student's Handbook*. Edinburgh University Press.

Bernstein, P. L. (1996). *Against the Gods: The Remarkable Story of Risk*. Wiley.

Bono, E. de. (2009). *Lateral Thinking: A Textbook of Creativity*. Penguin.

Branson, R. (2011). *Screw Business as Usual*. Virgin.

Broad, W. J. (2007). *The Oracle: Ancient Delphi and the Science Behind Its Lost Secrets*. Penguin.

Buffett, W. (2012, March 1). *Berkshire Hathaway 2012 Annual Report – Chairman's Letter*. Retrieved from *Berkshire Hathaway*: http://www.berkshirehathaway.com/letters/2012ltr.pdf.

Buffett, W. & Olsen, Max (editor). (2013). *Berkshire Hathaway Letters to Shareholders*. Max Olsen.

Burns, P. (2006, January 13). *Random Portfolios for Evaluating Trading Strategies*. Retrieved from *SSRN*: http://ssrn.com/abstract=881735.

Burton, S. R. (2004). *The Arabian Nights: Tales from A Thousand and One Nights (English translation)*. Random House Inc; Modern Library edition.

Clare, A. & Motson, N. (2010, September). Do UK Retail Investors Buy at the Top and Sell at the Bottom? *Cass Business School Working Paper*. Retrieved from *Cass Business School*: http://www.cass.city.ac.uk/__data/assets/pdf_file/0003/69933/Do-UK-retail-investors-buy-at-the-top-and-sell-at-the-bottom.pdf.

Clark, I. (2010). *Foreign Exchange Option Pricing: A Practitioner's Guide*. Wiley.

Clark, I. (2014). *Commodity Option Pricing: A Practitioner's Guide*. Wiley.

Dougherty, M. J. (1998, June 29). *Why Are We Getting Taller as a Species?* Retrieved from *Scientific American*: http://www.scientificamerican.com/article/why-are-we-getting-taller/.

Dubnov, S. (1968). *History of the Jews: From the Roman Empire to the Early Medieval Period (Volume 2)*. Thomas Yoseloff.

Durant, W. (1944 (reprint 1994)). *Caesar and Christ: A History of Roman Civilization and of Christianity from Their Beginnings to A.D. 325 (Story of Civilization)*. Fine Communications.

Elder, P. T., Bostock, J. (trans), & Riley, H. (trans). (1855). *The Natural History*. Taylor and Francis.

Encyclopaedia Britannica. (2013, October 16). *The Thousand and One Nights*. Retrieved from: http://www.britannica.com/EBchecked/topic/593514/The-Thousand-and-One-Nights.

Faith, C. (2007). *Way of the Turtle: The Secret Methods That Turned Ordinary People into Legendary Traders*. McGraw-Hill Professional.

Foxhall, L. (2007). *Olive Cultivation in Ancient Greece: Seeking the Ancient Economy*. Oxford University Press.

Frazzini, A., Kabiller, D., & Pedersen, L. H. (2013, November 21). *Buffett's Alpha*. Retrieved from *Yale Economics*: http://www.econ.yale.edu/~af227/pdf/Buffett's%20Alpha%20-%20Frazzini,%20Kabiller%20and%20Pedersen.pdf.

Fulton, R. (2013, January 20). *Plato's Black Swan*. Retrieved from *Curse of Socrates*: http://curseofsocrates.blogspot.co.uk/2013/01/platos-black-swan.html.

Galland, A. (2004). *Les Mille et Une Nuits (I–III)*. Flammarion.

Goetzmann, W. N. & Rouwenhorst, K. G. (2005). *The Origins of Value: The Financial Innovations That Created Modern Capital Markets*. Oxford University Press.

Haire, M. (2009, July 1). *A Brief History of the Walkman*. Retrieved from *Time*: http://content.time.com/time/nation/article/0,8599,1907884,00.html.

Hansen, V. (2012). *The Silk Road: A New History*. Oxford University Press.

Hawkinsin, T. (2007, April 27). *Zimbabwe Moves Devalue Currency by 95%*. Retrieved from *Financial Times*: http://www.ft.com/cms/s/0/12120486-f45c-11db-88aa-000b5df10621.html.

Herodotus & Holland, T. (trans). (2013). *The Histories*. Penguin.

Herodotus & Macaulay, G. C. (trans). (1890). *The History of Herodotus*. Macmillan and Co.

Hunt, P. (2011). *Late Roman Silk: Smuggling and Espionage in the 6th Century CE*. Retrieved from *Philolog*: http://traumwerk.stanford.edu/philolog/2011/08/byzantine_silk_smuggling_and_e.html.

Iamblichus & Taylor, T. (trans). (1818). *Iamblichus' Life of Pythagoras*. JM Watkins.

Ilmanen, A. (2011). *Expected Returns: An Investor's Guide to Harvesting Market Rewards*. Wiley.

Jaeger, L. (2008). *Alternative Beta Strategies and Hedge Fund Replication*. Wiley.

James, C. (2007). *Cultural Amnesia: Notes in the Margin of Time*. Macmillan.

Jenkins, I. F. (2013, March 22). *Alternative Beta has a Wide Umbrella*. Retrieved from *Financial Times*: http://www.ft.com/cms/s/0/70b6b6ea-7f6a-11e2-97f6-00144feabdc0.html#axzz2hEgCRXho.

Kahneman, D. (2012). *Thinking, Fast and Slow*. Penguin.

Kaminska, I. (2013, July 23). *Explaining the Commodity Warehouse Trade with Scripture*. Retrieved from *FT Alphaville*: http://ftalphaville.ft.com/2013/07/23/1578802/explaining-the-commodity-warehouse-trade-with-scripture/.

Kapuscinski, R. (2002). *The Shadow of the Sun*. Penguin.

Kapuscinski, R. (2008). *Travels with Herodotus*. Vintage.

Kerouac, J. (2011 (reprint)). *On the Road*. Penguin Modern Classics.

Kay, J. (2011). *Obliquity*. Profile Books.

Laertius, D. & Hicks, R. (trans). (1925). *Lives of Eminent Philosophers*. Harvard University Press.

Landler, M. (2007, December 2). *U.S. Credit Crisis Adds to Gloom in Norway*. Retrieved from *New York Times*: http://www.nytimes.com/2007/12/02/world/europe/02norway.html.

Lawson, J. N. (1994). *The Concept of Fate in Ancient Mesopotamia of the First Millennium: Towards an Understanding of "Shimtu" (Orientalia Biblica et Christiana)*. Harrassowitz Verlag.

Lichtblau, E. & Sanger, D. E. (2004, April 10). *August '01 Brief Said to Warn of Attack Plans*. Retrieved from *The New York Times*: http://www.nytimes.com/2004/04/10/us/august-01-brief-is-said-to-warn-of-attack-plans.html.

Markowitz, H. (1959). *Portfolio Selection: Efficient Diversification of Investments*. Wiley.

Mason, R. (2010, June 30). *How a Broker Spent $520m in a Drunken Stupor and Moved the Global Oil Price*. Retrieved from *The Telegraph*: http://www.telegraph.co.uk/finance/newsbysector/energy/oilandgas/7862246/How-a-broker-spent-520m-in-a-drunken-stupor-and-moved-the-global-oil-price.html.

McEwan, G. F. (2006). *The Incas: New Perspectives (Understanding Ancient Civilizations)*. ABC-CLIO Ltd.

Melis, E., Pollet, M., & Siekmann, J. (2006). Reductio ad Absurdum: Planning Proofs by Contradiction. *Reasoning, Action and Interaction in AI Theories and Systems Lecture Notes in Computer Science*, 4155, 45–58. http://link.springer.com/chapter/10.1007%2F11829263_3

Mieroop, M. V. (2004). *King Hammurabi of Babylon: A Biography*. Wiley-Blackwell.

Morris, A., Balakrishnan, S., Rushton, G., Aggarwal, S., & Rajendran, T. (2013, February 18). *Returns Focus: The Substance in Styles: Why Alternative Return Sources Should Become Standard in Fixed Income*. Retrieved from *Nomura*: http://www.nomuranow.com/research/globalresearchportal/getpub.aspx?pid=596809.

Murphy, P. (2012, July 13). *Time for Regulator to Move on Retail FX Trading*. Retrieved from *Financial Times*: http://www.ft.com/cms/s/0/93a462f2-cd03-11e1-b78b-00144feabdc0.html#axzz2hEgCRXho.

Narang, R. K. (2009). *Inside the Black Box: The Simple Truth About Quantitative Trading*. Wiley.

Nekritin, A. & Peters, W. (2012). *Naked Forex: High-Probability Techniques for Trading without Indicators*. Wiley.

Newcomb, T. (2011, December 14). *Where's the Must Have Toy of 2011?* Retrieved from *Time*: http://newsfeed.time.com/2011/12/14/wheres-the-must-have-toy-of-2011/.

Nordvig, J. (2013). *The Fall of the Euro: Reinventing the Eurozone and the Future of Global Investing*. McGraw-Hill.

O'Grady, P. (2002). *Thales of Miletus: The Beginnings of Western Science and Philosophy*. Ashgate.

O'Grady, P. (2004, September 17). *Thales of Miletus*. Retrieved from *Internet Encyclopedia of Philosophy*: http://www.iep.utm.edu/thales/.

Panchenko, D. (1994). Thales's Prediction of a Solar Eclipse. *Journal for the History of Astronomy*, Vol. 25, pp. 275–288.

Plato & Jowlett, B. (trans). (1892). *The Dialogues of Plato*. Oxford at the Clarendon Press.

Plato & Jowett, B. (trans). (2000). *The Republic*. Dover. https://archive.org/details/dialoguesplatov00platgoog.

Preis, T., Moat, H. S., Bishop, S. R., Treleaven, P., & Stanley, H. E. (2013, November 5). *Quantifying the Digital Traces of Hurricane Sandy on Flickr*. Retrieved from *Scientific Reports*: http://www.nature.com/srep/2013/131105/srep03141/full/srep03141.html.

Procopius & Dewing, H. B. (trans). (1989). *History of the Wars: Bks.VII, xxxvi–VIII v. 5*. Loeb.

Puhvel, J. (1994, Summer). The Origin of Etruscan Tusna ("Swan"). *The American Journal of Philology*, 105(2), 209–212.

Reed, C. M. (1999). *Maritime Traders in the Ancient Greek World*. Cambridge University Press.

Reinhart, C. M. & Rogoff, K. (2011). *This Time Is Different: Eight Centuries of Financial Folly*. Princeton University Press.

Roberts, K. (2011). *The Origins of Business, Money, and Markets.* Columbia University Press.

Rumsfeld, D. (2013). *Known and Unknown: A Memoir.* Penguin.

Rumsfeld, D. & Myers, G. R. (2002, February 12). *DoD News Briefing – Secretary Rumsfeld and Gen. Myers.* Retrieved from *U.S. Department of Defense*: http://www.defense.gov/transcripts/transcript.aspx?transcriptid=2636.

Russell, B. (1999 (reissue)). *Conquest of Happiness.* Liveright Books.

Schroeder, A. (2009). *The Snowball: Warren Buffett and the Business of Life.* Bloomsbury Publishing.

Sharpe, W. (1990, January 1). *William F. Sharpe – Biographical.* Retrieved from *nobelprize.org*: http://www.nobelprize.org/nobel_prizes/economic-sciences/laureates/1990/sharpe-bio.html.

Shea, A. (2007, July 5). *Jack Kerouac's Famous Scroll, 'On the Road' Again.* Retrieved from *NPR*: http://www.npr.org/templates/story/story.php?storyId=11709924.

Silver, N. (2012). *The Signal and the Noise.* Allen Lane.

Smith, A. (1776). *The Wealth of Nations.* W. Strahan and T. Cadell.

Smith, W. (1875). *A Dictionary of Greek and Roman Antiquities.* John Murray.

Sorkin, A. R. (2010). *Too Big to Fail: The Inside Story of How Wall Street and Washington Fought to Save the Financial System and Themselves.* Penguin.

Stempel, J. & Ablan, J. (2013, May 4). *Berkshire Hathaway's Annual Meeting of Shareholders.* Retrieved from *Reuters*: http://www.reuters.com/article/2013/05/04/us-berkshire-agm-quotes-idUSBRE94308B20130504.

Strachman, D. A. (2004). *Julian Robertson: A Tiger in the Land of Bulls and Bears.* Wiley.

Taleb, N. N. (2007). *Fooled by Randomness.* Penguin.

Taleb, N. N. (2008). *Black Swan.* Penguin.

Taleb, N. N. (2013). *Antifragile.* Penguin.

Thorp, E. (1973). *Beat the Dealer.* Random House.

Thubron, C. (2012). *Shadow of the Silk Road.* Vintage Digital.

Trenerry, C. F. (2010 reprint). *The Origin and Early History of Insurance Including the Contract of Bottomry.* The Lawbook Exchange Ltd.

Tsang, G. C. (1995, June 20). *Textile Exhibition: Introduction.* Retrieved from *AsianArt*: http://www.asianart.com/textiles/intro.html.

Tzu, S. & Giles, L. (trans). (1910). *The Art of War.* Project Gutenberg.

Whaley, R. E. (2006). *Derivatives: Markets, Valuation, and Risk Management.* Wiley.

Wikipedia. (2013, October 9). *Decathlon.* Retrieved from *Wikipedia*: http://en.wikipedia.org/wiki/Decathlon.

Wikipedia. (2014, January 15). *Occam's Razor.* Retrieved from Wikipedia: http://en.wikipedia.org/wiki/Occam's_razor.

Winkler, M. (1999). *Foreign Bonds an Autopsy.* Beard Books.

Wright, R. (2006). *A Short History of Progress.* Canongate Books.

Zuckerman, G. (2010). *The Greatest Trade Ever: The Behind-the-Scenes Story of How John Paulson Defied Wall Street and Made Financial History.* Penguin.

Zurawski, A. & D'Arcy, P. (2009, March). *Japanese Retail Investors and the Carry Trade.* Retrieved from *Reserve Bank of Australia*: http://www.rba.gov.au/publications/bulletin/2009/mar/pdf/bu-0309-1.pdf.

Zymler, S., Kuhn, D., & Rustem, B. (2013, January). Worst-Case Value at Risk of Nonlinear Portfolios. *Management Science*, 59(1), 172–178.

Index

Printed and bound by CPI Group (UK) Ltd, Croydon, CR0 4YY